Climate Change and Gender Justice

Climate Change and Gender Justice

Edited by Geraldine Terry
Series editor Caroline Sweetman

Published by Practical Action Publishing in association with Oxfam GB.

Practical Action Publishing Ltd
Schumacher Centre for Technology and Development
Bourton on Dunsmore, Rugby,
Warwickshire, CV23 9QZ, UK
www.practicalactionpublishing.org

ISBN 978 1 85339 693 9

© Oxfam GB, 2009

Since 1974, Practical Action Publishing (formerly Intermediate Technology
Publications and ITDG Publishing) has published and disseminated books and
information in support of international development work throughout the world.
Practical Action Publishing Ltd (Company Reg. No. 1159018) is the wholly owned
publishing company of Practical Action. Practical Action Publishing trades only
in support of its parent charity objectives and any profits are covenanted back to
Practical Action (Charity Reg. No. 247257, Group VAT Registration No. 880 9924 76).

Oxfam is a registered charity in England and Wales (no 202918) and Scotland (SCO
039042). Oxfam GB is a member of Oxfam International.

Oxfam GB,
Oxfam House, John Smith Drive,
Oxford, OX4 2JY, UK
www.oxfam.org.uk

Cover photo: Women wading through flood water with their emergency shelter kits
received from Oxfam; Pakistan, 2007. Credit: Iqbal Haider/Oxfam.

Indexed by Andrea Palmer
Typeset by S.J.I. Services
Printed by Hobbs The Printers Ltd
Printed on FSC 100% post-consumer waste recycled paper.

Contents

Figures

Tables

CHAPTER 1
Introduction

Geraldine Terry

Melting ice-caps, freak storms, the search for 'green' forms of transport and the international carbon trading system; superficially, both the impact of human-induced climate change and the policies adopted in response to it may seem gender-neutral. In reality though, there are complex and dynamic links between gender relations and climate change, as the chapters in this book show. These connections exist whether we are discussing human vulnerability to climate change's effects, how to adapt to those effects, or ways of reducing the levels of greenhouse gases (GHGs) that are causing climate change. Awareness of these gender dimensions is growing fast in Gender and Development (GAD) circles and among women's rights activists, but in mainstream policies they still tend to be overlooked. In part, the absence of a gender perspective in climate change debates is due to a lack of information and evidence. The chapters in this book help to fill this serious knowledge gap.

Challenges to gender analysis

Until recently, the interactions between gender relations and climate change have been obscured. There are several reasons for this. First, the mainstream policy discourse is stereotypically masculine: what we tend to read and hear about are complicated computer models; neoclassical economic approaches such as carbon trading; and searches for quick-fix technologies, such as environmentally friendly cars. It is true that various alternative approaches for thinking through the social aspects of climate change, such as sustainable development, climate justice, human rights or ethics, have been put forward. However, until now, gender equity has not been prominent in these alternative paradigms either.[1] Secondly, climate change is not happening in a vacuum. As several authors in this book mention, it is one trend interacting with many others, including economic liberalization and the world's present economic crisis; globalization; population growth; conflict; and unpredictable government policies, all of which threaten poor women and men in the global South. Even in a single community, trying to tease out the many inter-linked forces that shape people's lives can be daunting. For instance, in the Ugandan village where I have been conducting research, intense rainstorms often damage crops and property, but this is only one of a host of factors that combine to create and sustain poverty there. Thirdly, it is not always possible to blame specific events such as hurricanes, or even climate trends, on human-induced climate change. On the other hand, even if we cannot say that all the climate shocks and stresses we experience now are due to climate change caused by humans, at the very least they indicate what we can expect in years to come. We can learn from what is happening now to support adaptation in the future, as several of these chapters help us to do.

What do these chapters cover?

The following 12 chapters here are drawn from two issues of the journal *Gender and Development*. The first was published in 2002 (volume 10:2) and the second in 2009 (volume 17:1). The earlier of these issues broke new ground and laid the foundations for thinking about climate change in a Gender and Development context. The later issue showcases some of the progress that has been made since then in applying a gender lens to climate change.

The volume ranges over locations in Asia, Africa, Latin and Central America and the Pacific region. The chapters cover a wide spectrum of climate change-related topics: gendered vulnerability; disaster-preparedness and adaptation; mitigation initiatives; and finally, advocacy aimed at influencing climate policies. These differences in contexts, topics and themes are overlaid by distinct conceptual approaches and strategies. The authors are drawn from a variety of NGOs, academic institutions, and official development aid organizations, but they all derive their analyses from experience, sometimes presented here in the form of case studies. Several of the papers will be of particular interest to GAD practitioners and staff of development organizations wondering how to address gender and climate change in development programmes and projects on the ground.[2] That is because the writers present entry points for addressing gender issues, as well as describing practical activities such as the creation and use of new tools. On the other hand, all the chapters will help readers to think through climate change's gender dimensions and get up-to-date with recent initiatives in this field.

In the rest of this introduction, I will outline how each chapter individually contributes to our understanding of the gender and climate change nexus, while at the same time highlighting themes that crop up repeatedly through the collection. I will do this by considering what the authors have to say about these four important areas: vulnerability to climate change's effects; adapting to climate shocks and stresses; reducing GHGs (technically known as mitigation); and finally, advocacy efforts aimed at influencing public policy at various levels.

Gendered vulnerability

A person's vulnerability to climate change depends in part on gender roles and relations; rural women in developing countries are one of the most vulnerable groups (IPCC 2007). This is because they are often dependent on natural resources for their livelihoods, do most of the agricultural work, and are responsible for collecting water and fuel. Climate change is widely predicted to affect all these areas of women's lives adversely. For instance, increased climate variability is making agriculture more unpredictable, and continuing desertification in some regions exacerbates the domestic fuel crisis. In urban areas, on the other hand, poor women are likely to bear the brunt of health problems caused by 'urban heat island' effects, increases in vector-borne diseases like malaria and, for cities situated in dry zones, water shortages (United Nations Population Fund 2007). The different effects of climate change on women and men will alter gender relations, but we cannot yet predict exactly how these changes will play out.

When gender issues are mentioned at all in discussions of climate change, it is usually with reference to women's gendered vulnerability. But there is a tendency to present women as victims, rather than as agents capable of contributing to solutions, and to make broad generalizations that lump together all women in the global South. Demetriades and Esplen (2008) call for more nuanced and context-specific analyses that can be used to identify appropriate responses. On the other hand, in some countries at least, the message of women's gendered vulnerability has not yet got through and still needs to be communicated to national policy makers (Zahur 2008).

There is a divide in the academic climate change literature between, on the one side, those who think of vulnerability in terms of physical exposure and sensitivity, and on the other side, researchers who are more interested in how social differences such as class, gender, and ethnicity shape people's vulnerability. As might be expected of a book such as this one, the chapters here are mainly interested in the social components. For instance, Sara Ahmed and Elizabeth Fajber argue that vulnerability to natural hazards in India arises from poverty and marginalization, not simply to the physical effects of the hazards in themselves. Similarly, Stephanie Buechler writes that people's 'social location' is an important influence on their vulnerability. Political factors play a part, too. For Rosa Rivero Reyes, the severity of El Niño's impact on poor women and men's livelihoods in the Piura region of Peru in 1997–8 was due to their 'political invisibility' in national social and political processes, not just the damage caused by this notorious phenomenon. She points out that these rural communities had been consistently side-lined in Peru's development plans, in favour of more developed lowland and coastal areas.

Against this backdrop of social vulnerability affecting whole communities, what creates and sustains women's gendered vulnerability? In particular, a question runs through several of the papers here; how far is women's vulnerability due to their poverty and how far to non-economic factors, notably cultural norms? In the second chapter for instance, Terry Cannon raises this question when he discusses women's vulnerability to cyclones and floods in Bangladesh. He speculates that broad social and cultural changes that have improved Bangladeshi women's social status, such as reductions in fertility, may have reduced their vulnerability to disasters. On the other hand, Marlene Roy and Henry David Venema stress poverty as a key factor in women's vulnerability, although they also acknowledge that non-economic factors play an important part. They outline some of the ways climate change is likely to affect India, including through sea-level rises, flooding in the Himalayan catchment and declining water availability. The resulting losses of farm income are likely to have serious effects on the livelihoods of female agricultural labourers and smallholders, which will be compounded by their low social status. Reyes identifies the roots of women's vulnerability during the 1997–8 El Niño as poor access to education and healthcare, and lack of control over resources such as food. In turn, those inequalities made women vulnerable to the diseases that swept through the communities. The general import of these chapters is that, when analysing women's vulnerability, it may not always be possible to disentangle poverty from other types of gender inequality.

In any case, Sara Ahmed and Elizabeth Fajber show how woman's vulnerability depends on a whole range of intersecting social factors, not gender alone. In the area of Gujarat of which they write, cyclones are predicted to increase in strength and recent monsoon rains have been more intense than in the past. Although participatory research has found that women are generally more vulnerable to the effects of these changes than men, gender differences are cross-cut by class, caste and other distinctions. One of the highlights of this paper is the authors' account of the development and use of a new tool, the Vulnerability Capacity Index, which they say is designed to take the many different dimensions of vulnerability into account. The chapter by Valerie Nelson and Tanya Stathers, who are working with an aid-funded agricultural adaptation initiative in Tanzania, also illustrates how generalizations about women's vulnerability do not always tell the whole story. While they do not discuss differences among women, they comment that the impact of climate change has had positive, as well as negative, effects for women farmers in Dodoma. Many of them have reacted to changes in the climate by switching to different crops, and although that has increased their workloads, it has also brought them the benefits of higher independent earnings.

Stephanie Buechler analyses the gendered vulnerability of women in Sonora, Mexico in some detail; women there are likely to be particularly affected by water depletion related to climate change. Their vulnerability arises from their dependence on growing and processing fruit and vegetables, which in turn is linked to the fact that local cultural norms exclude them from the labour market. Meanwhile, in parts of Fiji, mangrove forests that provide protection from storm surges are being damaged, with men cutting trees for firewood and women stripping bark to make ceremonial clothing. Ruth Lane and Rebecca McNaught provide this interesting example of how local vulnerability can arise, in part, from gendered patterns of natural resource use. Whether we are male or female, we all play an active role in socio-ecological systems, for better or for worse.

Gender justice in adaptation strategies

Even if northern governments made massive cuts in carbon emissions today, the effects of climate change would still be felt for several decades, due to the time-lag between emissions being made and their impact felt (H.M. Treasury 2007). So individuals and societies need to adapt. Adaptation is different from short-term coping. While people's coping strategies may ensure immediate survival, they might fail to protect them in the long-term and could even make the situation worse. Effective adaptation, on the other hand, reduces people's vulnerability to climate shocks and stresses in the future. The term 'adaptation' covers a wide range of responses, from big government projects such as building sea-walls, to the changes people make on their own initiative, such as changing the crops they grow, taking out insurance, or finding ways to make a living that are less sensitive to the weather.

Since women in the global South are especially vulnerable, from the point of view of gender justice, adaptation resources should be channelled towards them. Women's full involvement in adaptation efforts is also essential to make sure they are effective. In sub-Saharan Africa, for instance, it is women who carry out many farming tasks, so their exclusion from adaptive innovations is highly counter-productive. As some chapters here mention, such as Lane and McNaught's, women have a vital role to play in adaptation because of their gendered knowledge, for instance in managing water resources. There are two main questions; what do women need to enable them to adapt to climate change effectively, and how can we support adaptation that is gender-just as well as effective?

On the whole, these chapters are not concerned with specific technical adaptations to environmental change, such as tree-planting or building embankments. Of course, such initiatives have an important place in the spectrum of adaptive behaviour. However, they are associated with an approach that sees vulnerability and adaptation primarily in physical, rather than social, terms. Instead, many of the writers here take a broader approach derived from analyses of unequal gendered power relations. Marlene Roy and Henry David Venema, for instance, find Amartya Sen's 'capabilities framework' useful in this context (Sen 1999). They emphasize that poor rural women in India lack basic political freedoms and are marginalized from decision-making. For them, an appropriate response to climate change is to find ways to strengthen women's voices in community-level environmental management.

On the subject of adaptation, Rosa Rivero Reyes' chapter is an interesting complement to Roy and Venema's, because she goes some way to showing how women's capacity as adaptation agents can be supported in practice. Like Roy and Venema, she sees women's ability to exercise their political rights as a crucial element of both effective adaptation and the wider process of sustainable development. Discrimination against women in Piura, Peru is a barrier to their involvement in policy formulation, so the organization CEPRODA MINGA decided to help them take part in local decision-making, and demand accountability from their regional representatives. A key point here is that, as well as being involved in deciding how to adapt to climate change, women must also have a say in setting overall development priorities and strategies. This is an important message that recurs throughout the book and is taken up in the conclusion. Like Marion Khamis et al. (see below), Reyes is keenly aware of the need to 'scale up' these local advocacy initiatives. She describes how CEPRODA MINGA took the lead in regional advocacy on gender issues, incorporating local women's demands. Rather than focusing narrowly on disaster prevention or adaptation, they prioritized equal rights at work, reducing gender-based violence and improving girls' access to education, none of which would normally be classed as adaptation, or even sustainable development, issues.

Like Reyes, Sara Ahmed and Elizabeth Fajber are also concerned with what they call community-based 'disaster governance', and like her they stress the involvement of both women and men in decision-making. One distinctive element in their approach to building adaptive capacity is their emphasis on the role of underlying systems, such as communications, transport or financial services. Poor women's and men's adaptive capacity can be strengthened both by putting good systems in place and ensuring their access to them. They document practical initiatives such as the construction of raised sanitation units in flood-proof localities, an example of adaptive infrastructure.

For Valerie Nelson and Tanya Stathers, adaptation policy should aim to develop women and men's generic ability to manage uncertainty. This derives from the idea of thresholds in the world's climate system, beyond which the climate may suddenly 'flip' from one state to another. According to some climate scientists, that could lead to drastic changes, irreversible except over unimaginably long time-scales. Only adaptive capacity in the widest sense would equip women and men to deal with such a rapid transformation in conditions.

With her focus on livelihoods, Stephanie Buechler identifies improving women's access to the labour market as the key to successful gender-sensitive adaptation in Sonora. Calling for a holistic approach, she advocates job creation and training for women and improving their access to secondary education, as well as adaptive agricultural innovations.

The Pacific region is acutely vulnerable to rising sea levels that threaten the very existence of some small islands. Lane and McNaught's chapter is full of examples of how agencies working in the region have tried to take a gender-sensitive approach to both adaptation and disaster responses. Their focus is on coastal protection, agriculture and fisheries, and they describe how gendered local knowledge can provide the basis for successful adaptation.

Gender aspects of mitigation strategies in the global South

The world needs to make a drastic and rapid cut in its greenhouse-gas emissions, to stabilize the global climate and avoid reaching a 'tipping point' beyond which very damaging consequences cannot be reversed. Greenhouse-gas emissions can be reduced in several ways: switching to renewable sources of energy and using fossil fuels more efficiently; slowing the rate of deforestation; adopting more efficient agricultural practices; and, last but not least, transforming consumption patterns in industrialized and rapidly-industrializing countries. The use of biofuels, championed by the European Union, has been widely denounced as a false solution that is already harming poor people in developing countries (e.g. Oxfam 2008a); this message also comes across loud and clear from Nidhi Tandon's chapter here. But while biofuels are a particularly iniquitous example of supposed mitigation activities that harm women's interests, in fact all the strategies listed above have the potential to affect gender relations in one way or another. Conversely, mitigation policies that aim to change behaviour in any of these areas will need to be based on a sound understanding of gender relations if they are to succeed.

Emily Boyd is interested in the potential synergy between the use of forest 'sinks' to soak up excess carbon and the promotion of gender equality. In her paper, she asks how far the Noel Kempff Climate Action Project in Bolivia contributed to meeting local women's gender needs. She observed that the project did meet some of their practical, immediate requirements, for instance by providing them with improved seeds, but that it did not address the more fundamental problem of their low social status. In their chapter, Marion Khamis, Tamara Plush and Carmen Sepúlveda Zelaya argue that if women themselves are involved in setting a project's agenda, they often start by focusing on here-and-now necessities but later go on to tackle the deeper issues that underlie their daily problems. Boyd found, though, that local women were excluded from decision making about the Noel Kempff project, so they never had a chance to make such a transition. She ends by describing it as a 'lost opportunity' for women's participation and empowerment.

One of the most stimulating aspects of Boyd's paper is that she does not confine her analysis to a single project. Rather, she attributes its failings to the mainstream model of sustainable development itself, which for her is riddled with masculine bias. To some readers her call for an alternative, 'feminine' approach to sustainable development will be controversial, because of its suggestion that all women share the same qualities and interests, and the way she seems to imply that 'feminine' and 'feminist' mean the same thing. There is a long-standing debate between two camps of female academics and women's rights activists: on one side are those who characterize men's and women's relationship to the natural world in terms of supposedly intrinsic masculine and feminine characteristics; on the other side are those who are interested in gendered social relations and the complexity of people's gendered identities. The first approach has the effect of glossing over distinctions and divisions among women. Yet, in the paper immediately after Boyd's, Sam Wong points out how a project in Bangladesh affected women in different ways because of factors such as class; a 'feminine' approach could obscure such differences.

Energia, the gender and sustainable energy network, advocates improving women's access to clean energy services, on the grounds that it could promote women's empowerment at the same time as reducing carbon emissions (e.g. ENERGIA/DFID Collaborative Research Group on Gender and Energy 2006). In his paper, however, Wong shows that this synergy cannot be taken for granted, even when organizations declare a commitment to women's empowerment. He analyses the organizational, institutional and technological changes associated with a small solar lighting project, noting how they interacted with women and men's livelihoods and power relations in the target community. Perversely, one of the project's unintentional outcomes was to increase some women's work burdens compared with men's. Wong puts forward a gender-sensitive framework for the governance of such interventions.

Nidhi Tandon's chapter repeats a rhetorical question that is implied in many of the chapters in this book: who is making the decisions about climate change mitigation and adaptation? Take the stampede into biofuel production. For Tandon, it is a gender issue; she attacks this rapidly expanding and unregulated industry as a threat to poor women's livelihoods in Africa and Asia. In general, such women have little say in how land is used, largely because of their customary exclusion from land ownership. If they were consulted, Tandon plausibly argues that they would prioritize food production over biofuel cultivation. As an alternative to growing biofuels, she calls for support to organic subsistence farming, in which women traditionally play an important role. She contrasts this approach with mainstream sustainable development policies that see livelihood diversification as the way forward for farmers in developing countries. It would need to be accompanied by other changes, such as giving women independent access to farm land and more of a say in how land is used, but she claims that these combined strategies would help women to adapt effectively to climate change.

Influencing the debate

In Tandon's view, women in the global South should 'lead change in the fields and at the grass-roots'. For her, protests are a last resort for bringing about policy change when all else fails. Chapters 12 and 13 are both concerned with how women can get policy makers to hear their adaptation and mitigation priorities. The advocacy initiatives they describe are very different, but potentially complementary.

Khamis et al. discuss a participatory video project designed to help empower poor and marginalized Nepalese women to claim their rights in a context of increasing floods, storms and droughts. The initiative followed research during which poor women from various parts of the Ganges River Basin were asked how they were dealing with erratic monsoons. The women were quite clear about the support they wanted to help them adapt to the changing climate, mentioning among other things training, information, and agricultural extension advice (ActionAid and Institute of Development Studies 2007). Action Aid and its local partner Bheri Environmental Excellence then decided to seek a way for such women to engage with, and assert themselves in, relevant policy processes. Although the video-making process turned out to be a powerful empowerment tool at the local level, the authors frankly point out the challenges of using participatory video in national and international policy debates. They also identify some ways the barriers might be overcome.

Minu Hemmati and Ulrike Röhr are also struggling to get women's voices heard in climate policy making, but they are using a different strategy. They are founding members of the GenderCC Network, and for years have regularly attended international climate negotiations, lobbying for gender issues to be mainstreamed in agreements and their practical mechanisms. The international climate protection system, set out in the UN Framework Convention on Climate Change (UNFCCC) and its protocols, aims to stabilize greenhouse-gas concentrations in order to prevent dangerous interference with the climate. Up to now, the UNFCCC's approach has combined national emissions targets, carbon emissions trading and the 'clean development mechanism'. It has assigned a crucial role to markets, confronting feminist lobbyists such as Hemmati and Röhr with a considerable challenge. Their historical account of how campaigners have tried to put gender issues on the table at a succession of annual conferences is especially useful for readers unfamiliar with these important negotiations. Although it has been hard for them to find a gender foothold on this policy rock-face, their chapter ends on a positive note. They report a growing interest in the gender justice perspective, and suggest entry points for advocacy.

Together, these chapters provide a rich and variegated resource, drawn as they are from very diverse experiences and regions. They deal with the gender implications of both climate change itself as well as the major policy and practice areas concerned with it. They highlight a range of gender issues within these areas, discuss key analytical concepts and frameworks, and show how they can be put into operation. For readers who want to promote gender justice within the climate change agenda, they will provide ideas and examples to inform, guide and inspire their own initiatives.

Notes

1. For instance, consider this sentence from a briefing paper on human rights and climate change (Oxfam 2008b); 'Over 20 years, [rich countries'] contributions to multilateral climate funds for technology transfer have been on average $437m annually: western Europeans spent ten times that much buying vacuum cleaners last year.' There is a clear masculine bias in singling out vacuum cleaners, which are associated with women's reproductive work, as symbols of inequitable energy consumption rather than, say, computer-game consoles or power drills, which are associated with men's leisure.

2.   See the articles by; Sara Ahmed and Elizabeth Fajber, Rosa Rivero Reyes, Ruth Lane and Rebecca Mcnaught and finally, Marion Khamis, Tamara Plush and Carmen Sepúlveda Zelaya.

References

ActionAid and Institute of Development Studies (2007) 'We know what we need: South Asian women speak out on climate change adaptation', London: ActionAid and Brighton: IDS.
Demetriades, J. and E. Esplen (2008) 'The gender dimensions of poverty and climate change adaptation', *IDS Bulletin* 39(4).
ENERGIA/DFID Collaborative Research Group on Gender and Energy (CRGGE) (2006) 'From the millennium development goals towards a gender-sensitive energy policy: Synthesis report', Leusden: ENERGIA and London: DFID.
H.M. Treasury (2007) *Stern Review: The Economics of Climate Change*, Cambridge: Cambridge University Press.
IPCC (Inter-governmental Panel on Climate Change) (2007) 'Fourth Assessment Report' (Synthesis Report), www.ipcc.ch/ipccreports/ar4-syr.htm [accessed 9 June 2009].
Oxfam (2008a) 'Another inconvenient truth: How biofuel policies are deepening poverty and accelerating climate change', Oxfam Briefing Paper 114, Oxford: Oxfam International.
Oxfam (2008b) 'Climate wrongs and human rights: Putting people at the heart of climate-change policy', Oxfam briefing paper 117, Oxford: Oxfam International.
Sen, A. (1999) *Development as Freedom*, New York: Knopf.
UNFCCC (United Nations Framework Convention on Climate Change) (n.d.) 'Emissions Trading', www.unfccc.int [accessed 9 June 2009].
UNFPA (2007) *State of World Population 2007: Unleashing the Potential of Urban Growth*, New York: UNFPA, http://www.unfpa.org/public/publications/pid/408 [accessed 19 June 2009]
Zahur, M. (2008) 'Pakistan: Climate Change and the Gender Implications', www.gdnonline.org

About the author

Geraldine Terry is researching gender aspects of climate risk in Uganda. She is based at the School of International Development at the University of East Anglia and is affiliated to the Tyndall Centre for Research on Climate Change and the Makerere Institute of Social Research, Kampala. She is the author of *Women's Rights*, published by Pluto Press, and editor of *Gender-based Violence* (Oxfam GB), also in the 'Working in Gender and Development' series.

CHAPTER 2
Gender and climate hazards in Bangladesh

Terry Cannon

This chapter first appeared in *Gender and Development* 10(2), pp. 45–50, 2002.

Bangladesh has recently experienced a number of high-profile disasters, including devastating cyclones and annual floods. Poverty is both a cause of vulnerability, and a consequence of hazard impacts. Evidence that the impacts of disasters are worse for women is inconclusive or variable. However, since being female is strongly linked to being poor, unless poverty is reduced, the increase in disasters and extreme climate events linked with climate change is likely to affect women more than men. In addition, there are some specific gender attributes which increase women's vulnerability in some respects. These gendered vulnerabilities may, however, be reduced by social changes.

To many from outside, Bangladesh is almost synonymous with disasters. In a country smaller than Britain, and with more than twice as many people, around one-third of the land is flooded every summer. The monsoon rains cover the low-lying land, and swell the three major river systems that struggle to find outlets to the sea. In some years, such as in 1998, nearly half of the land area of Bangladesh is under water. Tropical cyclones strike the coast at least once a year, bringing rainwater floods, salt-water incursions, and wind damage. Since the 1991 cyclone disaster, effective warning systems, coupled with the use of many more cyclone shelters, have reduced the toll to a fraction of earlier tragedies, and now the number of deaths each year is usually less than a thousand.

The inland rain and riverine floods have attracted considerable foreign attention and aid, as evidenced by the Flood Action Plan (FAP) of the early 1990s. Yet, paradoxically, the deaths caused by these events rarely exceed a few thousand – in contrast to the death toll of cyclones – and never reach tens of thousands. Floods are very visible and may appear to be a disaster, even though they are vital to the livelihoods of almost all of the rural population. Therein lies a second paradox: most of the rural population actually considers it a disaster when there is no flood. Without the annual cycle of inundation and silt, the fertility of fields is diminished, and they produce a much lower yield as a result of lack of water. Moreover, fish breeding is disrupted and output diminished when flooding does not create ponds and interconnections between waterways. This is a severe disadvantage to the poor who depend on fish as their main source of protein (and sometimes income).

This does not mean that floods should always be regarded as beneficial, or that people do not lose lives, assets, or become even poorer as a result of them (for example, those who lose land from erosion by the shifting of river channels in floods). However, while a flood can produce an obvious deepening of poverty, its absence has invisible consequences that may be just as bad. A distinction is made in Bengali between 'good' and 'bad' floods to reflect the difference. In general, the majority of the rural population would lose out rather than benefit from the prevention of flooding, by engineering measures such as embankments and river containment, envisaged in the FAP. The benefits of 'good' floods outweigh the disadvantages of the 'bad' (Blaikie *et al.* 1994). In a rare sample survey of rural people's attitudes to floods, 86 per cent of households were satisfied with the way that they adjusted to normal inundation, and did not want any change to that situation (Leaf 1997).

Climate change, hazards, and their gender dimensions

The principal climatic hazards affecting Bangladesh – floods and cyclones – are likely to increase in frequency, intensity, duration, and extent. The summer monsoon rainfall is projected to increase, swelling the main river systems in the wider catchment, and boosting the rainfall impact within the country. More rapid glacial melting in the Himalayan headwaters will also increase spring and early summer flows, further increasing the flood risk. In winter, problems of drought will increase. The current winter dry season (which already limits agriculture and particularly affects poorer farmers who cannot afford to irrigate) is likely to become significantly worse (World Bank 2000). Cyclones are low-pressure systems, which means that as well as causing rainfall flooding and wind damage, they raise sea levels and bring storm surges that flood the coast with salt-water. With rising sea levels, it is estimated that within a century the coastline will retreat by, on average, about 10 kilometres, causing the loss of 18 per cent of the country's land area. This will mean that the impacts of cyclones will be felt further inland than they have been to date (*op. cit.*, ii).

How these increased hazard impacts will affect women in particular, is extremely difficult to predict. The link between poverty and vulnerability is clearly crucial, and affects women disproportionately. If there is no serious progress in reducing poverty, then it can be assumed that women will become increasingly affected by the impact of intensified hazards, in terms of their ability to resist and recover from them. This outcome may be modified if there are more general reductions in economic inequalities between men and women.

It is also important that non-economic ('cultural') factors which produce gender inequality are also addressed – for instance, so that women can adequately seek shelter without shame and harassment, and are not condemned to poverty and increased vulnerability when widowed or divorced. These are issues that are already on the sustainable development agenda, and so it could be argued that reducing women's vulnerability to hazards will follow from this agenda. However, such an approach does not adequately address the specific gender dimensions of disaster preparedness. Evidence from Schmuck (2002), German Red Cross (1999), Baden *et al.* (1994), Rashid and Michaud (2000), Enarson (2000), Enarson and Morrow (1997), and Khondker (1996), all suggest that there are specific gendered factors which it is essential to take into account in order to reduce the vulnerability of women.

Understanding disasters and vulnerability

Disasters happen only when a natural hazard impacts negatively on vulnerable people. The severity of a disaster is therefore a reflection both of the location and intensity of the hazard, and of the number of people of given levels and types of vulnerability. For instance, tropical storms of similar intensity affect the USA and Bangladesh, but with very different outcomes. In 1992, Hurricane Andrew struck Florida, and caused more than 28 billion pounds' worth of damage, but killed fewer than 20 people (Morrow 1997). The year before, the cyclone that struck the south-east coast of Bangladesh killed 140,000 people, and ruined the livelihoods of millions (German Red Cross 1999). This does not mean that the people of Florida were unscathed and that they did not suffer (physically and mentally) from loss of homes, schools, jobs, and possessions. But the illustration shows how the impact of an equivalent hazard on different communities is related to differing levels of social vulnerability. This vulnerability can be considered to have five components, which vary from higher to lower levels according to political and social factors affecting different groups of people: namely, the initial conditions of a person, the resilience of their livelihood, their opportunities for self-protection, and their access to social protection and social capital (Cannon 2000; Blaikie *et al.* 1994). These differ hugely between the contexts of Bangladesh and the USA.

To understand a disaster, we need to understand the components of vulnerability of different groups of people, and relate these to the hazard risk (Cannon 2000; Blaikie *et al.* 1994). Vulnerability differs according to the 'initial conditions' of a person – how well-fed they are, what their physical and mental health and mobility are, and their morale and capacity for self reliance. It is also related to the resilience of their livelihood – how quickly and easily they can resume activities that will earn money or provide food and other basics. The hazard itself must be recognized, and the fact that vulnerability will be lower if people are able to put proper 'self-protection' in place – e.g. the right type of building to resist high winds, or a house site that is raised above flood levels. People also usually need some form of 'social protection' from hazards: forms of preparedness provided by institutions at levels above the household. These supplement what people cannot afford or are unable to do for themselves, and provide opportunities to implement measures that can only be provided collectively (e.g. codes to improve building safety, warning systems).

Social protection depends on adequate government or non-government systems being in place, while self-protection generally relies on people having an adequate income, knowledge of the hazard, and propensity and capacity to take precautions. In many hazardous places, people's vulnerability is also reduced if they are able to draw on adequate social capital. People may need to rely on each other, on family, and on organizations, at all stages of a disaster – from search and rescue after impact, to coping and sharing in the recovery period. Social capital may not always be neutral and benign: there are examples of disaster recovery where some people identified in a particular social group received assistance not made available to others, as after the Gujerat earthquake of 2000 (Vidal 2002).

Gender inequality, women's status, and capacity for protection

How are these components of vulnerability affected by gender relations, and how different are the vulnerabilities of men and women in relation to disasters in Bangladesh? From an analysis of existing gendered vulnerabilities, can we project what may happen in terms of climate change and the possible increase in frequency and intensity of climate hazards? Vulnerability in Bangladesh correlates strongly with poverty, and it is widely accepted that women make up a disproportionate share of poor people. How much of women's vulnerability to hazards can be apportioned to them being poor, and how much is due to specific 'gendered' characteristics of self protection, social protection, and livelihood resilience? And how will this be affected by climate change?

In fact, it is difficult to separate these two aspects of female vulnerability, precisely because gender plays a significant role in determining poverty. A recent Asian Development Bank report suggested that over 95 per cent of female-headed households are below the poverty line. The proportion of female-headed households in Bangladesh was officially reported as ten per cent, but other evidence cited suggests that a more realistic figure is 20–30 per cent (Asian Development Bank 2001). Many of these households consist of women who have been divorced or widowed, and who are culturally discouraged from remarrying. Ninety per cent of those who are single as the result of bereavement or divorce are women (*ibid.*). As a result, vulnerability to hazards involves a complex interaction between poverty and gender relations, in which women are likely to experience higher levels of vulnerability than men.

Women's nutritional status and coping capacity

Women's poorer nutritional status is a key aspect of their reduced capacity to cope with the effects of a hazard. In Bangladesh, women of all ages are more calorie-deficient than men, and the prevalence of chronic energy deficiency among women is the highest in the world (del Ninno *et al*. 2001). Although this study of the 1998 flood found no evidence of any increase in discrimination against females, it is clear that the situation is potentially disastrous. 'Given the already precarious nutritional state of large numbers of girls and women in Bangladesh... any further increase in discrimination against females in food consumption would have serious consequences.' (*op. cit.*, 64). Women also receive less and poorer-quality healthcare in comparison with men. Bangladesh is one of the few countries in the world where men live longer than women, and where the male population outnumbers the female (Asian Development Bank 2001).

Women's domestic burden and increased hardship

There is evidence that floods increase women's domestic burden. The loss of utensils and other household essentials is a great hardship, and floods also undermine women's well-being in general because of their dependence on economic activities linked to the home (Khondker 1996). In their study of gender in Bangladesh, Baden *et al.* found that women are likely to be less successful, and find it more difficult to restore their livelihoods, after a flood. Losses of harvest and livestock have a disproportionate impact on women, many of whom rely on food processing, cattle, and chickens for their cash income (Baden *et al.* 1994). Fetching water becomes much more difficult, and it may be contaminated. Water-borne illness might be expected to be more widespread among women, who are nutritionally disadvantaged. Women are likely to suffer increased mental strain, and bear the brunt of certain social constraints, for instance, they are shamed by using public latrines, or being seen by men when in wet clothing (Rashid and Michaud 2000).

Women's reduced ability to provide self-protection

Poverty is a key factor affecting people's ability to provide adequate self-protection, and it is likely that in female-headed households, the ability of women to create safe conditions in the face of impending floods or cyclones is reduced. The quality of housing, a location on raised ground, adequate storage for food – all are crucial to self-protection, but are more difficult for poor women to achieve. Both self- and social protection are also affected by gender issues related to 'culture'. During cyclones, women are handicapped by fear of the shame attached to leaving the house and moving in public. It may be too late when they eventually seek refuge. Societal attitudes restricting interaction between men and women make women more reluctant to congregate in the public cyclone shelters (raised concrete structures that protect from wind and flood) where they are forced to interact with other men. However, NGO activities to increase understanding and make warnings more effective seem to have improved this over the past ten years (German Red Cross 1999). Women's mobility is restricted as a result of their responsibility for their children. Their clothing restricts their mobility in floods, and in addition, women are less likely than men to know how to swim. It is estimated that 90 per cent of the victims of the 1991 cyclone disasters were women and children (Schmuck 2002).

Social change: a glimmer of hope?

There is evidence that some aspects of social change in Bangladesh are improving women's lives and reducing gender inequalities. The average number of children that a woman bears has declined significantly over the last 20 years, from 6.34 in 1975 to around 3.3 in 2001 (BBC 2001). This has significantly reduced women's child-care burden. It has also made their lives safer: more women die as a result of childbirth in Bangladesh than anywhere else in the world. Whether the significant cultural shifts inherent in this decline in fertility rates can have any impact in other areas of society, including on gender differences in vulnerability to climate hazards, is impossible to predict. If progress continues to be made in improving women's lives and reducing gender inequalities, through other initiatives such as micro-credit schemes for women, and associated empowerment activities by NGOs, then there is potential to reduce women's unequal vulnerability as the hazards increase with climate change.

References

Asian Development Bank (2001) 'Country Briefing Paper: Women in Bangladesh', Manila: Asian Development Bank.

Baden, S., C. Green, A.M. Goetz, and M. Guhathakurta (1994) 'Background report on gender issues in Bangladesh', *BRIDGE Report* 26, Sussex: Institute of Development Studies.

BBC (2001) 'Family planning in Bangladesh', World Service, 1 October, http://www.BBC.co.uk/worldservice/sci_tech/highlights/011001_bangladesh.shtml [accessed 9 June 2009].

Blaikie, P., T. Cannon, I. Davis, and B. Wisner (1994) *At Risk: Natural Hazards, People's Vulnerability and Disasters*, London: Routledge.

Cannon, T. (2000) 'Vulnerability analysis and disasters', in D.J. Parker (ed.), *Floods*, London: Routledge.

del Ninno, C., P.A. Dorosh, L.C. Smith, and D.K. Roy (2001) 'The 1998 floods in Bangladesh: disaster impacts, household coping strategies, and response', *Research Report* 122, Washington DC: International Food Policy Research Institute.

Enarson, E. (2000) 'Gender and natural disasters', *Working Paper* 1 (Recovery and Reconstruction Department), Geneva: ILO.

Enarson, E. and B.H. Morrow (1997) 'A gendered perspective: the voices of women', in W.G. Peacock *et al.* (eds.), *Hurricane Andrew: Ethnicity, Gender and the Sociology of Disasters*, London: Routledge.

German Red Cross (1999) 'Living with cyclones: disaster preparedness in India and Bangladesh', Bonn: German Red Cross.

Khondker, H.H. (1996) 'Women and floods in Bangladesh', *International Journal of Mass Emergencies and Disasters*, 14(3): 281–92.

Leaf , M. (1997) 'Local control versus technocracy: the Bangladesh Flood Response Study', *Journal of International Affairs* 511: 179–200.

Morrow, B.H. (1997) 'Disaster in the first person', in W.G. Peacock *et al.* (eds.), *Hurricane Andrew: Ethnicity, Gender and the Sociology of Disasters*, London: Routledge.

Rashid, S.F. and S. Michaud (2000) 'Female adolescents and their sexuality: notions of honour, shame, purity and pollution during the floods', *Disasters* 241: 54–70.

Schmuck, H. (2002) 'Empowering women in Bangladesh', http://www.reliefweb.int [accessed 9 June 2009].

Vidal, J. (2002) 'Helping hands', *The Guardian*, 30 January 2002 World Bank (2000) 'Bangladesh: climate change and sustainable development', Report no. 21104 BD, Dhaka: South Asia Rural Development Team.

About the author

Terry Cannon is a Visiting Fellow at the International Institute for Environment and Development (IIED), working with the Climate Change Group.

CHAPTER 3

Reducing risk and vulnerability to climate change in India: the capabilities approach

Marlene Roy and Henry David Venema

This chapter first appeared in *Gender and Development* 10(2), pp. 78–83, 2002.

This chapter argues that the ability of women to adapt to climate change pressures will be enhanced by using the 'capabilities approach' to direct development efforts. By using this approach, women will improve their well-being, and act more readily as agents of change within their communities. This argument is supported by previous research on gender and livelihoods, and a study conducted in rural India. Examples are based on the experiences of poor, rural women in India, who are particularly vulnerable to climate change impacts. Their survival is dependent on their being able to obtain many essential resources from their immediate environment. Yet these women lack many of the requirements for well-being, such as access to healthcare, literacy, and control over their own lives. Gaining these would reduce their vulnerability to their changing environmental circumstances.

The need to respond and adapt to climate change has become widely recognized, and people will have to deal with its impacts, with or without the help of government. The roles and activities of women and men are socially constructed, and gender-differentiated. Climate adaptation and mitigation strategies need to appreciate the different realities of women and men, in order to identify positive solutions for both. As Amartya Sen and others have shown, poor rural women in India generally have fewer rights and assets than men. They experience inequalities in such areas as healthcare and nutrition; are more likely to suffer sex-selective abortion or infanticide; are less likely to receive an education; have lower access to employment and promotion in occupations; lack ownership of homes, land, and property; and take disproportionate responsibility for housework and child-care (Patel 2002). This asymmetrical division of labour, rights, and assets leaves women more vulnerable to – and less able to cope with – the additional stress and deprivation brought about by climate change.

The situation of poor rural women in India

Rural men and women in India are historically bound to its agrarian land-scape, with which they have co-evolved throughout centuries of change. Today, unprecedented challenges, including a growing population, environmental hazards in the form of climate change and land degradation, and the globalization of markets, are driving the need for fundamentally different social arrangements.

The millions of rural income-poor of India, of whom 50 per cent are concentrated in the states of Bihar, Madhya Pradesh, and Uttar Pradesh, are caught in the middle of this sea-change without compass or rudder (UNDP 1997, 51). Since 1950, they have been rocked by the privatization of communal land, the Green Revolution, and the introduction of often expensive agricultural technologies, and have been pushed onto marginal land, resulting in decreased yields and increasing out-migration to non-farm employment, particularly amongst men.

Marginalization of poor rural women

Increasingly, women are sustaining their livelihoods as farm labourers rather than as cultivators, with their knowledge and labour largely marginalized as a result of mechanization and other technical interventions, which they are traditionally excluded from using. In addition, their workload has increased, as the switch to high-yielding varieties of grains has created fewer crops and animal wastes for animal fodder and household fuel, the provision of which is largely the domain of poor peasant and tribal women (Venkateswaran 1995; Agarwal 1997). Moreover, the traditional usufruct rights that women held to community land were lost after land reforms, thus denying them access to these lands where, 'the landless and landpoor [had] procured over 90 per cent of their firewood and satisfied 69-89 per cent of their grazing needs' in the 1980s (FAO 1997; Agarwal 2001, 1625).

Women's labour linked to household welfare and income

Of the total Indian female work force, 89.5 per cent works in rural India, and contributes extensively to household welfare and income (FAO 1997). According to Venkateswaran, women are estimated to contribute on average between 55 to 60 per cent of the total labour of farm production (Venkateswaran 1995, 20). They often start contributing to household economic activities before they are 15, with some putting in a full day's work by the time they are ten. They undertake the bulk of work necessary to maintain the home, contribute manual labour to the cultivation of plots, and care for farm animals (Venkateswaran 1995, 24). There is some variation within India, however. For example, in both hill and mountain regions, and in arid and semi-arid areas where forests have disappeared and agriculture remains poor, women spend between six and ten hours daily collecting the resources they need to meet their basic survival needs (Centre for Science and Environment 1999). Those in the rich plains areas, where forest biomass has been replaced by agriculture biomass, spend less time on these tasks, though poor women in these areas who don't own land or whose landholdings are slight, find themselves at the mercy of major landowners to meet their fuel and fodder needs (*op. cit.*).

High female illiteracy rates

Rural women have few options, especially with the loss of usufruct rights to community land. Education, which could increase their choices and opportunities, remains limited or non-existent. Even though there has been an increase in the literacy rate for Indian women overall, over 161 million rural women (approximately 70 per cent) are still illiterate (Government of India 2001). While many children attend school until the age of ten, girls usually drop out earlier to help at home. In addition, rural Indian women have little power within the household, and their contribution, especially in family enterprises, is often hidden from public awareness (Simmons 1997). This lack of power extends beyond the family, as women rarely participate in community-level decision making, and are consequently less able to act as agents of change to better their situation.

The impacts of climate change on the rural poor

Low-caste, tribal, and poor rural women, dependent as they are on their natural environment for water, fuel, fodder, and food, are immediately and adversely affected by all forms of environmental degradation, including climate change impacts. The Intergovernmental Panel on Climate Change (IPCC) considers India, with its large, agrarian population, to be acutely vulnerable to the impacts of climate change, and recent extreme weather events such as the cyclones in Orissa in 1999, and the severe drought in northern and central India in 2000, support this view. In addition, a 1998 World Bank report on the impacts of climate change on Indian agriculture maintained that these impacts would be region-specific, and could be significant for poor people living on marginal land.

While severe weather events such as cyclones, monsoons, and drought cannot be directly attributed to climate change, they do, nevertheless, illustrate the very real and probable impacts of climate change on the rural poor. The drought in Orissa, for example, forced many small and marginal farmers to give part of their landholdings to moneylenders, with unofficial estimates indicating that another half million people were forced into distress migration.

According to a briefing paper presented to the Indian Parliament by the Centre for Science and Environment in 2000, climate change manifestations in India will include increased temperatures, sea level rise along coastal regions, changes in monsoon rain patterns such as a decline in summer rainfall, increased flooding in the Himalayan catchment, and water resource problems in arid and semi-arid regions (Agarwal 2000; IPCC 2001). These impacts will affect agriculture and forestry, as well as human health. Agriculture, in particular, will experience decreased yields, as crop cycles shorten (for rice between 15–42 per cent and for wheat between 25–55 per cent), rainfall decreases, and conditions more conducive to pest infections, are created by rising temperatures. Consequently, researchers have made conservative estimates that farm incomes will decrease by 8.4–12.3 per cent (Sanghi 1997; Kumar and Parikh 1998).

A decline in farm-level income alone will have deleterious effects on the rural poor, particularly women, who are among the lowest-paid agricultural labourers (Venkateswaran 1995). In addition, women whose livelihoods depend on cultivating small plots and gathering fodder and fuel will be even more vulnerable as climate change advances, as they do not presently have access to the necessary resources or social status within households and communities (Adger and Kelly 1999). What can be done to reduce their vulnerability and help them adapt to their changing circumstances?

Increasing capabilities and reducing risk

According to Amartya Sen, there are five instrumental freedoms that, if present, and if women have access to them, will provide opportunities for women to act in their own self-interest and reduce their vulnerability. Access to these instrumental freedoms, namely political freedom, economic facilities, social opportunities, transparency guarantees, and protective security – is necessary for women to gain a better quality of life and acquire the capabilities they need to act as their own agents of change (Sen 1999).

Commonly referred to as the 'capabilities approach', Nussbaum (2000) describes this approach as, 'an approach to the priorities of development that focuses not on preference-satisfaction but on what people are actually able to do and to be'. Central to this approach is the idea that freedom is more than citizens having rights 'on paper': it also requires that citizens have the resources to exercise those rights. Thus, the capabilities approach goes beyond asking about satisfaction of people's preferences to ask what women's opportunities and liberties actually are, as well as how the available resources work or do not work in enabling women to function.

According to Sen, this 'capabilities approach' to development has considerable potential for enabling and empowering poor rural women.

> These different aspects (women's earning power, economic role outside the family, literacy and education, property rights and so on) may at first sight appear to be rather diverse and disparate. But what they have in common is their positive contribution in adding force to women's voice and agency – through independence and empowerment. (Sen 1999, 191–2)

REDUCING RISK AND VULNERABILITY TO CLIMATE CHANGE IN INDIA   **23**

Development in Kerala and the capabilities approach

The state of Kerala in southern India provides some insight into the usefulness of Sen's approach, as several aspects of Kerala's development path bear similarities to those advocated as part of the capabilities approach. Despite its low per capita income, Kerala is notable because it has the lowest birth rates, highest literacy rates, and longest life expectancy in India and, hence, is a low-consumption economy that delivers a high quality of life. Civil rights campaigns and caste reforms began in Kerala during the nineteenth century. Equitable access to education spread in the early twentieth century, and again in the 1960s, and the success of a campaign for universal literacy resulted in the newly literate writing letters to government offices demanding better services such as paved roads and hospitals (McKibben 1996).

Affordable healthcare is also widely available in Kerala, along with nutrition programmes. In addition, there appears to be much less gender discrimination, and a robust media and political structure. Recently, the government started a 'land literacy' programme known as the 'People's Resource Mapping Program', in which local villages map their local resources. These community maps are then combined with scientific maps to guide local environmental and social planning, with villagers taking and implementing the decisions (McKibben 1996).

Village women as agents of change

The provision of Sen's five instrumental freedoms is, however, dependent on cultural norms and rules that are manifested in a myriad of ways, including through roles and responsibilities within families, and through policies, practices, and legislation at community and state level. In India there exist numerous formal and informal arrangements and institutions that shape the different capabilities of men and women. One well-known example is the caste system, which is still prominent in many areas of rural India, and which greatly influences individuals' access to rights. For example, people from scheduled castes form 'the weakest economic segment of rural society with limited access to education and financial institutions, and little effective voice' (Simmons and Supri 1997, 311).

Informal institutional reform, whereby individuals at the community level become agents of change, appears to be a good option for increasing the ability of the poor to adapt to climate change. Chopra and Duraiappah (2001) indicate how vested interests work to prevent institutional change. They argue that the best development approach is through improved environmental and land management in communities, based on Sen's concept of five freedoms, which challenges the status quo. Two case studies conducted in Bihar and Rajasthan indicate that this type of development can be successful (Chopra and Duraiappah 2001). In Bihar, an informal institution called 'Chakroya Vikas Pranali' was formed to negotiate a set of rules to govern the use of local land

and water resources. The success of Chakroya Vikas Pranali was attributed to transparency in decision-making and sharing benefits, risk minimization, and increased protective security through the distribution of economic and social opportunities amongst individuals over time.

Certainly, better environmental management at the community level is seen by many experts as essential to efforts aimed at minimizing climate change impacts. However, women may not benefit from such community-led change unless these local and informal institutional arrangements are shaped by the specific and often different needs, roles, and responsibilities of men and women. Research conducted by Agarwal (2001) on participation in joint forestry management projects indicates that while women may be active in all-women community groups, their participation in other community-based organizations is generally low. In some cases, women were actively excluded by men even though spaces were reserved for women on the local councils. This lack of participation by women indicates that political freedom, one of Sen's five freedoms, is not generally available to women, thus restricting what they are able to do and to become. Moreover, the absence of political freedom is critical, as it is a prerequisite for many of the changes necessary for women to take an active part in shaping rural development that meets their needs (Chopra and Duraiappah 2001).

Conclusions

By using the capabilities approach to direct land and environmental management changes in communities, the well-being of the rural poor can be improved. This has the potential to go a long way towards reducing their vulnerability to the risks of climate change. Poor rural women, who are already among the most vulnerable, must be specially considered in such development efforts, however, and their right to participate in decision-making must be promoted and protected.

References

Adger, W.N. and P. Kelly (1999) 'Social vulnerability to climate change and the architecture of entitlements', *Mitigation and Adaptation Strategies for Global Change* 4(3–4), 253–66.

Agarwal, A. (2000) 'Climate Change: a Challenge to India's Economy. A Briefing Paper for Members of Parliament', occasional paper, Centre for Science and Environment, New Delhi : CDE, http://www.cseindia.org/html/cmp/cse_briefing.pdf [last checked by author April 2002].

Agarwal, B. (1997) 'The gender and environment debate: lessons from India', in N. Visvanathan et al. (eds.), *The Women, Gender and Development Reader*, London: Zed Books.

Agarwal, B. (2001) 'Participatory exclusions, community forestry, and gender: an analysis for South Asia and a conceptual framework', *World Development* 29(10): 1623–48.

Centre for Science and Environment (1999) *State of India's Environment: The Citizen's Fifth Report*, New Delhi: CDE.

Chopra, K. and A.K. Duraiappah (2001) 'Operationalizing capabilities and freedom in a segmented society: the role of institutions', paper presented at a conference on 'Justice and Poverty: Examining Sen's Capability Approach', Cambridge, UK, June 2001, Winnipeg: International Institute for Sustainable Development.

FAO (1997) *SD Dimensions: Asia's Women in Agriculture, Environment and Rural Production: India*, http://www.fao.org/sd/WPdirect/WPre0108.htm [accessed 9 June 2009].

Government of India (2001) *Census 2001* (provisional), http://www.censusindia.net/results/2001_Census_Data_Release_List.htm [last checked by author April 2002].

IPCC (2001) *Climate Change 2001: Impacts, Adaptation, and Vulnerability*, Geneva: Intergovernmental Panel on Climate Change.

Kumar, K. and J. Parikh (1998) 'Climate change impacts on Indian agriculture: the Ricardian approach', in Dinar et al., *Measuring the Impacts of Climate Change on Indian Agriculture*, World Bank Technical Paper 402, Washington DC: World Bank.

McKibben, B. (1996) 'The enigma of Kerala', *Utne Reader*, March–April: 103–12.

Nussbaum, M. (2000) 'Women and work – the capabilities approach', *The Little Magazine* 11, http://www.littlemag.com/martha.htm [accessed 9 June 2009].

Patel, V. (2002) 'Of famines and missing women', *Humanscape* 9(4), http://humanscapeindia.net/humanscape/new/april02/culturematters.htm [last checked by author April 2002].

Sanghi, A. (1997) 'Global warming and climate sensitivity: Brazilian and Indian agriculture', unpublished PhD thesis, Department of Economics, University of Chicago, Chicago IL.

Sen, A. (1999) *Development as Freedom*, New York: Anchor Books.

Simmons, C. and S. Supri (1997) 'Rural development, employment, and off-farm activities: a study of rural households in Rurka Kalan Development Block, north-west India', *Journal of Rural Studies* 13(3): 305–18.

UNDP (1997) *Human Development Report*, New York: UNDP.

Venkateswaran, S. (1995) *Environment, Development and the Gender Gap*, New Delhi: Sage Publications.

About the authors

Marlene Roy is a researcher on gender and sustainable development at the International Institute for Sustainable Development, Winnipeg, Canada. Henry David Venema is Program Director, Sustainable Natural Resources Management at the International Institute for Sustainable Development, Winnipeg, Canada.

CHAPTER 4

Gendering responses to El Niño in rural Peru

Rosa Rivero Reyes[1]

This chapter first appeared in *Gender and Development* 10(2), pp. 60–69, 2002.

Climatic disasters are a recurrent problem in Peru. The impacts of disasters differ between and within regions and communities. Rural upland communities, largely dependent on small-scale agriculture and natural resources for survival, are particularly vulnerable to the negative effects of extreme climate events. Government policies have not only failed to mitigate this vulnerability, but have served to exacerbate it. Women face particular vulnerabilities in the context of extreme climate events. Traditional analysis and government policy approaches have served to obscure these. This chapter reflects on the gender-specific lessons learned by the Centre for Andean Advancement and Development, CEPRODA MINGA, during its work with poor rural communities in the Piura region of Peru in the aftermath of the 1997-8 El Niño phenomenon. It focuses on the ways in which rural communities, and women in particular, have traditionally been excluded from policy creation, and considers how they can become influential social and political actors creating their own strategies for sustainable development and disaster mitigation and preparedness.

Disasters are a recurrent problem in Peru. Over the past five years, around one million Peruvians have been directly affected by major disasters, and perhaps the same number again have experienced the negative effects of smaller scale events (Villarreal 2002). One of the major disasters to take place in recent years was the 1997–8 El Niño phenomenon. El Niño is a regular climatic occurrence. It takes place every five years or so, when the cold Humboldt current that flows north from Antarctica along the coast of Chile and Peru is replaced with a warmer, southern-flowing current from the tropics. This new current raises sea temperature, and causes heavy rainfall, floods, and landslides in some areas, and drought in others. The severity of El Niño's impact varies from year to year, and from place to place.

While the relationship between global processes of climate change, and specific climate events like the 1997–8 El Niño remains unclear, one of the predicted outcomes of climate change is that extreme climate events will occur with greater frequency and severity. Existing experiences of responding to climate-related disasters, particularly those amongst more vulnerable populations, can offer important lessons for informing disaster prevention and mitigation in the future.

In Peru, the impacts of the 1997–8 El Niño phenomenon were particularly severe. Over 100,000 homes were either damaged or destroyed by floods and landslides, affecting around half a million people. Three-quarters of those affected were from rural areas (Villarreal 2002).

The Centre for Andean Advancement and Development, CEPRODA MINGA, is an NGO working in the Piura region of northern Peru. This mountainous, predominantly rural area is particularly vulnerable to the negative impacts of El Niño events. CEPRODA MINGA works with local communities to build women's and men's capacities as social and political actors, and to strengthen local institutions. CEPRODA MINGA undertakes participative planning with the region's rural communities in order to influence the formation of local, regional, and national policies for sustainable development and disaster prevention. A principal objective of this work is to develop a 'gender policy agenda' for the region, and to mainstream an understanding of gender relations into all policy formation for sustainable development.

Differential impacts of the 1997–8 El Niño phenomenon in the Piura region

The impacts of the 1997–8 El Niño phenomenon varied considerably within and between regions in Peru. While agriculture in the coastal areas of Piura benefited from improved climatic conditions, its upland areas experienced heavy rainfall causing soil, forest, and crop degradation, and leading to decreased agricultural production and capacity (Torres 1998).

Small-scale agriculture and natural resources represent the principal source of food and income for rural upland communities in the Piura region. Repeated experience of severe El Niño events over recent decades, with inadequate environmental, economic, and social recovery in-between, has diminished these communities' abilities to prepare for, and cope with, disaster. Food insecurity is an ongoing problem in the region, exacerbated, rather than created, by El Niño. The absence of an agrarian development policy with a focus on small-scale agriculture has led to food insecurity, increased rural-urban migration, and environmental degradation. In addition, before the disaster, national economic policies had favoured developments in coastal areas over those in the rural uplands. As a result, communities in upland areas found themselves in a doubly vulnerable situation at the time of El Niño. To survive in these conditions, small-scale agriculturalists have to exert considerable pressure on woods and other natural resources in order to supplement diminishing returns from agriculture. This negative cycle leaves their least powerful members increasingly vulnerable to loss, damage, and food insecurity (CLADEM 2001).

The losses and damages sustained during the El Niño event caused household income to fall dramatically during 1997, and increased the exposure of rural households to acute food insecurity. During the most critical period of El Niño, when many rural communities were flooded or cut-off, food supplies were extremely scarce, and prices increased to levels beyond the incomes of the poorest households.

Analysing the gender-differentiated impacts of El Niño

While the scientific community has developed a better understanding of, and ability to predict, El Niño events, this research has not prioritized a social analysis of the effects of El Niño, or a gender differentiated understanding of El Niño's impacts. Where social data have been collected, these have often been aggregated in a way that obscures gender differences. The observations below have arisen from CEPRODA MINGA's work with rural communities in Piura.

Discrimination against women means that women in rural Piura typically have low access to education, specialist technical assistance, healthcare, or control over the family's productive resources. These widespread and profound inequalities put poor women (and their children) in a situation of particular vulnerability to food insecurity during El Niño. Gender inequalities in food distribution and consumption within households were common, including during periods where households as a whole appeared to have sufficient food. Widespread malnutrition also exposed women and children disproportionately to epidemics (acute respiratory and diarrhoeal infections, malaria, dengue, and cholera), which increased significantly during El Niño. Pregnant women were at particular risk from malaria, which causes serious complications during pregnancy, and other peri- and post-partum illnesses.

Increased migration of men out of the area into the coastal valleys and cities in search of employment increased the numbers of temporarily female-headed households. Female-headed households faced particular challenges in their attempts to survive the effects of El Niño. Women heads of households were typically not recognized as such by the major rural community organizations (largely led by men).[2] Equally, the increased burden of household and agricultural work placed on women in the absence of men posed an acute limitation to their ability to seek paid employment.[3] Nonetheless, as we shall see, women in Piura were able to develop various survival strategies and capacities with which to tackle the problems generated by El Niño.

Government responses to El Niño and disaster prevention in Peru

The El Niño policy context

Peruvian regional authorities have barely acknowledged the differentiated effects of El Niño in the Piura region. This differentiation has political implications, and is connected with regional processes of development. Over the past 50 years, regional development models have favoured the development of agro-export industries (cotton and rice) in the coastal valleys, along with the development of major oil industry and irrigation infrastructure projects. Communities in rural upland areas have largely been excluded from these processes of development, and have suffered from the absence of an agrarian development policy focused on the needs and realities of subsistence farmers. National economic policy is dependent on primary exports of minerals, fish, and agricultural products, tending to marginalize considerations of environmental protection, sustainability, or small-scale production for local consumption. The concentration of economically important industry in the coastal region also entailed that the majority of emergency and reconstruction interventions taking place during and following El Niño were focused on coastal areas.

Understanding and responding to disasters – the failure of top-down responses

The mainstream view of El Niño events is to consider them as isolated and bounded disasters, arising from natural causes, which must be scientifically understood, predicted, controlled, and prevented using large-scale technical interventions (Wilches-Chaux 1998). The Peruvian government's response to the threat of El Niño has typically been to prioritize the construction of preventative physical infrastructure and other technical responses, and to focus this on regions of greater national economic importance. A view of disasters as isolated occurrences creates an approach to civil defence that is restricted and temporary, and prevents its institutionalization as a part of everyday life. There has been little attempt to mobilize the population in disaster prevention. The 1997–8 El Niño event highlighted the gross weaknesses in the National Civil Defence System, as local and regional actors had practically no involvement in decision-making processes. The inevitable result of this has been the creation of a widespread sense among the population that disaster response is a matter for the state, and not for communities themselves to confront (Rivero and Cuba 2001).

A contrasting approach, taken by CEPRODA MINGA and others, is to view El Niño and other disasters as the outcome of long-term social and political processes. These disasters expose the vulnerability of people faced with environmental threats, caused by natural events or human activities. This approach accounts more effectively for the pattern of differentiated effects of El Niño, within and between communities and households. It also accounts for the long-term accumulation of vulnerabilities amongst rural upland communities that have been repeatedly affected by disasters, with little opportunity or assistance to rebuild their capabilities. The political invisibility of these communities has left them excluded from wider development processes. This, combined with repeated severe El Niño shocks, the lack of a powerful civil defence movement, and a lack of access to government emergency responses, has locked both men and women, and particularly women, into a cycle of environmental degradation of increasingly marginal lands, and resulting continual food insecurity (CEPRODA MINGA 1999).

El Niño events are an inevitable aspect of the Peruvian climate. They bring both opportunities and threats in accordance with their severity, and the geography of specific places. It is essential for communities to adapt to these in order to survive and to develop sustainably.[4] In the view of CEPRODA MINGA, this can only come about through the transformation of the social and political processes that generate disasters into processes creating sustainable development. This requires the full participation of all community members (CEPRODA MINGA 2001).

Mainstreaming gender in development work and humanitarian response

While it is clear that there have been efforts on the part of public and private institutions in Piura to incorporate a gender perspective into their work, this has commonly been treated as a technical aspect of the planning and analysis of development projects. This approach impedes the development of a better understanding of women's empowerment as a social and political process aimed at transforming the unequal relationships between men and women, within households, communities, and society at large.

Women organizing locally for survival

During recent decades, women in the Piura region have been active in forming a range of women's organizations locally; these include the *Comités de Vaso de Leche* ('glass of milk committees'), *Comedores Populares* (canteens), and *Clubes de Madres* ('mothers' clubs'). All of these forms of organization are intended to improve food security and nutrition within rural communities. Within these organizations, women members have full participatory rights to vote and voice their opinions.

During the critical period of El Niño, women leaders from Alta Piura assumed a decisive role. They took a lead in rehousing families who had lost homes, managing the distribution of emergency aid, and forming local work groups. There were many opportunities for women to demonstrate their skills as community leaders and protectors, despite their increased vulnerabilities.

However, this process of formation of women's survival organizations, and their high profile during the disaster, was only very weakly linked with wider processes of political or social empowerment of women (Rivero, Afonso, and Eggart 2002). While women were active in leading interventions locally, they were largely absent from institutions at the district, provincial, and regional levels. While they were accustomed to having voice and vote within the dedicated women's organizations, the 'principal' community organizations like the *Comunidades* and *Rondas Campesinas* (civil guards) only gave voting participation to widows, single women, and other women without a man to represent them. Although women's contributions to community survival within the emergency context were widely recognized, men held all the technical, management, and decision-making roles in the civil defence committee, the principal organization charged with responding to the disaster.

While disasters like El Niño can offer women opportunities to assume new leadership roles and activities at a local level, the experience of the 1997–8 El Niño event showed that this increased local visibility was not translated into wider transformations in gender relations. When combined with the increased pressures and vulnerabilities that poor rural women in particular faced during the El Niño crisis, there is a real danger that women are simply burdened with extra tasks for no political or social reward. Project planners in disaster situations need to take care that encouraging women's greater participation in community-level initiatives does not load them with additional tasks and responsibilities, while failing to accord them with greater power and access to formal political bodies and national development processes.

CEPRODA MINGA realized that in the context of disasters, women's needs change. This is a result of the ways in which women's increased role as protagonists within the emergency response combines with the disproportionate risk that women will suffer chronic malnutrition or illness (see Table 4.1).

CEPRODA MINGA – developing strategies for civil defence

CEPRODA MINGA considers that the management of disaster risk is one of the central concerns of disaster prevention. When disasters are viewed as the result of long-term imbalances between societies and their environment, disaster risk management also becomes a long-term commitment. This approach emphasizes the management of risk and vulnerability *before* disaster occurs (Rivero and Cuba 2001). We use the term 'disaster risk management' to refer to the technical and political capacity of women and men, and their organizations and institutions, to transform the social processes that generate disasters and convert them into processes of sustainable development. Democracy is essential to this transformation.[5]

Capacity-building with rural people to enhance their full participation in political and social processes, and particularly in the creation of regional development policy, has been the main focus of CEPRODA MINGA's work following the El Niño event. We have been able to take advantage of wider political changes in Peru that have followed the end of the Fujimori government, including a renewed emphasis on democracy and decentralization, and the strengthening of national civil defence systems. From the outset, we knew that overcoming discrimination against women would be crucial if women, and poor women in particular, were not to be excluded from the benefits of these changes.

The CEPRODA MINGA interventions

The CEPRODA MINGA capacity-building projects were implemented during the reconstruction period following the 1997–8 El Niño, in Chalaco, a very remote mountain district in Piura. The outcomes of El Niño in this district included forest and crop destruction, increased soil erosion, and an increase in illnesses as a result of food insecurity and shortages of clean water.

CEPRODA MINGA initiated participatory planning processes within the Chalaco communities. These processes were intended to go beyond technical discussions of disaster prevention and management to consider how communities might build new kinds of social and political relationships and institutions. These relationships and institutions would involve all their members in decision making and consensus-building.

Creating sustainable risk-management mechanisms among disaster–ridden communities is dependent upon 'social capital': the intricate web of social relations and networks that characterize those communities. One aim of the participatory planning processes was to identify these relationships and networks, and to enable communities to use them as a basis for the development

Table 4.1 Capacities and vulnerabilities of rural women in the context of the 1997–8 En Niño disaster

	Vulnerability	*Capacity*
Citizenship and social organization	• Increased numbers of women face a double burden of responsibility, as both income generators and carers for children and the elderly. • Women frequently do not have control of resources (water, land, housing). As such, they may be limited in their ability to make decisions in these areas during an emergency. • Women have limited access to training, information, or education. • Domestic violence is frequent and widespread, as a result of economic difficulties. • Women often feed their families in preference to themselves and are thus at increased risk of malnutrition. • Women are not able to participate in the 'principal' decision-making organizations.	• Educators • Social sensitivity and capacity for solidarity • Transparent management of resources • Willingness to learn and to share
Psychological attitude	• Women perceive themselves to be dependent on their husbands. • Women experience increases in stress as a result of food insecurity and epidemics. • Women perceive themselves to be marginalized.	• Women have a strong sense of family and community responsibilities. • Women have the capacity to mobilize their organizations. • Women exhibit strong pragmatism.
Physical and material factors	• Pregnancy • Illness • Lactation in a context of widespread malnutrition	• Women as protectors of their community • Women search for means of survival

of strong rural institutions. Another aim was to explore and value different forms of local knowledge and culture, and to consider how this 'cultural capital' might be valuable in the management of disaster risks.

The importance of mainstreaming gender relations into participatory planning

Gender perspectives were integrated into all stages of the planning process, as part of the process of valuing different kinds of knowledge and cultural and social capacities. However, we noted from the early stages of our intervention that when men and women interact, women have a tendency to subordinate their gender specific needs and demands within the wider discussion. Through the intervention we learned that it was necessary to empower women in articulating their gender-specific needs to enable them to negotiate solutions in participatory decision-making fora.

While women have been able to participate in decision-making bodies at the level of their community or district, they have typically been absent from other, higher, levels of decision-making. We realized that local-level plans to articulate and respond to women's gender-specific needs would fail unless they were linked to higher-level changes in public policy. For this reason, we realized that, in addition to the local participatory planning processes, it would be important to create a 'gender policy agenda', with the aim of influencing and creating gender policies at the regional level. A key aspect of this is the empowerment of women to demand accountability in relation to these policies, to ensure that gender policies are not simply reduced to empty declarations of principles or tools for technical analysis, or filed away in the offices of bureaucrats.

A key part of the promotion of the regional gender policy agenda, which is ongoing, involves building on the base of women's widespread local organizational processes to create regional representatives who can negotiate gender-specific demands in decision-making fora at all levels. Currently, CEPRODA MINGA is promoting the 'gender policy agenda' at a regional level in an electoral context: for the first time, regional elections are being held in all regions of Peru. Through consultation with public and private institutions, CEPRODA MINGA is supporting a regional centralization process for women's organizations. It sees these as important emerging actors in the country's democratic transition.

However, we realize that we need to create a permanent regional-level gender post if the gender policy agenda is to become reality.

Increasing women's participation in local organizations

The participatory planning processes, and the development of women's capacities to articulate their strategic gender needs, are beginning to increase women's visibility in community decision-making spaces. Women are increasingly participating in decision-making spaces that would have been 100 per cent masculine just a few years ago. Men have increasingly learned to listen to and take into account women leaders' opinions as a result of the consultation and participatory processes. As a result, the women of Piura have made significant advances in participating in wider development processes, and ensuring that their needs and interests are being included in development strategies. Local systems for sustainable development and disaster prevention have been strengthened through women's participation.

From the beginning of our interventions, existing women's organizations such as the 'glass of milk' committees, mothers' clubs, and the *Rondas Campesinas Femeninas*, actively participated in meetings, guaranteeing the representation of their households and localities. In some cases, women have taken on major responsibilities, for example in the hamlet of Nogal Chalaco, where for the first time in history a woman was elected president of the Committee for Small-Scale Producers of Coffee and Sugar Cane.

There have been changes within local level community organizations, where women have taken on more leadership positions representing women's interests, and gained voting powers and a voice in district assemblies. There has also been greater recognition of women's rights in local judicial systems. In the 'principal' local organizations like the District Assembly of the Chalaco *Rondas Campesinas*, women and men now both have a right to vote, with women also assuming some leadership roles. Where the *Rondas Campesinas* are involved in local judicial processes, there have been advances in their willingness and ability to recognize women's rights, something which has not taken place widely in the formal justice system.

In mixed organizations like the small scale coffee and sugar-cane producers' committees, women have became more conscious of their role as producers and citizens. In Peru, as elsewhere, there is a widespread devaluation and lack of recognition of women's role in productive activities. This is considered at most as a supportive role within the traditional household division of labour. Women have traditionally considered the productive activities that they undertake to be a form of support to male producers. Typically, women who under take agricultural activities declare themselves to be housewives or petty traders at the time of the census. As a result, women's role in productive activities has been invisible in registers and statistics, and has not been widely recognized or appreciated.

Since the beginning of the CEPRODA MINGA interventions, women have begun to make themselves more visible within these organizations, as producers involved in all aspects of production. Increasingly, women are assuming leadership posts in the central directive, and promoting technological innovation in their smallholdings, which is in turn strengthening the capacities of new female leaders.

Rural women – from survival strategies to regional development

For rural women there has been a significant shift from focusing on survival strategies within local community groups to engaging in wider development processes. Women have moved from expressing demands linked to their practical needs, such as improvements in feeding programmes and service delivery, to making their 'strategic' gender needs and their role as social actors increasingly visible in local consultation processes. Today, women are demanding to be considered as workers equal to men, within development programmes; they express the need to build capacity in the exercise of their rights in order to confront situations of gender violence and abuse, and to challenge instances of unjust rulings and decision-making by authorities in favour of men. According to statistical data from the area, boys and girls have now got equal access to public education, which is an important change compared with 1990 when girls had very limited access.

Conclusions

Sustainable development in Piura will be a long-term process. Similarly, we realize that there is a long way to go in achieving real equality between women and men in all areas. Nonetheless, as a result of the CEPRODA MINGA interventions, a better understanding of disaster prevention has developed within the Chalaco communities. Where, previously, the idea of rural development was associated with physical infrastructure and centralized decision making, CEPRODA MINGA's interventions have contributed to the creation of a widespread new understanding of how people can develop their own capacities to transform their situation. At an assembly meeting, both male and female participants spoke of how they now felt able to talk directly with authorities, whereas before they went through intermediaries. This, they felt, had enabled them to claim their rights as citizens and take their proposals to larger political fora that have hitherto been considered as excluding and ignoring rural people's concerns. Importantly, the participative planning process has enabled rural people – women and men – to create and promote their own proposals for democratic government and local development in a context of decentralization.

Notes

1. This chapter has been translated from Spanish and adapted by Kate Kilpatrick.
2. These organizations typically only recognize women who do not have a man to represent them, such as single women and widows. When a woman's husband is absent from the community for migratory work or some other reason, she is not usually recognized by these organizations as the acting household head.

3. Rural women who migrate to the larger towns in the region usually obtain income through domestic work or through petty commerce. During El Niño, these opportunities decreased considerably as households across the region were affected by the disaster.
4. In fact, communities in Peru were previously better-adapted to El Niño events than they are today. Agricultural changes and humanitarian aid packages have created widespread dependence on external inputs, displacing traditional native plant varieties (for example, the yacon *(Smallanthus sonchifolius)*, and native bean and potato species), which are often better adapted to the climatic conditions.
5. The communities that displayed a better organizational response to El Niño were those where participative processes and grassroots NGOs were in existence long before the disaster. These institutions and communities appeared to emerge strengthened rather than undermined from the El Niño emergency and reconstruction period. Those communities and institutions with scant experience of popular participation typically fell prey to welfarism and clientelism.

References

CEPRODA MINGA (1999) 'Plan Estratégico para el Desarrollo Sostenible y la Gestión de Riesgos de Desastres de la Microcuenca Nogal Chalaco', Piura, Peru: CEPRODA MINGA.

CEPRODA MINGA (2001) 'Plan Estratégico del Distrito de Chalaco para el Desarrollo Sostenible y la Gestión de Riesgos de Desastres', Piura, Peru: CEPRODA MINGA.

CLADEM (2001) 'Perú Diagnóstico de la Situación de los Derechos Sexuales y los Derechos Reproductivos 1995-2000', Lima: CLADEM Peru.

Rivero, Rosa and Severo Cuba (2001) '"Primero es la Gente": Prevención de Desastres, Borrador de Documento de Sistematización', Piura, Peru: CEPRODA MINGA.

Rivero, Rosa, Klara Afonso, and Luisa Eggart (2002) *Guía Metodológica: Const ruyendo una Agenda Politica de Genero en la Region Piura: Los Derechos Humanos de las Mujeres*, Piura, Peru: CEPRODA MINGA.

Torres, F. (1998) 'Efectos de "El Niño" en Cultivos y la Productividad Primaria Vegetal en la Sierra Central de Piura', paper presented at a workshop on '"El Niño" in Latin America: its Biological and Social Impacts. The Basis for Regional Monitoring', 9-13 November 1998.

Villarreal, L.A. (2002) 'Vulnerabilidad, desastres y desarrollo en el Perú', in *Pobreza y Desarrollo en el Perú*, Lima: Oxfam GB.

Wilches-Chaux, Gustavo (1998) *Guía de la Red para la Gestión Local del Riesgo*, Lima: ITDG Peru and Red de Estudios Sociales en Prevención de Desastres en América Latina.

About the author

Rosa Rivero Reyes is the Technical Secretary of the La Red Risk Management and Climate Change Group in north-east Peru. She is responsible for risk management and climate change at the NGO CEPRODE MINGA.

CHAPTER 5

Engendering adaptation to climate variability in Gujarat, India

Sara Ahmed and Elizabeth Fajber

This chapter first appeared in *Gender and Development* 17(1), pp. 33–50, March 2009.

Most policy makers and practitioners have now started to recognize the different ways in which climate change impacts on poor, vulnerable, and socially excluded women and men. However, making adaptation policies and programmes sensitive to gender issues does not simply mean 'adding on' a concern for women. It also requires a nuanced understanding of gendered forms of vulnerability, and a stronger commitment of resources – financial, technical, and human – to address specific gendered priorities. Drawing on insights from coastal Gujarat, in India, this chapter illustrates how researchers and practitioners can collaborate to strengthen learning across communities and regions. Simple and practical tools for assessing vulnerability, as well as empirical research and documentation, can further and support advocacy on climate-resilient development policies.

Introduction

The recently announced National Action Plan on Climate Change (NAPCC) in India recognizes that climate change has different effects on women and men, due to gender relations and roles, and it affects relations between them too. To quote the Action Plan: 'With climate change there would be increasing scarcity of water, reductions in yields of biomass, and increased risks to human health with children, women and the elderly in a household becoming the most vulnerable. With the possibility of decline in the availability of food grains, the threat of malnutrition may also increase. All these would add to deprivations that women already encounter and so in each of the Adaptation programmes special attention should be paid to the aspects of gender' (Government of India 2008, 12).

For the first time in India, a high-level policy document has acknowledged the significance of gendered impacts of climate change, and the need to address gender concerns in adaptation interventions. Unfortunately, this understanding has not been translated into the NAPCC's assessment of the effects of climate change or its outlines of mechanisms that could support people to adapt. Partly, this has to do with the lack of gender/sex-disaggregated data on climate risks, and the relatively poor documentation of adaptation programmes, or the lessons they can provide, in terms of building resilient communities. More to the point, however, is the fact that disaster risk-reduction in India, and indeed in much of the developing world, has focused on relief and rehabilitation, rather than long-term climate-resilient development. Intense climate events, such as drought, floods, cyclones, and storms have largely been seen as *natural* disasters, to which humanitarian response is often the only answer; technological solutions (for example, embankments in flood-prone areas), or administrative machineries (despite attempts at decentralization), have failed to respond adequately.

Where adaptation activities do exist, they are *ad-hoc* and uncoordinated at different scales and levels, neglecting the need simultaneously to create conditions that enable and support adaptive strategies, based on a clear analysis of differential vulnerability. In India – and across South Asia – gender identity intersects with other social stratifiers, including class, and discrimination based on caste or religion. These shape people's experience of poverty, which denies millions of people – women and men – their basic human and livelihood rights. Not only are poor, rural women and men faced with an agrarian landscape which is being challenged by environmental hazards, but the economic opportunities created by structural reforms have not trickled down. Meanwhile, the social fabric underlying collective mobilization by civil society continues to be deeply embedded in the politics of identity. Thus, climate and disaster risks often overlay conflicts between different identity groups – making it even more difficult for vulnerable women and men to voice their concerns, or to participate in participatory processes of planning for change.

It is in this context of climate variability, contestation, and institutional complexity that collaborative partnerships between researchers, development practitioners, and policy advocates become so critical in terms of both laying a framework for adaptation and equally, trying to engender it. ISET (the Institute of Social and Environmental Transition) is an organization which represents a unique attempt at crossing interdisciplinary and geographical boundaries, and building knowledge located in both theory and practice, while being committed to solidarity with poor and vulnerable people. Drawing on insights from coastal Gujarat, this chapter looks at how ISET members and partners have worked together to (i) identify differential vulnerabilities, and (ii) facilitate initiatives to strengthen the adaptive capacity of poor women and men, such as participatory livelihood diversification and decentralized disaster governance.[1] We begin with a brief introduction to ISET, outline our conceptual understanding of adaptation and vulnerability, and then move on to examine our learning from ongoing adaptation pilots.

ISET: collaborative partnerships which respond to change

Built over the past decade, ISET is an innovative collaboration between organizations, which involves researchers and development practitioners. It seeks to evolve a framework for shared learning through dialogue. Empirical research by ISET is used to inform policy debates critically, and to respond to basic societal needs, through supporting sustainable, gender-just policy interventions.[2] ISET has members, individuals and organizations (NGOs, research institutes) and partners in South Asia (India, Pakistan, Nepal), North America, Europe, and, more recently, South-East Asia. They work as a community of practice, linked virtually, rather than physically. From its earlier work on the politics of water management in South Asia, ISET has been trying to build an approach towards both understanding adaptation and facilitating small adaptation pilots based on participatory, iterative methodologies for assessing vulnerability and the benefits and costs of disaster risk-reduction measures.[3] Both authors are senior associates of ISET, and have been working to support gender and vulnerability analysis in ISET research and practice. This support is both conceptual and methodological.

Understanding adaptation

Our understanding of adaptation moves beyond conventional notions of 'coping'. Rather, we view adaptation as 'the capacity of social actors to *shift* livelihood strategies under stress, and to develop supporting systems that are resilient and *flexible* to absorb and respond to the impacts of [climate] change' (ISET forthcoming 2008, 6).[4]

Adaptation can be defined as either autonomous or planned, although in practice, both strategies are often interconnected:

- *Autonomous* adaptation depends on underlying systems that enable people and organizations to take advantage of opportunities available in the new environment, or constrain their ability to shift livelihood strategies as conditions evolve.
- *Planned* adaptation depends on the ability to:
  o proactively identify, and respond to, emerging constraints and opportunities;
  o enable autonomous adaptation processes by supporting the development of flexible, resilient, and accessible social and physical infrastructure systems; and
  o establish social protection systems capable of ameliorating the impact of climate change on vulnerable groups.

ISET has undertaken extensive action research in South Asia, which has led us to identify a variety of systems that enable poor women and men to adapt – in both planned and autonomous ways. These include communication, public infrastructure, transport (mobility), and finance (Moench and Dixit 2004;

2007). Underlying these systems are social and power relations that facilitate *access* for different socio-economic groups, men and women, including rights and entitlements to productive resources or assets (land, water, labour, credit), social networks, capacity-building, and the transfer of new knowledge to support livelihood diversification. Governance considerations, such as accountability, transparency, and the informed participation of vulnerable women and men in community decision-making on disaster management, are equally important to ensure that those directly affected can negotiate access to discussions and decisions, and ultimately build their capacity to adapt.

Understanding vulnerability

Central to adaptation is vulnerability, which is not the same as poverty, and is often more difficult for policy makers to understand (Ahmed and Mustafa 2007). We follow the Hyogo Framework 2005–2015,[5] in defining vulnerability as a 'set of conditions determined by physical, social, economic and environmental factors or processes which increase the susceptibility of a community to the impact of hazards,' (adopted by the UN at the World Conference on Disasters in 2005). This emphasizes the need to look at vulnerability not simply as a result of, or response to, environmental extremes (Cutter 1996; Vincent 2004). Rather, vulnerability is rooted in the construction of *everyday* social space or social existence; that is, vulnerability needs to be seen as context (for example, unequal access to opportunities) rather than outcome (Bohle *et al.* 1994).

Analysing vulnerability requires us to recognize how different factors – physical, social, and attitudinal – are interconnected. These factors combine to affect the degree to which hazards affect individuals or communities, and also define their ability to adapt. Across South Asia – and particularly in India, given its huge population, more than 80 per cent of whom live on less than $2 per day (UNDP 2007) – women, children, and elderly people carry disproportionate 'vulnerability bundles', and these place them in the category of highest risk (Ariyabandu and Wickramasinghe 2003; Wisner *et al.* 2004). In our own research, this is borne out in women's discussions of their vulnerability to food insecurity. Poor women in flood-prone villages in eastern Uttar Pradesh described the difficulty in accessing food after floods as living with 'half-full stomachs' (focus-group discussion, Gorakhpur, November 2006). Women in semi-arid villages in Kutch, Gujarat changed this metaphor slightly, to state that 'drought lives in our stomachs' (focus-group discussion, Bhuj, October 2007).

Measuring vulnerability

If we understand vulnerability to be a relative term with multiple dimensions, can we really measure who is vulnerable – and vulnerable to what? Vulnerability analysis tends to be based on the experience of past hazards/disaster events and can only be, at best, predictive (looking at an individual or community's *likely* susceptibility). However, if vulnerability is viewed as a dynamic process, this takes into account the *risk* of exposure and susceptibility. Equally, this enables us to assess the strength of different responses, and/or the potential for building people's capacity to adapt. Then, we may have a better indication of *who* is vulnerable, *when*, and *how*. We can also look at opportunities for addressing vulnerability, and enhancing adaptive capacity.

Given the complexities of what makes people vulnerable, some factors are easy to identify and measure (such as the location of physical settlements, buildings at risk, or environmental degradation). Others are less visible, and sometimes more difficult to assess, such as resource tenure, or changes in attitudes. Ideally, research into vulnerability should include both a qualitative understanding of the context, and a quantitative assessment, based on well-defined indicators of change.

Phase 1 of ISET's approach to vulnerability assessment in coastal Gujarat (2006–2007) began with participatory assessments of vulnerability, drawing on various frameworks for assessing the three dimensions of vulnerability – physical, social, and attitudinal (Anderson and Woodrow, 1989; ActionAid 2005). Information/data was collected through participatory exercises, often with women and men separately, such as historical time-lines of disasters or seasonality calendars to identify monthly variations in food, water, and livelihood security.

Over the past year, in a parallel ISET project on disaster risk-assessment, we have developed – and are testing – the Vulnerability Capacity Index (VCI), a simple quantitative vulnerability index based on 11 'drivers of vulnerability', with some modification between household and community levels, and rural/urban communities (Mustafa and Ahmed 2008). Scores are attached to the different indicators, and the three dimensions of vulnerability are then weighed to come up with a composite score. The index is not comprehensive; it is, rather, indicative – and the main drivers of vulnerability are consistent with similar quantification exercises by others (e.g. Bosher *et al.* 2007).

Limitations of space make it difficult to discuss the VCI and methodological challenges in more detail, but Table 5.1 illustrates the parameters and indicators with which we are working.

Vulnerability assessments have been supported by shared learning dialogues at different levels – community, district, and state. Shared learning dialogues are essentially well-facilitated dialogues between government functionaries, disaster-prone communities, NGOs, and representatives from financial and market-based institutions to understand different perspectives on climate change (Moench and Dixit 2007). They have often led to consensus around possible and innovative adaptation measures, and provided opportunities for networking and collaboration between different social actors.

In the next section, we look at how vulnerability and shared learning dialogues have helped in the identification of gendered strategies for strengthening

Table 5.1 Indicators of vulnerability at the rural household level (illustrative)

Material Vulnerability Weightage: 35%	Institutional Vulnerability Weightage: 50%	Attitudinal Vulnerability Weightage: 15%
• Income source – local/ non-local, and or non-land based • Educational attainment, particularly for women • Assets – fungibles • Exposure to risk – distance from river, coast, landslide zone	• Social networks • Extra-local kinship ties – response at times of adversity • Infrastructure – access to roads, water, sanitation, electricity, health services, communication • Proportion of dependants in household • Reliability of early warning systems • Belonging to the disadvantaged – caste, religious or ethnic minority	• Sense of empowerment, derived from: • Access to leadership at different levels – community, regional, national • Knowledge about potential hazards

Source: Drawn from Mustafa and Ahmed, 2008

adaptive capacity and building resilient communities, by ISET's NGO partner, Utthan, in drought- and flood-prone villages in coastal south Gujarat.

Exploring the physical aspects of vulnerability: a case from coastal Gujarat

Gujarat has the longest coastline (1,600km) among all the Indian states. It is a coast which is rich in biodiversity, but also very prone to many hazards, including extreme cyclones, and salinity intrusion, or ingress (the gradual seeping of salt into the soil and into freshwater aquifers), flooding, and drought. Salinity ingress, though not directly attributable to climate change, affects nearly 30 per cent of the land area of the state (GHDR 2004: 92) and in turn, has an impact on agricultural productivity and the quality of drinking water available. While data on climate variability is mixed, cyclones are likely to increase in strength and intensity, though perhaps not in frequency. This may lead to more wind damage to crops, buildings, and other infrastructure. There have also been some changes in rainfall patterns. Over the last two years, the monsoon season has been characterized by short periods of intensive rainfall, often leading to floods, followed by increasing gaps in the number of rainy days. These changes, in turn, are causing more surface runoff (overland flow of excess water that can not be absorbed by the ground), soil erosion, and sedimentation of tanks. This makes it more difficult to store water in small dams which fill with sediments or do not adequately capture water, and increases the probability of flash floods. On the other hand, increase in summer temperatures and short heat-wave conditions, as well as shorter winter months and an increase in average winter temperatures, could have a positive impact on the amount of plants providing ground cover, and the amount of organic matter breaking down into the soil. This is important to reduce erosion, buffer the effect of storms, and assist groundwater to recharge or replenish itself.

The effects of climate change in coastal Gujarat are aggravated by growing populations, urbanization, and the recent political demarcation by the state of large coastal areas as Special Economic Zones for industrial development, posing a challenge to livelihood security and natural resource-management interventions.

Utthan and its work

Utthan, which means 'upliftment' in Hindi, was formed in 1987 to facilitate participatory, community-led, and gender-sensitive development in drought- and conflict-prone villages in Gujarat. Under an ISET project, funded by the International Development Research Centre (IDRC),[6] Utthan has initiated adaptation pilot projects in three villages in the coastal district of Bhavnagar: Sartanpar, Tarasara, and Katpar. All three villages are affected by periodic drought, salinity ingress, cyclones, and water-logging, during the monsoons, when there are floods caused by intensive rainfall, coupled with storm surges or high tides. Little protection is afforded by the village embankments. The pilot projects are based on Utthan's participatory assessment of vulnerability and collective identification with village members and other stakeholders through shared learning dialogues, of strategies to strengthen adaptation. The VCI is actually being used by Utthan now as a monitoring tool; earlier assessments of vulnerability and coping were largely through participatory appraisals – time-lines of disasters, seasonal calendars on food and income security, and so on.

Utthan has also set up a People's Learning Centre for Livelihood Security and Disaster Mitigation in Coastal Communities (PLC-Coastal). The intention is to make this a space for integrating diverse voices, concerns, and experiences within coastal communities susceptible to drought, salinity, and cyclones.[7] PLC-Coastal also addresses patterns of social discrimination, with a focus on integrating rights and experiences of the most vulnerable women and men. Utthan and PLC-Coastal were key partners in the implementation of this project.

Social dimensions of vulnerability in project villages

The participatory vulnerability assessments also yielded important information about the social dimensions of vulnerability. Gujarat has a relatively better history of collective mobilization compared with other states in India, and this is visible in the effective functioning of a variety of local institutions, including temple groups, self-help groups (SHGs), *panchayats* (elected local village councils), disaster committees, and a range of community natural resource-management institutions, facilitated by NGOs. Both Sartanpar and Katpar have active *sarpanches* (elected *panchayat* leaders), and strong women's participation in local community institutions. They have been able to negotiate with district-level government departments for basic primary health facilities, a secondary school particularly for girls, and better roads. In Tarasara, in contrast, there is a distinct lack of community organizations, and the village is clearly divided by factional politics.

Caste intersects with gender in all three villages to determine who is vulnerable, where they live, and their access to resources, including communication and information systems. In Sartanpar, for example, poor tribal groups reside in low-lying, flood-prone areas on the outskirts of the village, making it difficult for them to access relief, or get information on impending disasters. The village temple provides the only safe sanctuary for people during floods and cyclones, but space is limited, and it is possible, though difficult to prove, that lower-caste groups are denied access because of social practices – ritual pollution – that discriminate against them.[8]

Most of the households are dependent on farm labour – which is seasonal, and also insecure – or high-risk activities, such as fishing and salt farming, which are affected by dangerous storms or annual flooding. Those who have managed to diversify their livelihoods, or migrate, are households which have relatively good recourse to social networks, skills, and capacities (for example, some education).

Fall-back mechanisms in the event of climate-change-related disasters include social networks, extended family support, and dependence on moneylenders after a disaster event, but the degree to which people can rely on these varies from household to household and the extent or magnitude of the calamity.

The participatory research showed women in all three villages to be more vulnerable than men from the point of view of gender identity, but the experience of gender inequality is mediated by other aspects of social identity. Hence, the vulnerability of individual women varies, according to their socio-economic group and access to entitlements. For example, women from small and marginal landholding families, where male migration is high, often do not have clear legal title over land, either in their name, or jointly with their husbands, despite land reforms and changes in the property law. This makes it difficult for women to access various resources which could help with adaptation; for example, water for irrigation, or credit and extension services, which are often tied to land ownership where land serves as collateral, and recognition as a 'farmer' or 'head of the household'.[9] In addition, water-supply systems are unreliable, insufficient, or brackish, and not accessible when the villages are waterlogged, thus increasing women's workload as they have to walk further to find and fetch potable water.

Gender inequality also affects women's access to information and communications which could ensure their safety, and the safety of their dependants. In the event of an emergency such as a flood, access to early-warning information is 'gendered'. This information often comes through communication media such as television, radio or, in some pilot activities, mobile phones, which are more frequently used by men than by women. According to the vulnerability assessments in the villages, most women cannot swim, whereas at least 40 per cent of the men can. In many rural communities in Gujarat (and elsewhere in India), girls and women are not encouraged to learn how to swim, largely for reasons of cultural appropriateness or modesty. Those women who can swim, or at least keep themselves afloat, are from the traditional fishing communities, who literally walk into the water, using their hands or simple nets to fish.

Facilitating adaptation: gender, livelihoods, and governance

As stated above, based on the information gained in the participatory research, Utthan, together with PLC-Coastal, is facilitating adaptation pilots in three villages. These pilot activities address the systemic factors we outlined in our earlier definition of adaptation: namely, access to resources and knowledge to support livelihood diversification, adaptive infrastructure, and capacity-building of poor women and men, to ensure that they are able to participate in decision-making processes.

1. Livelihood diversification

   Given increasing salinity and declining agricultural productivity, the shared learning dialogues facilitated by Utthan and ISET clearly indicated the need for poor women and men in these villages to look for alternative livelihoods.

   The coastal belt of Gujarat is suitable for spiny or rock lobsters which are commonly found along rocky shores. With the support of the non-profit company, the Coastal Salinity Prevention Cell,[10] pilot demonstration projects on lobster fattening were implemented by Utthan at two selected sites. This involved women and men from two self-help groups (within which 70 per cent of the members come from households below the poverty line). Prior to Utthan's intervention, the majority of lobsters caught in this area used to fetch a lower price in the market as they weighed only around 100 grams. After one project cycle of six months, the fattened lobsters (weighing 150 grams) could command a better price in the market.

   This programme so far has directly benefited 48 families, and has generated employment for 120 people-days per household in a year. Loans of about $130 were provided to each participating family for a one-time investment in the cages, or pits, in which lobsters are reared. The recurring cost associated with feeding the lobsters is primarily for the fish, which women and men catch locally. While lobster-rearing is done by both women and men, marketing is almost entirely women's responsibility – mostly in local markets and nearby villages. However, over time they have been able to negotiate better prices from buyers as a collective. The buyers are now coming directly to the sites to buy from them, saving them the trouble and cost of travel; public transport is limited, and private options are costly.

Following this pilot demonstration, the National Centre for Sustainable Aquaculture and the Marine Products Export Development Authority have both shown interest in copying and scaling up this activity in other coastal villages. The first round of loans to the self-help groups has been repaid, and a federation of self-help groups involved in fishing is in the process of being registered. Training on the technical, marketing, and management aspects of lobster-rearing is being planned for fisherfolk from the three adaptation pilot villages, and another ten villages.

In Katpar village, many small and marginal farmers, and some fisher families, are involved in rope-making from mill cotton waste, as a source of supplementary income. Recently, an exposure visit was organized for a group of 11 men and four women from Tarasara. The Katpar families are ready to help them initiate this activity, and have suggested that the Tarasara group take the raw material and market it through Katpar's existing contacts initially, prior to making their own contacts. Efforts are also being made to engage women's self-help groups in rope-making by linking them up with Area Level Federations of self-help groups,[11] so that they can give them training on rope-making, and help facilitate access to raw materials and to markets.

2. Adaptive infrastructure for water and sanitation
Access to appropriate sanitation facilities and potable drinking water are two priorities consistently raised by women in flood-prone areas, as women are largely responsible for domestic water collection, and need safe and secure spaces to meet their sanitary and hygiene needs with dignity. Under the state sector reforms programme, Utthan is supporting *pani samitis* (village water committees) to work in partnership with the government Water and Sanitation Management Organization (WASMO). Together, they are developing infrastructure and management mechanisms to ensure access to safe drinking water for all. Women are actively involved in these committees, but their roles and responsibilities on the committees need to be explored and critiqued from a gender perspective.

Pilot community-sanitation units have also been implemented: one each in two villages (Katpar and Sartanpar), with each elevated unit having two latrines. These are cement structures, designed for coastal areas prone to salt-water erosion. They have been designed with technical support from Utthan's engineering team, and are primarily meant for the families who live in the low-lying flood-prone areas. At the moment, the toilets are only used by women and children, and are kept clean by the participating households.

3. Capacity-building for disaster governance
Village-Level Disaster Committees (VLDCs) have been formed in all the three pilot villages – a process that took some six months to a year, with extensive discussions on roles and relationships with the local *panchayat.*

The VLDC has sub-committees for various tasks, and these are outlined in Table 5.2. Each sub-committee has six members (though this number varies), half of whom are meant to be women. At least two of the six members are supposed to come from vulnerable groups in the village. In practice, however, the representation of women on the sub-committees is nominal – there are no women on the Rescue and Relief committees, and no women on the committees for Temporary and Permanent Shelter. Women's absence from the former is not surprising, given that most women cannot swim. However, the committee is responsible for the distribution of relief, and the lack of women on the committee raises a number of gender concerns regarding the distribution of food between and within households. Women's absence from the Temporary and Permanent Shelter committee raises other gender concerns about the question of women's safety and security in temporary shelters, particularly that of adolescent girls (Ahmed 2006).

There are no women as yet on the Water and Sanitation Committees, except in Sartanpar village, where there is a water-supply project being implemented under the state sector reforms programme.[12] Not surprisingly, women *are* present on the sub-committees for health in each village – although not in the numbers that they should be – while there are also a few women on the Communication committee. This is both a technical function – accessing information about impending disasters from district functionaries – as well as one of outreach to others in the

Table 5.2 Women's representation in sub-committees for disaster management

Committee	Responsibilities	No. of Members			No. of Women		
		T	S	K	T	S	K
Communication	Collect and share information on impending disasters with village, close contact with government functionaries	4	6	6	0	1	3
Health	Trained in first-aid, awareness of communicable diseases during/post disasters, coordinate with Primary/ community health centres	6	6	3	1	2	0
Rescue and Relief	Knowledge of various provisions used during disaster emergencies, awareness of safe place to shift people to, access to necessary equipment	5	5	5	0	0	0
Water and Sanitation	Knowledge of water availability and quality which can be accessed, sanitation...	3	5	5	0	4	0
Temporary and Permanent Shelter	Trained to construct temporary shelter provisions during emergency, ability to explain importance of retrofitting houses _ earthquakes, cyclones	*	9	3	*	0	0

Source: Drawn from Utthan/PLC Report, August 2007 – January 2008.
Note: T_Tarasara; S_Sartanpar; K_Katpar * No sub-committee formed yet

village. Women can perform an important role here, in terms of quickly identifying and reaching vulnerable elderly people, widows, and children with early warnings.

Initial insights: implications for policy and practice

As the activities described are in initial stages and the projects are still under way, it may be too early to discuss 'lessons' as such. However, these experiences do generate initial insights and point to – or reinforce – areas that need to be strengthened in policy and practice more widely in order to engender adaptation efforts. These areas are outlined below:

The importance of simple and practical tools to understand vulnerability

The complexity and interconnectedness of social, physical, and behavioural factors that contribute to vulnerability make it a difficult concept to capture and assess. At the same time, understanding these complexities is crucial in order to support and enable effective adaptation strategies of the most vulnerable people. The conceptual tools that we need to do this must be simple and manageable, and we need practical indicators that can be used by different stakeholders in communities to gather data. Tools such as vulnerability mapping, and the VCI used in this project, are steps in this direction, though they need more refinement. Already they have helped communities to broaden the way they understand vulnerability, beyond physical exposure to risks, and to understand better how women, men, children, and different social groups may be affected differently by climate change, or may have more limited ability to adapt. Of course, to understand gender differences, it is important also to use these tools at intra-household levels.

Strengthening social networks as fall-back mechanisms for women

Social networks can be key factors in building resilience and reducing vulnerability to climate-change impacts (Fussel 2007; Twigg 2007), providing financial and social safety nets at times of need. This was well-illustrated in the quantitative vulnerability assessment for the VCI conducted by ISET and Utthan in Sartanpar village in 2007. There, an agricultural labourer, Tappuben, who lives in a low-lying area of the village, has identified strong-social support networks within and beyond family relations as important to helping her at times of adversity. Her active involvement in several village organizations, including the Disaster Management Committee and the Village Water Committee, has helped her gain confidence and articulate her views in decision-making (Mustafa and Ahmed 2008). Apart from only *recognizing* the importance of social networks, we feel that it is important to explore mechanisms that can *strengthen* these networks to enhance women's access to information, financial resources, and social support. For example, these networks may also be used to channel information on climate or disaster preparedness, or on alternative livelihood options.

Enhancing gender-equitable access to information and capacity development

Individuals, families, and communities that have diversified livelihood strategies are better able to manage risk and cope with impacts of climate change. Their strategies may include diversification into non-farm livelihoods less sensitive to climatic variability, such as the expansion of rope-making in Katpar and Tarasara villages. Alternatively, they may also include the identification of agriculture or aquaculture opportunities that enable people *to take advantage of* changing climate conditions and their associated effects, such as the case of lobster-breeding in increasingly brackish water systems. Development of these livelihood options requires access to training and skill development, and information on technologies and ways of adding value to create a profit. Apart from technical support, poor women and men also need to develop market linkages, facilitate business planning, and enhance their capacity to negotiate for better prices. This also requires access to credit, which can be a significant challenge for poor women, given the changing macro-policy environment on micro-finance in India.[13]

However, 'extension systems' – that is, systems to deliver training and other inputs – often perpetuate a male bias in agriculture and aquaculture, privileging and predominantly reaching men (see Duvvury 1998; Kelkar 2007). Alternative strategies and gender-sensitive extension systems are needed to target, engage, and support both women and men in accessing the skills and resources they need for successful livelihoods. Strengthening informal social institutions, such as co-operatives or self-help groups, may be one vehicle to improve economies of scale and negotiate power structures, thereby enhancing potential returns from smaller-scale enterprises.

Innovations and dedicated resources to respond to women's priorities

The research which underpinned the project discussed in this chapter suggests that local authorities need to identify and validate women's priority needs in flood, drought, and intense storm conditions. Validation must be translated into attention to women's interests and needs, and resources (financial, human, and technological) need to be channelled to women to enable them to meet their needs in ways which support greater gender equality. Innovations, such as the example of providing toilets which are specially adapted to function in low-lying flood-prone areas, can have tremendous impact on women's security and dignity, and even on managing health and the spread of disease. However, scaling up these pilots to ensure a wider impact requires resources and partnerships with other organizations. In this case, Utthan is exploring such partnerships with WASMO and private-sector actors.

Strengthening gendered participation and voice in disaster governance

Strengthening community-based institutions for co-ordinated planning for managing disasters and impacts from extreme climate events is an important step towards enhancing adaptation. Village Disaster Committees, such as those in Tarasara, Sartanpar, and Katpar, can facilitate access to climate information in order to manage water more effectively. They can also plan agricultural activities; plan and deliver health services; improve early warning for extreme events; and facilitate relief efforts. But despite facilitation by a gender-sensitive NGO like Utthan, it is still a challenge in these villages to encourage women's participation in management committees, despite this being a very important element in ensuring that women's priorities are met. Political actors, NGOs, and civil society need to facilitate the participation of both women and men in community disaster governance, to ensure the voices of both sexes are heard. Strengthening women's confidence in their own knowledge, and in learning more about climate change and adaptation through awareness-raising activities and the community efforts described above are steps towards this. Training to promote the leadership skills of women may also help them to be more active in community organizations.

Concluding remarks

As our experiences in Gujarat demonstrate, engendering adaptation strategies in India is an ongoing challenge. Initial efforts in Gujarat by Utthan, ISET, and partners are generating preliminary insights that point to directions for policy and practice that can help us move towards this goal. These reflections need to be supplemented by ongoing documentation and learning from pilot initiatives, such as the ones outlined in this chapter, in order to promote gender-sensitive and gender-inclusive adaptation. In the case of Gujarat – and globally – explicit attention to engendering climate-change adaptation 'on the ground' is still relatively new, and there is a need for rigorous documentation and analysis *with communities* on successes and challenges.

At the same time, there is a need to scale up these lessons to policies and practice at state and national levels. But first, more emphasis needs to be placed on ways to engender the processes and strategies for adaptation to reach and respond to women's and men's differing priorities and needs in various communities. That is, the focus should extend beyond scaling up specific interventions – in this case, lobster-fattening, adapting sanitation structures, and facilitating disaster management committees – although there is the potential to reach a much larger population with these initiatives, and this should not be understated. However, state actors and civil society also need to ensure gender issues are integral to their approaches and explicitly engage women and men of different social groups in priority-setting and development of interventions most relevant to their situation. This also involves building gender concerns into the underlying systems that have been identified as necessary to enhance adaptation: livelihood diversification, infrastructure, communication, access to skills and knowledge, and community-based disaster governance. Furthermore, the current disjunctures between the disaster risk-reduction and development sectors must be bridged, to ensure that strategies are both short-term to address immediate impacts, but also long-term to reduce vulnerability and risk, and enhance more climate-resilient development.

All of these efforts require strengthening the capacities of communities, sector agencies, development actors, and policy makers to understand climate change and adaptation, and gendered impacts and strategies. At ISET, we are moving towards this by building capacity to use the VCI as a simple monitoring tool to provide baseline data about the different physical, social, and attitudinal vulnerabilities of women and men in households and communities, and to assess changes resulting from adaptation interventions. The Shared Learning Dialogues are also broadening our understanding of the issues, and facilitating active engagement in developing strategies and interventions. Finally, we ourselves, together with Utthan and other partners, are continuing to build our own capacities in understanding gendered adaptation needs and priorities of communities, in order to develop practical strategies, methods, and tools to address these, and to communicate lessons to inform policy and debates.

Notes

1. While this chapter builds on insights from two specific ISET projects (namely, one funded by DFID (Department for International Development, UK) on the costs and benefits of disaster risk-reduction measures and the other funded by IDRC (International Development Research Centre) on understanding vulnerability and adaptation to climate variability), it also draws on other ISET climate-change projects. The authors would like to thank the Utthan team, as well as ISET colleagues, for sharing their work with us.
2. See www.i-s-e-t.org (last accessed November 2008)
3. See www.climate-transitions.org (last accessed November 2008)
4. Our understanding of adaptation draws on ISET's collective analysis and conceptual framework which is rooted in research and practice around climate variability in South Asia.
5. The Hyogo Framework for Action 2005–2015: Building Resilience of Nations and Communities was adopted by participants (government, international organizations, civil society, scientific community) at the World Conference on Disaster Reduction held 18–22 January 2005 in Kobe, Hyogo, Japan. It outlines strategies and actions to guide governments and civil society on reducing vulnerability and improving resilience to disasters and environmental change. See www.unisdr.org/eng/hfa/docs/ Hyogo-framework-for-action-english.pdf (last accessed November 2008).
6. The project 'Adaptation and Livelihood Resilience', supported by the IDRC, is being implemented by ISET and partners in Gujarat, Uttar Pradesh, Chennai, and Nepal, from 2006–2009. A key component is the

development of pilot activities at community and state levels to enhance adaptation and resilience.

7. PLC-Coastal was established in 2006 with support from the American India Foundation to Utthan. See www.plccoastal.org/ (last accessed November 2008).

8. Groups of higher castes or higher social standing may perceive those of lower caste as being 'polluted' or 'dirty', and will not permit them to share social spaces such as temples, even in times of need.

9. For a full discussion on gender and land rights in India, see Agarwal (2003). Despite recent reforms in Hindu property laws to give women (wives, daughters) equal inheritance rights over land as men/sons, the implementation of such laws varies from state to state in India. In Gujarat, there is an active civil-society land-rights network, which Utthan is a part of, and which has successfully helped many small and marginal women farmers claim their just rights over land they had inherited.

10. See www.cspc.org.in (last accessed November 2008)

11. Self-help groups are small (10–15 people), voluntary groups, primarily of women, that were initially facilitated by NGOs with the intent of mobilizing collective savings and empowering women economically through access to credit, bypassing exploitative moneylenders. Gradually, self-help groups have been linked to banks for larger loans, and federations are being promoted to support micro-enterprises as well as raise larger gender-rights issues.

12. Women are actively involved in several village water committees, facilitated by Utthan under various decentralization programmes. They are not part of the water sub-committees as these are largely responsible for accessing safe water and sanitation after a disaster, rather than for daily water governance.

13. The proposed Micro-financial Sector (Development and Regulation) Bill (2007), which is still under consideration by Parliament, has been strongly opposed by civil society for its anti-poor and anti-women implications.

References

ActionAid (2005) *Participatory Vulnerability Analysis: A Step by Step Guide for Field Staff*, London: ActionAid International.

Agarwal, B. (2003) 'Gender and land rights revisited: exploring new prospects via the state, family and the market,' in S. Razavi (ed.) *Agrarian Change, Gender and Land Rights*, Oxford: Blackwell and Geneva: United Nations Research Institute for Social Development.

Ahmed, S. (2006) 'Gender, vulnerability and disasters: key concerns for policy and practice', *Disaster and Development* 11: 165–77.

Ahmed, S. and D. Mustafa (2007) 'Understanding vulnerability, building capacity', in M. Moench and A. Dixit (eds.) *Working with the Winds of Change: Towards Strategies for Responding to the Risks Associated with Climate Change and Other Hazards*. Boulder, CO: ISET, Kathmandu: ISET-Nepal, and Geneva: ProVention.

Anderson, M. and P. Woodrow (1989) *Rising from the Ashes: Development strate-gies in times of disasters*, London: Westview Press.

Ariyabandu, M. M. and M. Wickramasinghe (2003) *Gender Dimensions in Disaster Management: A guide for South Asia*, Colombo: Intermediate Tech-nology Development Group.

Bohle, H.G., T.E. Downing, and M.J. Watts (1994) 'Climate change and social vulnerability', *Global Environmental Change* 41: 37–48.

Bosher, L., E. Penning-Rowsell, and S. Tapsell (2007) 'Resources accessibili-ty and vulnerability in Andhra Pradesh: Caste and non-caste influences', *Development and Change* 38(4): 615–40.

Cutter, S. (1996) 'Vulnerability to environmental hazards', *Progress in Human Geography* 20(4): 529–39.

Duvvury, N. (1998) 'Women and agriculture in the new economic regime', in M. Krishnaraj, S.M. Ratna, and S. Abusaleh (eds.) *Gender, Population and Development*, New Delhi: Oxford University Press.

Fussel, H. (2007) 'Vulnerability: a generally applicable conceptual framework for climate change research', *Global Environmental Change* 17: 155–67.

GHDR (2004) *Gujarat Human Development Report*, Ahmedabad: Mahatma Gandhi Labour Institute.

Government of India (2008) *National Action Plan on Climate Change*, Prime Minister's Council on Climate Change, Government of India.

Hyogo (2005) *Hyogo Framework for Action 2005-2015: Building the Resilience of Nations and Communities to Disasters*, A/CONF.206/6, World Conference on Disasters Reduction, January 18-20, Kobe, Hyogo, Japan.

ISET (forthcoming 2008) 'From research to capacity, policy and action: En-hancing adaptation to climate change for poor populations in Asia through research, capacity building and innovation', London: DFID and Ottawa: IDRC.

Kelkar, M. (2007) 'Mainstreaming gender in agricultural research and exten-sion: how do we move beyond efficiency arguments', in S. Krishna (ed.) *Women's Livelihood Rights: Recasting Citizenship for Development*, New Delhi: Sage.

Moench, M. and A. Dixit (2004) *Adaptive Capacity and Livelihood Resilience: Adaptive strategies for responding to floods and droughts in South Asia*, Boulder, CO: ISET and Kathmandu: ISET-Nepal.

Moench, M. and A. Dixit (2007) *Working with the Winds of Change: Towards strategies for responding to the risks associated with climate change and other hazards*, Boulder, CO: ISET, Kathmandu: ISET-Nepal, and Geneva: ProVen-tion.

Mustafa, D. and S. Ahmed (2008) 'Pinning down vulnerability: From narra-tives to numbers', ProVention and ISET Working Paper No. 2, www.i-s-e-t.org or www.climate-transitions.org [last accessed November 2008].

Twigg, J. (2007) 'Characteristics of a disaster-resilient community: a guidance note', London: DfID Disaster Risk Reduction Inter-agency Coordination Group.

UNDP (2007) *United Nations Human Development Report 2007/2008*, http:// hdrstats.undp.org/countries/data_sheets/cty_ds_IND.html [accessed 9 June 2009].

Vincent, K. (2004) 'Creating an index of social vulnerability to climate change in Africa', Tyndall Centre for Climate Research, Working Paper No. 56, University of East Anglia, Norwich, UK.
Wisner, B., P. Blaikie, T. Cannon, and I. Davis (2004) *At Risk: Natural hazards, people's vulnerability and disaster*, London and New York: Routledge.

About the authors

Sara Ahmed taught gender, development and environmental courses at the Instiute of Rural Management, Anand, India before working as a senior associate with the Institute for Social and Environmental Transition (ISET) on climate change, adaptation and vulnerability issues in South Asia. In May 2009, she joined IDRC's (the International Development Research Centre) Rural Poverty and Environment Team.

Elizabeth Fajber's work as a Senior Associate with ISET involves research and development on challenges of adaptation, vulnerability, and gender in Asia. Previously, she was based in India for nine years as a senior program specialist with the International Development Research Centre (IDRC) of Canada, working on issues of gender and social equity, resource governance, and poverty alleviation. She is also an independent consultant engaged in action research and strategic planning on gender and adaptive management.

CHAPTER 6

Resilience, power, culture, and climate: a case study from semi-arid Tanzania, and new research directions

Valerie Nelson and Tanya Stathers

This chapter first appeared in *Gender and Development* 17(1), pp. 81–94, March 2009.

Rapid changes to the climate are predicted over the next few years, and these present challenges for women's empowerment and gender equality on a completely new scale. There is little evidence or research to provide a reliable basis for gender-sensitive approaches to agricultural adaptation to climate change. This chapter explores the gender dimensions of climate change, in relation to participation in decision-making, divisions of labour, access to resources, and knowledge systems. It draws on insights from recent research on agricultural adaptation to climate change in Tanzania. The chapter then explains why future gender-sensitive climate-adaptation efforts should draw upon insights from 'resilience thinking', 'political ecology', and environmental anthropology – as a way of embedding analysis of power struggles and cultural norms in the context of the overall socio-ecological system.

Introduction

Poverty and vulnerability to climate risks are not the same, but there are significant overlaps. It is very likely that climate change will have different effects on women and on men, exacerbating poverty and existing inequalities. Increased vulnerability is predicted for millions of smallholder farmers in the South, due to the effects of climate change on agricultural production (Easterling *et al.* 2007; Huq and Ayers 2007; Ziervogel *et al.* 2008). This is particularly the case in Africa, although the climate predictions describe a complex and diverse set of potential outcomes for the continent (Christensen *et al.* 2007). The goal of tackling gender inequalities and supporting women's empowerment has been a part of international development for some time, as has the exploration of the gender, poverty, and environment nexus in academia. However, the scale of projected climate change presents challenges on a completely new level.

More attention to gender and power analysis is urgently required in un-derstanding how the impacts of climate change will play out in poor people's livelihoods, but also to identify the secondary impacts of initiatives imple-mented by governments, NGOs, and the private sector in response to perceived risks. First, this chapter explores some of the gender and equity dimensions of climate change and some of the concepts that can guide gender-climate research. Second, it applies a gender lens to some initial findings from an agricultural-climate innovation project in a semi-arid area of Tanzania. Third, it sets out some new directions in climate-change research and describes how these relate to gender studies.

Gender, equity, and climate change

The gender and equity dimensions of climate change are likely to be many, as climate change will affect all parts of the world. It is therefore useful to consider the scope of these (interrelated) dimensions: (i) the gender and de-velopment inequalities that underpin the functioning of the carbon-based global economy; (ii) the gender impacts of climate change in different parts of the world and in diverse agro-ecosystems; (iii) the gender dimensions of participation in climate negotiations; (iv) the gender impacts of mitigation activities, such as promotion of biofuels, carbon trading, and labelling; and (v) the gender-differentiated impacts of adaptation initiatives and processes (e.g. migration).

To date, there has not been adequate attention given to gender analysis in any of these areas. For example, the impacts of climate-mitigation activities are far from speculative, as the effects are already being widely felt, but the empirical evidence is limited. The expansion in first-generation liquid biofuels creates gendered risks in food insecurity, pressures on resource access and bio-diversity, and employment discrimination (Rossi and Lambrou 2008).

Similarly, on adaptation, there is a rapidly increasing amount of research on farmer observations of climate change (see a recent survey of farmers in ten African countries: Maddison 2006, 25) and documenting existing coping and adaptation strategies for managing climate risks (e.g. IUCN 2007). But rarely do these give sufficient attention to how these impacts and strategies may be gendered or differentiated along other lines of social difference.

Existing gender norms and ability to adapt to climate risks

Existing gender norms and power inequalities shape the ability of men and women to adapt to climate risks (Rossi and Lambrou 2008). These include: (i) participation in decision-making and politics; (ii) the division of labour, (iii) resource access and control, and (iv) knowledge and skills. Culture and knowledge systems shape all of these norms, influencing what is deemed ap-propriate in a particular society – although this is contested and reworked in everyday life (Long and Long 1992).

Achieving greater gender equality and women's voice in decision-making is critical in climate negotiations, and in national/sub-regional mitigation and adaptation planning. More creative ways of supporting women's direct advocacy in this arena should be developed, using community research and communication (e.g. through the use of participatory video, as discussed elsewhere in this issue (Nelson and Braden 1999)). Gender analysis in adaptation plans is lacking. There is no gender differentiation of interests or possible impacts discernable in Tanzania's National Adaptation Programme of Action (NAPA) on climate change – it refers only to 'vulnerable communities'. This is still a plan and things could change in implementation. But the aim should be to develop more integrated and participatory multi-tiered approaches in adaptation planning, providing space for less powerful voices (Paavola, in Adger *et al.* 2006, 217).

The gender-based division of labour leaves men and women with different levels of exposure to climate risks and opportunities (Rossi and Lambrou 2008). It is possible that there will be whole shifts in agricultural patterns, as the biophysical patterns of feasibility of crop production change. As a consequence, the range of livelihood options open to households may disappear, although others may open up and men and women will be differently exposed to new and existing climate-related risks. Positive outcomes could also occur as gender norms are challenged. But a critical issue for community adaptation will be how rapidly such 'system'-level shifts will occur, and who will be worst affected in situations of sudden change.

Livelihood resource access and control is gendered. This is the case for the whole range of resources (e.g. land, water, trees, social networks, income, credit, government social protection and safety nets, infrastructure, education, health facilities, political power, etc.). Men and women are likely to have different options and 'safety nets' for coping with climate change (Rossi and Lambrou 2008). Social safety nets and support mechanisms will become more important, but are also gendered. For example, climate index-based insurance schemes are being trialled in different parts of the world, and while these could provide important support in times of hardship, such market-based mechanisms could also undermine existing indigenous webs of obligation and support. As substantial climate-adaptation financing becomes available, how easily will women and men be able to access these resources or influence how they are invested? Social turbulence could provide avenues for women's empowerment, but increased resource conflicts could have the opposite effect.

Women and men may have both common and distinct forms of knowledge and skills, because of the differing responsibilities they have in production, reproduction, and trade. Women's knowledge about climate and agriculture has often been overlooked in rural development in the past, but social-science studies have amply illustrated women's role in agriculture. African women's indigenous agricultural knowledge supports household food security, especially in hard times (e.g. drought and famine), where they can use their knowledge of drought and pest-tolerant plants (Ramphele 2004 and Eriksen 2005, cited in IPCC 2007, 457) and seed selection to cover diverse conditions in a growing season (Easton and Roland 2000, cited in IPCC 2007, 457).

Recognition of these gendered knowledge systems and skills may provide a rich resource for coping with climate change (Rossi and Lambrou 2008). A Bolivian agricultural development project is building on the specialist climate-prediction and agricultural knowledge of particular men and women in Aymara communities, known as *yapachuris* or 'sowers' (ISDR 2008). The international NGO InterCooperation, a Bolivian NGO called PROSUKO, and UNAPA (a farmers' organization) are providing financial and technical services to members for agricultural development and risk management, mainly by supporting the *yapachuris* to share their knowledge through farmer-to-farmer extension. The high-altitude plains around Lake Titicaca are characterized by climate hazards (frost, rain, and hailstorms, and conversely, extreme heat and dryness) – all of which are predicted to intensify due to climate change (*ibid.*). Women are usually responsible for storage, and female *yapachuris* store a broad range of potato varieties, grain seeds, and other species, including medicines. They can identify ways to manage risk for other women farmers, as they know the best conditions and locations for sowing each species and variety. They are also being trained in monitoring bio-indicators of climate and weather-related hazards (*ibid.*, 7) and in leading negotiations over long-term market access for local produce (*ibid.*, 5). Positive project achievements include reductions in crop losses from drought, hail, frost, and flooding, plus more stable market access for local crops. This instrumental use of women's knowledge must avoid assumptions that women are necessarily inherently 'closer to nature' than men (Nelson *et al.* 2002), as these kinds of knowledge differences are socially acquired. Climate-related initiatives must retain a solid focus on the dynamics of power relations and the equity impacts occurring – avoiding giving women extra work without additional support.

Gender, climate change, and agriculture in semi-arid Tanzania

A case study from Tanzania[1] draws on findings from an action research project (part of the Climate Change Adaptation in Africa programme (CCAA)). The project aims to strengthen agricultural adaptation to climate change through multi-stakeholder innovation and learning. Participatory situation analyses in two Tanzanian villages in Dodoma (Laikala, Kongwa district; Chibelela, Bahi district) were conducted, including key informant interviews, focus-group discussions, and individual interviews with men and women from different socio-economic and age groups. The project is at an early stage, but some interesting insights can be gained by analysing these findings using a 'gender lens'. The findings illustrate some of the complexities of analysing climate-change impacts in areas characterized by climatic variability – where farmers are already coping with uncertainty coupled with ongoing trends (e.g. endemic poverty, rapid population growth, etc.), which limit people's capacity to adapt (Thomas and Twyman 2005; Morton 2007).

Climate projections and agricultural scenarios for Tanzania

Generally speaking, it is thought that agriculture is likely to be affected by climate change in a number of ways (e.g. reductions in crop yields, size of areas for crop production and grazing, increases in pests and diseases). Predictions for East Africa are uncertain, but suggest that up to 10 per cent of Tanzanian grain production may be lost by 2080 (Parry *et al.* 1999; Downing 2002). In the Dodoma and Tabora central regions, maize yields may decrease by 80 per cent (Mwandosya *et al.* 1998). Below is analysis of the project findings from a gender perspective.

i) *There is a high degree of consensus in local observations of climate change across different social groupings.* Shortened and highly unpredictable rainfall season; extreme winds, which now blow all year round due to loss of vegetation cover; stronger winds forcing the rain clouds across the sky without letting them rain; more intense sunshine and heat. Increased drought was mentioned by both men and women as a result of less predictable and more intense sunshine and heat. Women in both villages identified a much colder period in June and July than in the past, whereas none of the men interviewed mentioned this; this was possibly mentioned more by the women because they lost poultry at this time. These local observations about climate change are consistent with scientific projections (Mwandosya *et al.* 1998; Hulme *et al.* 2001; IPCC 2001) which suggest that Tanzania will warm by between 2°C and 4°C by 2100. Changes in temperature and rainfall are likely to prolong dry seasons, and to worsen periodic droughts, particularly inland.

ii) *The increasing unpredictability of the rainfall season has led to more people having to use oxen ploughs.* Ploughing land using oxen is much faster than by hand, and this speed allows maximum use of the shortened, often intermittent rainy period for crop production. However, the poorest households can rarely afford to plough using oxen, and the wealthier owners prepare their own fields first. While the position of women varies, many said they were struggling with simultaneous increases in demands on their labour and the increased need to hire oxen ploughs.

iii) *There are crop failures, yield variability, migration, and heavy workloads.* Unpredictable rainfall, declining soil fertility, and increased incidence of some pest and disease problems are leading to more frequent crop failure and increased yield variability. Farmers are being forced to cultivate larger areas of land to obtain sufficient food, and this is increasing the trend for seasonal and (mainly) male outmigration – all of which is increasing the burden on women. Voluntary seasonal migration is not a new coping strategy in this region, but it is reported to be increasing, undermining family relationships and leading to the spread of HIV – particularly affecting women's wellbeing. Young people's perceptions of future rural livelihood opportunities are also being negatively affected. Male outmigration can have positive outcomes for women, challenging existing gender inequalities. It can lead to more freedom in decision-making for women over household cash, which can also increase due to remittances (Cleaver 2000). But, in other situations (echoed in people's accounts of life in Dodoma) more negative gender outcomes may occur.

Gender intersects with age and health as factors in determining vulnerability, according to the women's focus groups interviewed in Chibelela village. As might be predicted, they said that children, women, elders, widows and widowers, orphans, and the long-term sick people were the poorest and most vulnerable to climate change, because of their increasing inability to secure food in times of drought. Women in Dodoma with children are less able to take up labouring opportunities because of their child-care responsibilities and cultural norms. Increased food shortages were reported to be affecting the health of women, because they were eating fewer, poorer quality meals per day. It would appear that, in many ways, existing inequalities – created as they are by social norms and inequitable power relations – are already being compounded by increased climate variability in Dodoma.

iv) *There are changes in the crops grown and a need to replant more frequently.* Farmers in the two areas studied have changed the balance of crops grown, with greater cultivation of drought-tolerant crops. Farmers are choosing different faster-maturing sorghum varieties, because the rainy season is now so short that their traditional varieties cannot mature in time. Sesame and sunflower have been introduced following market demand and government advice – because they are more drought-tolerant. Cassava production has increased, because it is a drought-tolerant food crop. Farmers are changing the balance of crops grown due to climate, but also government advice and market signals. Chibelela women said that some crops (maize, groundnuts, bambara nuts, and cowpeas) are being grown more widely to earn cash, and because women received training on improving storage.

Changes to the mix of crops grown can alter men's and women's access to and control of the income, as well as workload, but the picture is mixed. Grain is typically sold by men, and women are less likely than men to control the cash that is received. Increased marketing of food crops (e.g. sorghum and maize) which are grown by women is increasing their workloads, despite the fact that they do not benefit from the profits. Conversely, the increased sale of groundnuts, bambara nuts, and cowpeas – traditionally sold by women – is providing women with more access to, and control of income. While the division of labour and norms about sale and control of income are relatively fixed for some crops, this is not the case for others. Also, the norms are negotiated differently from household to household. The introduction of sesame and sunflower may have led to more household income, but control of this cash is not always shared and these crops have led to more weeding work for women.

A more frequent need to replant annual crops is widely reported. Farmers have to replant bulrush millet and groundnuts more often, as rains are unpredictable, coming and then stopping abruptly, meaning that time and seeds are wasted, and the quality of the crops affected. The gender impacts are mixed: women tend to be responsible for groundnut cultivation in Dodoma, so they bear the brunt of having to replant, but, at the same time, women tend to have control of the groundnut income, so increased cropping and sales tend to benefit them.

v) *It is important to explore poverty and system resilience over time.* In times of hardship, such as prolonged extreme climatic events (e.g. drought), people are forced to sell assets to get food. Men in both villages reported reduced crop yields and had sold off assets (e.g. livestock) at low prices in hard times. This can lead to the inability to invest for the long term, and contributes to the inter-generational transfer of poverty (Tanner and Mitchell 2008). More analysis is needed of how climatic changes will interact with and possibly compound other trends affecting rural populations over time. Beyond cropping, other activities such as collecting firewood and water, which tend to be seen as 'women's work', are likely to be adversely affected by a changing climate, especially where this is compounded by localized environmental degradation. Decreased access to fuelwood was reported in the Dodoma studies – suggesting the probability of more work for women as they search further afield, leaving them less time to earn income, let alone rest or relax. As climate change occurs, there may be changes in the natural resource base upon which people rely for their livelihoods, and this will work in conjunction with social patterns of resource use. It is important to understand how localized environmental degradation, resource rights, and a changing climate will interact, while avoiding the over-simplifications of the past about environmental degradation by poor people.

How resilient is the agro-ecological system? Will the rich indigenous knowledge and coping strategies which exist in many places be enough to enable people to survive? In Dodoma, will the coping and adaptive strategies outlined above (such as replanting, crop switches, use of oxen ploughs) be sufficient to deal with climate change, particularly as the workload and responsibilities of (some) women increase? New directions in climate-change research highlight the fact that social and ecological changes will not necessarily occur in incremental ways.

New directions in climate-change research and gender

The scientific study of human-induced climate change has emerged from meteorological and biophysical sciences. Only latterly has there been greater engagement by (non-economic) social scientists and development practitioners in more interdisciplinary approaches. As a result, technological responses to climate change have been at the fore, with little thought given initially to the ways in which climate change affects human relations, or its impact on equality. Much of the early adaptation modelling and planning was quite top-down, but this is beginning to change, with greater emphasis now on participatory planning and action (Huq and Arendse, cited in Nelson *et al.* 2008). Some equity analysis is emerging in the climate-change research field (see for example Adger *et al.* 2006), but rarely is gender a central focus.

Early risk/hazards literature assessed biophysical threats and the exposure of specific places or sectors to those risks, but in the 1990s political economy/ ecology approaches showed that sensitivity and exposure to climate risks is shaped by socio-economic and political processes (Eakin and Luers 2006). Social research has shown how processes of negotiation, decision-making, and action shape development outcomes (e.g. Long and Long 1992). Resilience-based thinking can complement this analysis by showing how these processes influence the rest of the social and ecological system. Resilience thinking, an important new direction in climate-change research, emerged in the 1980s, with antecedents in the 'systems thinking' of the 1970s. It presents a fundamentally different view of how change occurs in complex and linked socio-ecological systems – and this has implications for development and gender policy and practice.

Change does not necessarily happen in a linear, incremental fashion, in ways intended by actors; yet development planners plan insufficiently for turbulence (Roche 1994; 1999). Change can be unpredictable and sudden, because of the ways in which complex systems work – via feedback processes and thresholds (Walker and Salt 2006, 32). Resilience is the ability of a system to absorb disturbance (e.g. market changes, fires, conflict) and maintain function, structures, and feedback processes. Socio-ecological complex systems can exist in different states or regimes (Eakin and Luers 2006), and their resilience is measured by distance from a threshold. The closer you are to a threshold, the less it takes to be pushed over. Sustainability is all about knowing if and where thresholds exist, and having the capacity to manage the system in relation to these thresholds (Walker and Salt 2006, 63). Once a system crosses a threshold (or multiple thresholds) it can behave in a different way, often with undesirable and unforeseen outcomes. Such a transition from one system state to another can be sudden and painful for vulnerable groups. Turbulent times can throw up opportunities to challenge constrictive social norms, but rapid system-level shifts bring real risks for all, particularly the least powerful.

This is not just an abstract field of enquiry. Such rapid shifts in systems from one state to another often come with unwelcome surprises (e.g. when a lake changes from clear water to persistent murky water (Walker and Salt 2006, 32)), or as illustrated by the current financial crisis or 'credit crunch'. Those with least resources and power are obviously the least likely to be able to adapt rapidly, to change their livelihoods and survive. Resilience analysis seeks to provide some pointers as to how to manage for resilience at a system level, although predicting where and how change will occur in a system is often impossible until it has already happened (Walker and Salt 2006).

Following through the principles of resilience requires a change in environmental governance from the traditional, 'managerialist', 'command-and-control' methods (optimizing efficiency in particular parts of the system and failing to consider the bigger system), to managing for uncertainty and building adaptive capacity. However, this may mean trade-offs, for example between reducing vulnerabilities now to specific perceived risks (as much adaptation currently aims to do), and developing sources of resilience and maintaining sufficient flexibility in the management system to cope with sudden surprises and shocks (Nelson *et al.* 2007). Resilience thinking does provide space for the agency of actors (*ibid.*), as 'desired outcomes' (the state in which a socio-ecological system is or should be) can be deliberated upon and worked towards. Yet who has a say in this process is clearly an important matter: 'Who decides what should be made resilient to what, for whom resilience is managed, and to what purpose?' (Lebel *et al.* 2006, cited in Nelson *et al.* 2007).

The understanding of development futures and gender in the light of climate change should also seek to draw upon the insights of environmental anthropology (e.g. that the Western notion of nature and society as separate entities is *not* a universal given (Croll and Parkin 1992)). In fact in many societies around the world, people's conceptions of how they relate to each other and the environment are much more complex. A key principle of resilience-based thinking is that we are all actors playing a role *in* socio-ecological systems; that we are all part of nature, with social and ecological systems linked in complex and dynamic ways. However, resilience scholars have not yet gone further in exploring how different societies construct ideas of climate, society, and environment, and what this means for adaptation decision-making.

The 'cultured climate' refers to how the meanings attached to climate vary across cultures and contexts (Roncoli *et al.* 2003; Strauss and Orlove 2003). This affects how they interpret scientific information (e.g. seasonal forecasting predictions). Religion and cosmologies can play an important role in shaping how people in different parts of the world view the landscape: 'Mountain communities in Costa Rica, Tibet and the Peruvian Andes see mountains as living beings or gods' or 'worship mosaics of landscapes consisting of rivers, peaks, valleys and agricultural landscapes' (Fabricius *et al.* 2007). Spirituality can shape landscape management, as sacred lakes, forests, and grazing areas can be protected and provide a reserve in times of crisis (*ibid.*). The causes of unfavourable climate events, such as failure of the rains, drought, or storms, can be seen as due to a failure by humans to appease deities. While religion and spirituality shape decision-making, statements about beliefs and practice can sometimes appear contradictory; forecasting can be seen in some religions as being an act of human vanity as the future is pre-determined, yet farmers also pray and take concrete, purposive actions to reduce risks (Roncoli 2006, 88).

Research on local observations of climate change is increasing, but social memory of climate is very unreliable from a scientific point of view. People remember what is important to them, which is influenced by their occupations and experiences. Discussion of weather and climate is a mechanism for constructing a shared understanding of the past and can have moral overtones and purposes. Cultural constructions of climate memories are as much to do with working out proper moral conduct as they are about economic goals and commemorating climate events. The British discuss the weather to avoid tensions and embarrassments related to strong social class divisions, and Tanzanian rainmaking rituals have gendered and symbolic meanings (Sanders, in Strauss and Orlove 2003).

Seasonal forecasting is one area of increasing focus in climate-change research, but scientific information cannot be pre-packaged. As it is delivered it inserts itself into existing power relationships and can catalyse these dynamics – for example, ethnic, gender, and seniority hierarchies were found to shape the processing of climate information amongst groups of Ugandan farmers discussing climate information (Orlove and Kabungo, cited by Roncoli 2006, 87). Local farmers will interpret the information they receive depending on their own worldview, concerns, culture, and accumulated experience of climate events (Roncoli *et al.* 2003, 197). Farmers in Burkina Faso were retaining only part of or completely different messages from those intended by scientific forecasters. Their interpretations depended largely on how they view rainfall, what they are interested in knowing about rainfall, and the risks they perceive – all of which may be gendered.

Perceptions of risk – including climate risks – can be gendered (Davidson *et al.*, cited in IPPC 2007, 457), and women's risk perceptions can be given less attention than those of their male counterparts. Understanding the cultural and gendered construction of climate, environment, and risks is thus an important part of climate adaptation – and has implications for climate and development policy, equity, and gender.

Conclusion

More empirical evidence from particular locations is needed to enable us to understand how the climate is changing and how this is interpreted and experienced in gendered ways. The case study from Dodoma gives a number of indications of how increased climate variability is influencing livelihood strategies, as well as the potential gender impacts, although the picture is still sketchy. A critical question is how far adaptation adjustments will suffice if there are rapid shifts in the socio-ecological system; who will be most affected; and what can be done in order to promote climate resilience in the overall system, in an equitable way. More gender-sensitive action research is needed as an integral part of adaptation efforts to find appropriate responses to climate change.

Note

1. The Tanzanian research was analysed by the authors. The original Tanzanian research was conducted by the CCAA project – led by Dr A. Majule and Dr E. Liwenga of the Institute of Resource Assessment, University of Dar es Salaam, Tanzania, with support from T. Stathers and R. Lamboll of the Natural Resources Institute, University of Greenwich. The project studies which have been analysed were:

    Stathers, T.E., Ngana, J.O., Katunzi, A., Swai, O.W., Kashaga, S.B., (2007) 'Climate Change Adaptations in More and Less Favoured Areas of Tanzania: Local Perceptions, Vulnerability and Current and Future Adaptation Strategies in Chibelela Village, Bahi District, Dodoma Region', Institute of Resource Assessment, University of Dar es Salaam, Tanzania. 81 pp.

    Stathers, T.E., Ngana, J.O., Katunzi, A., Swai, O.W., Kasanga, F.P.M., (2007) 'Climate Change Adaptations in More and Less Favoured Areas of Tanzania: Local Perceptions, Vulnerability and Current and Future Adaptation Strategies in Laikala Village, Kongwa District, Dodoma Region', Institute of Resource Assessment, University of Dar es Salaam, Tanzania. 80 pp.

    The project has been funded from June 2007 to March 2011. Project website http://www.ccaa-agrictama.org

References

Adger, W.N., J. Paavola, S. Huq, and M. Mace (2006) *Fairness in Adaptation to Climate Change*, Cambridge, MA: MIT Press.

Cannon, T. (2008) 'Reducing people's vulnerability to natural hazards: communities and resilience', WIDER Research Paper 2008/34, Helsinki: UNU-WIDER (United Nations University, World Institute for Development Economics Research).

Christensen, J.H., B. Hewitson, A. Busuioc, A. Chen, X. Gao, I. Held, R. Jones, R.K. Koli, W.T. Kwon, R. Laprise, V.M. Rueda, L. Mearns, C.G. Menéndez, J. Räisänen, A. Rinke, A. Sarr, and P. Whetton (2007) 'Regional climate projections. Climate change 2007: the physical science basis', in S. Solomon, D. Qin, M. Manning, Z. Chen, M. Marquis, K.B. Averyt, M. Tignor, and H.L. Miller (eds.) *Contribution of Working Group I to the Fourth Assessment Report of the Intergovernmental Panel on Climate Change*, Cambridge: Cambridge University Press, 847–940.

Cleaver, F. (2000) 'Analysing gender roles in community natural resource management: negotiation, lifecourses and social inclusion', *IDS Bulletin* 31(2): 60–7.

Croll, E. and D. Parkin (1992) *Bush Base: Forest farm. culture, environment and development*, London: Routledge.

Downing, T.E. (2002) 'Protecting the vulnerable: climate change and food security', in J.C. Briden and T.E. Downing (eds.), *Managing the earth: The Linacre lectures*, Oxford: Oxford University Press.

Eakin, H. and A. Luers (2006) 'Assessing the vulnerability of social-environmental systems', *Annual Review of Environment and Resources* 31: 365–94.

Easterling, W., P. Aggrawal, P. Batima, K. Brander, L. Erda, M. Howden, A. Kirilenko, J. Morton, J.-F. Soussana, J. Schmidhuber, and F. Tubiello (2007) 'Food, fibre and forest products', in M.L. Parry, O.F. Canziani, J.P. Palutikof, P.J. van der Linden, and C.E. Hanson (eds.) *Climate Change 2007: Impacts, Adaptation and Vulnerability. Contribution of Working Group II to the Fourth Assessment Report of the Intergovernmental Panel on Climate Change*, Cambridge: Cambridge University Press, 273–313.

Fabricius, C., C. Folke, G. Cundill, and L. Schultz (2007) 'Powerless spectators, coping actors, and adaptive co-managers: a synthesis of the role of communities in ecosystem management', *Ecology and Society* 12(1): 29.

Hulme, M., R. Doherty, T. Ngara, M. New, and D. Lister (2001) 'African climate change: 1900–2100', *Climate Research* 17(2): 145–68.

Huq, S. and J. Ayers (2007) 'Critical List: the 100 Nations most vulnerable to climate change', Sustainable Development Opinions Series, London: International Institute for Environment and Development.

Inter-governmental Panel on Climate Change (IPCC) (2001) *Climate Change 2001: Impacts, Adaptation, and Vulnerability*, Cambridge: Cambridge University Press.

Inter-governmental Panel on Climate Change (IPCC) (2007) *Climate Change 2007: Impacts, Adaptation and Vulnerability. Contribution of Working Group II to the Fourth Assessment Report of the Intergovernmental Panel on Climate Change*, Cambridge: Cambridge University Press.

ISDR (2008) 'Gender perspectives: Integrating disaster risk reduction into climate change adaptation: Good practices and lessons learned', Geneva: United Nations International Strategy for Disaster Reduction.

IUCN (2007) 'Climate change vulnerability assessment in Zambia', Climate Change and Development Project, Pilot Phase, Béatrice Riché – IUCN Forest Conservation Programme, Geneva: International Union for Conservation of Nature.

Leach, M., A. Sumner, and L. Waldman (2008) 'Discourses, dynamics and disquiet; multiple knowledges in science, society and development', *Journal of International Development* 20(6): 727–38.

Long, N. and A. Long (1992) *Battlefields of Knowledge: The interlocking of theory and practice in social research and development*, London: Routledge.

Maddison, D. (2006) 'The perception of and adaptation to climate change in Africa', Discussion Paper Series No. 10, Pretoria: Centre for Environmental Economics and Policy in Africa (CEEPA).

Morton, J.F. (2007) 'The impact of climate change on smallholder and subsistence agriculture', *Proceedings of the National Academy of Sciences of the United States of America* 104(50): 19680–85.

Mwandosya, M.J., B.S. Nyenzi, and M.L. Luhanga (1998) *The Assessment of Vulnerability and Adaptation to Climate Change Impacts in Tanzania*, Dar es Salaam: Centre for Energy, Environment, Science and Technology.

Nelson, D., W.N. Adger, and K. Brown (2007) 'Adaptation to environmental change: contributions of a resilience framework', *Annual Review of Environment and Resources* 32: 395–419.

Nelson, S. and Y. Lambrou (undated) 'People-Centred Climate Change Adaptation: Integrating Gender Issues', Food and Agriculture Organization Briefing Paper, Gender, Equity and Rural Employment Division (ESW), ftp://ftp.fao.org/docrep/fao/010/a1395e/a1395e00.pdf [last accessed November 2008].

Nelson, V. and S. Braden (1999) 'Communities meet policy-makers through video-supported analysis: Rural energy issues in Malawi', PLA Notes 34, London: International Institute for Environment and Development.

Nelson, V., R. Lamboll, and A. Arendse (2008) 'Adaptation, adaptive capacity and development', DSA-DFID policy forum background paper, http://climateanddevelopment.nri.org/background_papers/nelson_lamboll_and_arendse_climate_change_adaptation.pdf [accessed 9 June 2009].

Nelson, V., K. Meadows, T. Cannon, J. Morton, and A. Martin (2002) 'Uncertain predictions, invisible impacts, and the need to mainstream gender in climate change adaptations', *Gender and Development* 10(2): 51–9.

Parry, M., C. Rosenzweig, A. Iglesias, G. Fischer, and M. Livermore (1999) 'Climate change and world food security: a new assessment', *Global Environmental Change* 9(1): S51–67.

Redclift, M. and T. Benton (1994) *Social Theory and the Global Environment*, London: Routledge.

Roche, C. (1994) 'Operationality in turbulence', *Development in Practice* 4(3): 160–72.

Roche, C. (1999) *Impact Assessment for Development Agencies: Learning to Value Change*, Oxfam Development Guidelines, Oxford: Oxfam GB.

Roncoli, C. (2006) 'Ethnographic and participatory approaches to research on farmers' responses to climate predictions', *Climate Research* 33(1): 81–99.

Roncoli, C., K. Ingram, C. Jost, and P. Kirshen (2003) 'Meteorological meanings: farmers' interpretations of seasonal rainfall forecasts in Burkina Faso', in S. Strauss and B. Orlove, *Weather, Culture, Climate*, Oxford: Berg.

Rossi, A. and Y. Lambrou (2008) 'Gender and Equity Issues in Liquid Biofuels Production: Minimizing the Risks to Maximize the Opportunities', Rome: Food and Agriculture Organization, ftp://ftp.fao.org/docrep/fao/010/ai503e/ai503e00.pdf [last accessed November 2008].

Sen, A. (1990) 'Food, economics and entitlements', in J. Dreze and A. Sen (eds.) *The Political Economy of Hunger*, Oxford: Clarendon, 50–67.

Strauss, S. and B. Orlove (2003) *Weather, Culture, Climate*, Oxford: Berg.

Tanner, T. and T. Mitchell (2008) 'Entrenchment or enhancement: Could climate change adaptation help reduce chronic poverty?', Working Paper 106, Manchester: The Chronic Poverty Research Centre.

Thomas, D.S.G. and C. Twyman (2005) 'Equity and justice in climate change adaptation amongst natural-resource-dependent societies', *Global Environmental Change* 15(2): 115–24.

United Republic of Tanzania, Vice President's Office, Division of Environment (2007) National Adaptation Programme of Action (NAPA), http://unfccc.int/resource/docs/napa/tza01.pdf [accessed 9 June 2009].

Walker, B. and D. Salt (2006) *Resilience Thinking: Sustaining Ecosystems and People in a Changing World*, Washington DC: Island Press.

Ziervogel G., A. Cartwright, A. Tas, J. Adejuwon, F. Zermoglio, M. Shale, and B. Smith (2008) 'Climate change and adaptation in African agriculture', Stockholm: Stockholm Environment Institute.

About the authors

Valerie Nelson is a social development specialist at the Natural Resources Institute, University of Greenwich, and is currently working on climate anthropology and adaptation, as well as conducting fair and ethical trade research.

Tanya Stathers is a post-harvest, integrated pest-management specialist at the University of Greenwich. She has experience in innovation systems and is currently working on agricultural adaptation to climate change in Tanzania and Malawi.

CHAPTER 7

Gender, water, and climate change in Sonora, Mexico: implications for policies and programmes on agricultural income-generation

Stephanie Buechler

This chapter first appeared in *Gender and Development* 17(1), pp. 51–66, March 2009.

This chapter focuses on the sustainability of gendered agricultural income-generating activities in Sonora, near the Mexico–USA border, in the context of climate change. Farming, and fruit and vegetable home-processing enterprises, still predominate in the area. However, several types of fruits can no longer be produced in this area due to warmer temperatures. Climate change has implications for the sustainability of these activities, which will affect women and men differently, affecting control over their livelihoods and food security. The chapter makes recommendations for development policies and programmes, for these and similar agricultural communities worldwide.

Introduction

Low-income women in agricultural communities are among the world's poorest people. They are among the most vulnerable to the harmful impacts of climate change (Lambrou and Piana, 2006). These women are highly dependent on natural resources, such as water, for household tasks, and, frequently, for farming. They undertake farming either together with men, or alone as in the case of women's subsistence production, when men migrate, or when women are single or widowed (Buechler 2000; Buechler 2005). However, with warmer temperatures due to climate change, evaporation rates are higher, and water supplies are further strained by greater demand from competing sectors of the economy. Rainfall patterns are also less predictable due to climate change, and drought and flooding are more common. Higher rain intensities can also cause more run-off, which in turn tends to cause greater sedimentation (the settling of soil into surface-water bodies, such as rivers, that causes loss of some plant and aquatic life), as well as water pollution (Bierbaum 2008). This can harm crop yields and human health (Buechler and Devi Mekala 2005). These events can threaten women's livelihoods more than men's, due both to gendered responsibilities within the household and gendered constraints to labour-market participation. Men may increase migratory activities, and their absence increases women's workloads.

Two agricultural communities in north-west Mexico, in the state of Sonora, are the focus of an ongoing study on gender, climate change, and water.[1] Women and men in these communities process fruits and vegetables into canned and candied goods. For women, in particular, these activities allow them to earn and control income, and to maintain a degree of food self-sufficiency for their households. Women also use these processed goods to exchange as gifts, which help secure women's status in important social networks, including ones which extend across the border to the USA. These tight social networks, in turn, help ensure family members' co-operation in the production process, principally in the form of labour, the purchase of raw materials, and marketing. The networks are increasingly important because current government programmes cannot be relied upon to act as safety nets.

The study: context, aims, and methods

The two communities are located approximately 75 and 65 kilometres respectively from the border with the state of Arizona in the USA. The community of Terrenate, with a population of 343 people, is located closer to the border, near the city of Imuris, which has a population of 6,273 people. San Ignacio, with a population of 720 people, is located further from the border, near Magdalena – a city of 30,000 people (INEGI 2006b). Terrenate and San Ignacio are located approximately 10 kilometres from each other, along the Magdalena River, at an altitude of 800 and 780 metres respectively above sea level.

This study aimed to analyse how social location (gender, class, caste, ethnicity, and age), and physical and political location, influence people's access to – and management of – natural resources. It took a multi-disciplinary approach; I am a feminist social scientist, trained in political science, public policy, sociology, and anthropology, and influenced also by feminist geography. I incorporated knowledge gained from living, working, and conducting research on gender and poverty in central Mexico, south India, highland Bolivia, and central Honduras, as well as the south-west and north-east USA, to understand the complex effect of context on the processes examined in Sonora, Mexico.

In the research, I used feminist research methodologies, in order to facilitate dialogue between myself as researcher and the women, men, and children I interviewed. As the interviewees discussed particular aspects of their lives, I also shared with them aspects of my own life. Interviewees were thus able to think about me in relation to social contexts that were important to them; for example, my position in my immediate and extended family, in my community, and within my work/institution. Deeper conversations often evolved out of these dialogues, taking place in the course of frequent formal and informal meetings in different physical as well as social locations, such as orchards, vegetable fields, inside the home compound (on the patio, inside the home), and in the market. At some of these meetings, respondents were alone; at others, they had other family members present. New avenues of inquiry opened up through using these methods, as new interpretations of questions arose and new areas that were important to the women and men were discussed and then incorporated into future interviews.

The research was carried out as part of my work in an applied research institute at the University of Arizona. While preparing for a new graduate course entitled 'Gender and Natural Resource Management in Latin America' for the Latin American Studies programme, that included the topics of gender and water, and gender and climate change, I became aware of the scarcity of published research on gender and climate change.

In both central Mexico and south India, I had learned from women and men farmers, NGOs, and government bodies, about unequal access to water for agriculture for different social groups. This gave me a foundation for researching gender, water, and agriculture linkages in Sonora. However, it was only after conducting initial interviews, and visiting orchards, tree nurseries, and vegetable fields in Sonora, that I began to be aware of the influence of climate change on water and agriculture in this region. I also noted gender differences in agricultural livelihood activities. The effects of climate change on these activities were already evident to the community members. These effects are predicted to become even more pronounced in the near future, and mitigation and adaptation efforts are therefore likely to take on even greater urgency for community members.

The Sonora, Mexico–Arizona border area, and climate change

Latin America is heavily dependent on natural resources, and is thus likely to be affected to a significant degree by climate change (Eakin and Lemos 2006; Baethgen 1997; Working Group on Climate Change and Development in Latin America 2006). According to IPCC technical paper VI, titled 'Climate Change and Water', the connections between water resources and climate change have not been understood or addressed properly in either climate or water policy and management, despite the fact that: '[a]ccording to many experts, water and its availability and quality will be the main pressures on, and issues for, societies and the environment under climate change; hence it is necessary to improve our understanding of the problems involved' (IPCC 2008, 7).

Along the Sonora, Mexico–Arizona border, average rainfall is less than 100mm per year. Winter rains come from the north, and summer rains come from the monsoon. The rainfall and temperature in the region is very variable, because of strong El Niño/Southern Oscillation (ENSO)-related weather patterns. Due to climate change, Mexico may experience a decrease in summer precipitation as well as an increase in winter precipitation of as much as 10 to 20 per cent (Magaña and Conde 2003). Studies on soil and air temperature, and on rainfall, discovered that there is a more rapid rate of localized global warming in Sonora than across the border in Arizona, mainly because of desertification caused by land clearing, deforestation, buffelgrass invasion,[2] and overgrazing, that causes a loss of biodiversity and economic potential of the land that includes the production of food (Stoleson *et al.* 2005; Klopatek *et al.* 1997). Daytime temperature ranges on the Sonoran border were found to be increasing in the summer, and decreasing in winter and early spring, at a faster rate than on the Arizona side of the border (Balling *et al.* 1998). One study on climate change in the south-west of the USA predicted temperature increases of 2 to 3°C by 2030, and 4 to 7°C by 2090, and warned that this would put even more pressure on already scarce water resources, in part because of resulting higher evaporation rates (Sprigg and Hinckley 2000). Water-resource scarcity will affect irrigation, and warmer temperatures can harm plant health and agricultural productivity.

Agricultural policies and economic conditions, in addition to climate change, have a profound effect on the food security of regions, countries, and individuals. The World Bank and the International Monetary Fund have directed Mexico and many other developing countries to cut agricultural subsidies, in order to reduce budget deficits. This has discouraged production (Bradsher and Martin 2008). The involvement by the Mexican state in agriculture has diminished greatly since the 1980s; between 1981 and 1993, government investment in agriculture diminished by 81.8 per cent (Buechler 2001; Robles 2000). The budget for 2009 for the Secretary for Agriculture, Fishing and Livestock (Sagarpa) recommended by the President's office and sent to Congress in September 2008 was reduced by 9.4 per cent (La Reforma September 9, 2008). Mexico is a big importer of wheat, maize, and sorghum from the USA (Chapagain and Hoekstra 2008). From September 2007 to September 2008, wheat prices rose by 130 per cent, corn by 53 per cent, rice by 74 per cent, and soy by 87 per cent on the international market (FAO *et al.* 2008), affecting local food prices in Mexico. This set of dynamics, added to crop losses related to climate change, is likely to cause further price hikes. Low-income households, that include many agricultural producer families, are likely to be negatively impacted by these higher food prices since most purchase, rather than produce, the majority of their basic food items. Farming communities' food security is also affected by crop losses, since a portion of food grown is normally retained for household consumption.

Water, climate change, and agricultural production in the study areas

Water in the study areas

There are three water sub-regions along the Mexico–USA border; the area studied is located in the central surface border area of Sonora, Arizona, New Mexico, and Western Texas. This sub-region does not have any major river systems (unlike the Colorado river watershed to the West, and Rio Grande/Rio Bravo to the East), yet there are numerous growing cities with agricultural areas that surround them (Maganda 2005, 4). Competition for water from growing urban centres, industry, and agriculture is putting pressure on water resources in the state (Magaña and Conde 2003) and in the study area. This is typical of many other areas near urban centres throughout Mexico, and, indeed, throughout the world. Increasing pressures on water causes farmers to be more susceptible to climate change (Appendini and Liverman 1994; Ingram *et al.* 2008).

Water from the Los Alisos Basin/Magdalena River is piped to supply the nearby city of Nogales for domestic water supply, and this means less groundwater and surface water is available for agriculture in the communities studied. The cropped area in the state of Sonora has diminished by 40 per cent from 1996 to 2004 (Bracamonte *et al.* 2007). In this semi-arid, drought-prone region, which has an average rainfall of approximately 330mm per year, the majority of the agriculture is irrigated. Water for irrigation in the communities studied comes from springs channelled into irrigation canals, from wells, and from municipal domestic supply from groundwater (Buechler forthcoming).

Control and ownership of land

Agricultural land in both communities is mostly in the hands of men, due to a patriarchal and patrilineal system of land ownership (Buechler, fieldnotes, January–April 2008), and government policies that continue discrimination against women as property holders and farmers (Robles *et al.* 1993; Buechler and Zapata 2000; Deere and León 2001; Sachs 1996).

What is cultivated?

In San Ignacio, fruit production predominates. Orchards are common in many of the towns surrounding the cities of Magdalena and Imuris. Fruit production in the area has a long history. Jesuit missionary Eusebio Kino, soon after founding the mission of Santa Maria Magdalena de Buquivaba in 1688, taught the Pima Indians about raising and cultivating fruit trees.

The varieties of fruits that are grown are shifting. At present, mainly quince, peaches, persimmons, pears, and citrus fruits are produced. Plum and apricot production once predominated; however, these fruits have almost completely disappeared. Fig and olive trees have also become much rarer in the area. The producers in the area attributed these changes in cropping patterns to water scarcity (which has been particularly evident, they claimed, in the last seven years), to warmer average temperatures, and to nematode infections of the tree roots. Community members with tree nurseries noted that a higher number of saplings die due to higher temperatures, and some have decided to stop raising trees as a result. Farmers are also abandoning farming for other occupations in urban areas in Mexico or the USA. This has a negative impact on agricultural labour availability.

In Terrenate, vegetables are the main crops cultivated, although many farmers have some fruit trees located on the peripheries of their vegetable fields. Vegetable cultivation in the area has grown steadily; buyers often come to the fields with their trucks to sell the produce in the USA, directly from their trucks along the road. However, the cropped area is becoming smaller, due to internal – as well as international – migration, and off-farm employment in Magdalena and other surrounding cities, that alters labour availability. The cropped area is also being reduced, as land is taken out of production due to water scarcity and climate change. Water scarcity is manifested in falling water tables and less surface water in the river and from springs. Climate change is causing temperatures to rise, which causes higher rates of evaporation of this scarce water.

Processing and marketing the produce

In San Ignacio, and to a lesser extent, in Terrenate, fruits are canned (cooked with sugar then placed in air-tight glass jars) by women, or are made into jams or quince jelly by men and women. Women pickle and can a wide variety of vegetables in both San Ignacio and Terrenate. This production fostered tight social networks important for sustaining livelihoods. Irma explained that the main reason she engaged in canned fruit and jelly production with her husband and children was so that they could all work together.[3] Even in adulthood, sons and daughters often helped their parents during peak production periods; younger children took over housekeeping and child care. Women with migrant relatives living in the USA near the border often obtained used or new glass jars from them for the canned goods. Women thus enlisted aid for this production, even from family members across the border who might have become estranged, ceasing support for their Mexican relatives (Buechler forthcoming). Men tended to concentrate on the more commercial aspects of quince jelly and jam production, selling it to local and regional stores and municipal markets in the cities of Nogales and the more distant state capital, Hermosillo.

Canned fruit and pickled vegetable production also supported income generation. They are sold by the women to itinerant vendors, who come to the community to buy the products; these are then sold on stands along the highway. They are also sold to stores in Magdalena and Imuris, to people for home consumption, and to religious pilgrims who pass through the area in October. Carmen, a woman whose family members own vegetable fields and orchards in Terrenate, relayed that she gives a case of canned peaches to a relative who lives in Nogales, Arizona to sell. Women mainly used the income to purchase food and clothes, and to pay for their children's educational expenses. As Alicia, an agricultural labourer, exclaimed, '[m]en work in the orchards but women kill themselves doing these things [producing canned fruits and vegetables] so that their children can get an education' (field interviews, April 2008). Women emphasized using the products to support their daughters' education. In turn, educated children were expected to maintain their parents in their old age.

These agricultural products are also used by women to help secure social networks and household food security. Fruit and vegetable preserves are given as gifts to maintain reciprocal relationships with relatives and close friends, or given to important figures in the community such as the priest. Esperanza explained, 'I cannot give birthday gifts because of the cost, so I bring along a can of my peaches when I attend a birthday party'. Selena revealed that she held products in reserve for gift giving and home consumption:

> *I keep two boxes of canned peach jars and four boxes of quince jelly bars to give as gifts. I also keep one box of canned peaches and a few pieces of quince jelly but these are for my household. I keep some fruit to make fruit juice for my family and also to eat as snacks.*
> (Field interviews, March 2008)

These exchanges are important to women, because they depend on mutual aid arrangements in the form of reciprocal gifts, and women helping each other out by providing labour for agriculture and small-scale enterprises. Jars or bars of quince jelly are also often given to other family members in need, as in the example of a woman who gave her urban-based daughter-in-law canned fruits and vegetables to sell, to earn money for her sick husband's (the woman's son) medicines and doctor's visits. June Nash, an anthropologist who has studied gender and work in Latin America for over four decades, has helped to shed light on the underlying importance of such roles: 'Women's mediating positions linking families to communities and communities to larger political, economic and social circuits, become crucial to survival where global development processes have undermined social reproduction' (Nash 2005, 145). The necessity of this exchange in the communities studied is rooted in the poor remuneration of their urban-based offspring, and in the low incomes in general (Buechler forthcoming).

Sustainability of these livelihood activities in the context of water scarcity and climate change

The sustainability of this production and processing is unclear, however. There are already signs of growing water depletion, with lower water levels in the spring-fed irrigation channels and greater pressure on water resources, particularly in May to June, and November to December. This causes greater dependence on the springs for water for household use. In Terrenate, open wells were dug by the vegetable farmers to try to compensate for the decreasing spring-water levels. However, the pumping costs added to the rising costs of other inputs like fertilizer, seeds, and pesticides, and the low returns on their investments in terms of crop prices, make this production (as one woman farmer expressed it) *incosteable* (uneconomical). Many people in both the communities studied have migrated to the USA, though new migration has been made more difficult due to increased border surveillance. Maximum spring and summer temperatures are also rising, and these are already having a noticeably deleterious effect on fruit saplings and on vegetable production, and are causing farmers to reduce the area under production.

Climate variability is likely to intensify in the future, resulting in greater impact on farmers' livelihoods. Unseasonable frost in April 2008 was followed by very heavy wind and rain in May, first freezing and then blowing away many of the flowers that would have formed fruit on the fruit trees. When asked whether the government would compensate farmers for their resulting losses, José, a fruit farmer in San Ignacio, replied:

> *My friends and I were sitting yesterday in the plaza talking about our crop losses and had a good laugh. One friend said with a smile, 'I have insurance'. Another friend replied 'I have insurance too', and then I joined in and said 'I have insurance too – I have the assurance that when I die I will be carried down this street right here, on the way to the cemetery over there'.*
> (Field interviews, July 2008)

This seemingly easy banter between friends belies the serious consequences of weather-related crop loss, in a context in which the state suspended crop insurance to small farmers as early as 1990. With climate change, the need for crop insurance will increase.

Unpredictable, heavy rainfalls make the whole area near the border vulnerable to erosion and flooding (Vásquez-León and Bracamonte 2005). The communities studied are both located along the Magdalena River. In 1993, there was heavy flooding that ruined much of the land and the wells used in agricultural production on both sides of the Magdalena River. Climate variability is likely to increase with climate change, as is the frequency and intensity of extreme weather such as drought and flooding, placing the communities at greater risk of their fields flooding (homes are located on higher ground, therefore are usually spared). Women play more important roles in household water and fuelwood collection than men in Latin America as a whole (Byrne and Baden 1995), and in the study communities. After a flood, these responsibilities become more arduous, because community water sources often become polluted, necessitating travel to obtain water, or the often unaffordable option of purchasing water (Reyes 2002).

Water depletion and climate change will increasingly affect women, due to unequal gender power relations. Social networks that have been maintained in part by extended family members working together and exchanging or gifting these agricultural products within the community will be weakened. Weaker social networks will translate into reduced community cohesion and reduced control over community-development processes. Women's vulnerability is likely to increase in the absence of strong social networks that have functioned to act as a safety net extending between mothers and their children, women and their spouses, women and their neighbours, women and important community figures, and women and their relatives who are located within and outside community, regional, and national boundaries. Women depend to a greater extent than men do on these networks because most of their work entails larger labour (rather than scarce capital) expenditures; women's workload increases during crisis periods, creating a situation in which they have more work than they can perform by themselves, necessitating help by others. Women's economic autonomy is also at risk from climate change. The food-security status of women and their households will also become weaker without fruits and vegetables that they can retain for household food consumption, particularly in light of rising food prices. Women will be in a more vulnerable position in the face of these changes. As a result, their particular, gendered needs will need to be incorporated into planning at the policy and programmatic levels.

Policy and programmatic implications

A holistic approach to policy formulation and programme development is needed for these and similar agricultural communities. Gendered vulnerabilities to climate change and water scarcity should figure prominently in all climate-change-related initiatives. One of the main ways to improve women's adaptive capabilities is through employment creation and job training, in the nearby cities, and in the communities themselves. Another is to address some of the environmental conditions that harm agricultural livelihoods.

Mining is an activity that provides employment for men in the border area. Very few women are employed (Browning-Aiken, n.d.). One of the closest mines is near Cananea, Sonora, approximately 120 kilometres away from the communities studied. A van from the Cananea mine picks up and drops off miners from the study area. A new mining area is scheduled to open in 2009, near Magdalena. This will undoubtedly create employment options for young men in the two study communities and other areas. Male employment may help household livelihood security and provide alternatives to agriculture which, as discussed, will become an increasingly risky activity; in part, as a result of climate change and water scarcity. Mining activities require large volumes of water, that are then contaminated with metals. Peña Blanca Lake, near the Mexico–USA border and not far from the study area, is currently being drained and will then be dredged, due to mercury, lead, and arsenic contamination from long-abandoned mining operations in the vicinity (Davis 2008).

Maria, from San Ignacio, works as a maid, as a fruit and vegetable processor, and as an agricultural labourer, and has a son who works in mining. Shifts rotate so that he works night shifts one month, and day shifts the next. Shifts are 12 hours long, six days a week. Although health insurance and benefits are provided, Maria explained: 'my son wants to get out of this job because it is horrible work...he says that it is very dangerous' (field interviews, January

2008). She contrasted this work with her married daughter's work: 'my daughter lives in Terrenate. She is doing very well because she married a man with land there, and they have fruit trees, fodder and cows and she makes fresh cheese to sell and canned peaches for her family' (field interviews, 2008).

Industry is an important employer in Magdalena and Imuris. There are *maquiladoras* (assembly plants); one of the largest produces hospital equipment. A few people also work in *maquiladoras* in Nogales. Vans from the *maquiladoras* go to the two communities studied, to collect and drop off workers each day. Beverages, construction, and furniture production are other urban businesses. Greenhouses are located on the road to San Ignacio, as well as near Imuris on the Imuris–Nogales highway. Some of the better-educated sons and daughters are employed as accountants and managers in these greenhouses. Others work at jobs such as transplanting and maintenance there. The majority of the workers are men (field interviews, June–September 2008).

There are many limitations to the eligibility of most women for the higher positions in these assembly plants, since they require higher education, but there are also only a few positions at higher levels. Most positions are remunerated at a low level, and require long working days for six days a week. Job instability is high, with few long-term contracts offered, and a high closure rate. Because of these factors, the desirability of these jobs for many women, including women with children, is low. One woman, Carmen, said that her daughter and son-in-law both worked for three years in a *maquiladora* that makes hospital equipment; however, they migrated to Arizona because they could not make ends meet. Teresa, a woman who worked in a *maquiladora* until she had children, shook her head and said, 'they pay miserable wages, and everything costs so much' (field interviews, June 2008, author's translation).

Employment in the greenhouses is problematic for several reasons. Greenhouse employment has been documented in other areas of Latin America such as Colombia to be dangerous to the health of their mostly female workforce (Rodriguez and Silva 1988; Wright and Madrid 2007). Workers in the greenhouses near Magdalena have complained that the temperature often reaches 43°C and that low compensation is offered for long working hours. Women who work there are mainly migrants from southern Mexico, and in general, mainly men are employed there (field interviews, September 2008).

Alternative employment to agriculture must be created that pays a living wage, offers decent working conditions, and offers the possibility for advancement. Job training and education for women would help make them competitive for new jobs that were created. Reliance on agriculture might be able to be reduced if better jobs are available. Family members would also be able to stay in Mexico, rather than migrate, which entails great personal risk and sacrifice for the migrant and the family members they leave behind.

Replicating one particular grassroots project from another area of Mexico might help to overcome climate-change and water-related obstacles in agricultural production in the study area. Such an initiative might help to control future localized climate change that, as mentioned above, is worse in Sonora than in the neighbouring south-west US region, and has as its most probable cause land clearing, deforestation, buffelgrass invasion, and overgrazing. This type of project would also aid in erosion control and in the retention of water after a rainfall. The risk from flooding would also diminish.

In a project in eight villages in the Mixteca region of Oaxaca, Mexico, a farmer organization called the Center for Integral Small Farmer Development in the Mixteca (CEDICAM) has organized farmers to plant native, drought-tolerant trees (raised in local nurseries) in order to help prevent erosion; improve water filtration into the ground; provide carbon capture and green areas; add organic material to enrich soil and provide more sustainable, cleaner wood for wood-burning stoves. CEDICAM is also working with farmers to construct contour ditches, retention walls, and terraces, to capture rainfall that recharges groundwater and helps revive springs; the contour ditches also help to control erosion. Local production and use of organic fertilizers is also being undertaken, and crop rotation and local selection of seeds is encouraged. Women are taking part in the construction of these structures, and may start reaping some of the benefits (Reider 2006, 56).

In San Ignacio and Terrenate, such measures would help to retain/harvest water from rainfall to recharge aquifers, and might also increase flow in the springs used for irrigation. Such measures may also help to control erosion; erosion, as mentioned before, has been documented in other areas in Sonora, and is made worse by climate change (for example, from increased heavy rain). Erosion is also a problem in San Ignacio and Terrenate. Planting trees on hillsides would also produce wood for cleaner fuel for the wood-burning stoves that are used to produce the canned fruit and vegetables and the quince jelly, and for heating homes and cooking during the winter. This would make production cheaper in terms of the time, labour, and money involved in collecting and/or purchasing wood. The use of organic fertilizers instead of chemical fertilizers, and the production of less water-intensive crops, as well as a move away from monoculture, (particularly evident in vegetable production in San Ignacio and Terrenate) would also help in reducing the negative impacts that chemical and water-intensive agriculture have on climate (Shiva 2005). Women would likely benefit in many ways from such projects that might help make fruit and vegetable production and processing part of sustainable livelihoods.

Conclusion

Women's livelihoods are jeopardised by changes in climate and associated depletion of water resources in the Sonora border area. The agricultural production and processing activities described here for two communities near Magdalena and Imuris cities are widespread throughout the region. It is clear that women and men have differing dependence on these activities. Women, who dominate fruit and vegetable canning and pickling, use these products as gifts, to strengthen social ties; these ties are important to them, because they help them enlist the aid of family members in their household, in their community, and in urban areas in Mexico. They also use their geographical location near the border to draw migrant relatives in the USA into the production and marketing of the canned goods. The loss of this production due to climate change and water scarcity would place women in a more vulnerable position, partly because current employment alternatives require higher education, and do not pay a living wage.

To assist such communities to respond to the challenge of building sustainable livelihoods in the face of climate change, a combination of mitigation and adaptation strategies will be needed. Employment-creation and job-training programmes, and an integrated project that includes erosion control, water harvesting/retention, reforestation, and local seed and organic fertilizer use, would begin to address the gendered needs of women and men in climate-change and water-scarcity adaptation processes. More macro-level policies are also necessary, such as government support of improved secondary education and small-scale agricultural production, including support for agricultural extension and crop insurance, as well as subsidies of agricultural inputs such as seeds and safer pesticides.

Notes

1. I gratefully acknowledge the funding obtained for this study, that is part of an ongoing research project near the Mexico–USA border, from the Resource Center on Agriculture and Food Security (RUAF) Foundation in the Netherlands (November 2007–May 2008), the Magellan Circle Award from the University of Arizona (January 2008–May 2008), and a Fulbright Scholar Border award (August 2008–April 2009).
2. Buffelgrass (Pennisetum ciliare) is 'a shrubby grass to 1.5 feet tall and 3 feet wide.' It 'grows densely and crowds out native plants of similar size.' (www.desertmuseum.org/invaders/invaders_buffelgrass.htm, last accessed November 2008)
3. All names of interviewees are pseudonyms, to protect their identity.

References

Appendini, K. and D. Liverman (1994) 'Agricultural policy, climate change and food security in Mexico', *Food Policy* 19(2):149–64.

Baethgen, W.E. (1997) 'Vulnerability of the agricultural Sector in Latin America to climate change', *Climate Research* 9: 1–7.

Balling R.C., J.M. Klopatek, M.L. Hildebrandt, and C.K. Moritz (1998) 'Impacts of land degradation on historical temperature records from the Sonoran Desert', *Climate Change* 40(3/4): 669–81.

Bierbaum, R. (2008) 'Coping with climate change: a national summit', *Environment* 50(4): 59–64.

Bracamonte, A.S., N. Valle Dessens, and R. Méndez Barrón (2007) 'La Nueva Agricultura Sonorense: Historia Reciente de un Viejo Negocio', *Region y Sociedad* XIX, Número Especial: 51–70.

Bradsher, K. and A. Martin (2008) 'Hoarding nations drive food costs even higher', *New York Times*, 30 June, www.nytimes.com/2008/06/30/business/worldbusiness/30trade.html?_r=1&th&emc=th&oref=slogin [accessed 9 June 2009].

Browning-Aiken, A. (forthcoming) *Regional Development and Social Memory: Border Voices*.

Browning-Aiken, A., B. Morehouse, A. Davis, M. Wilder, R. Varady, D. Goodrich, R. Carter, D. Moreno, and E. Dellinger McGovern (2007) 'Climate, water management, and policy in the San Pedro Basin: results of a survey of Mexican stakeholders near the U.S.–Mexico border', *Climatic Change* 85(3/4): 323–41.

Buechler, S. (2000) 'El Trabajo de Mujeres, Niñas, Niños y Hombres en Parcelas Irrigadas de Guanajuato en Tiempos de Crisis', in S. Buechler and E. Zapata (eds.), *Género y Manejo de Agua y Tierra en Comunidades Rurales de México*, Serie Latinoamericana, México, D.F.: International Water Management Institute and the Colegio de Postgraduados, Montecillo.

Buechler, S. (2001) 'Water and Guanajuato's Ejido Agriculture: Resource Access, Exclusion and Multiple Livelihood Strategies', unpublished Ph.D dissertation, Department of Sociology, Binghamton University.

Buechler, S. (2005) 'Women at the helm of irrigated agriculture in Mexico: the other side of male migration', in V. Bennett, S. Dávila Poblete, and M. Nieves Rico (eds.) *Opposing Currents: The Politics of Water and Gender in Latin America*, Pittsburgh, PA: University of Pittsburgh Press.

Buechler, S. (forthcoming) 'Gender, water and climate change dynamics of fruit and vegetable production and processing in peri-urban Magdalena, Sonora, Mexico', in A. Hovorka, H. de Zeeuw, and G. Prain (eds.) *Women Feeding Cities*, Leusden: RUAF Urban Agriculture Programme, RUAF Foundation, and Ottawa: International Development Research Centre (IDRC).

Buechler, S. and G.D. Mekala (2005) 'Local responses to water resource degradation in India: groundwater farmer innovations and the reversal of knowledge flows', *Journal of Environment and Development* 14(4): 410–38.

Buechler, S. and E. Zapata (2000) 'Anduve Detrás de Todo a la Corre y Corre: Género y Manejo del Agua y Tierra en Comunidades Rurales de México', México, D.F.: International Water Management Institute, and Montecillo: Colegio de Postgraduados.

Byrne, B. and S. Baden (1995) 'Gender, Emergencies, and Humanitarian Assistance', Briefings on Development and Gender (BRIDGE) Report, November.

Chapagain, A.K. and A.Y. Hoekstra (2008) 'The global component of freshwater demand and supply: an assessment of virtual water flow between nations as a result of trade in agricultural and industrial products', *Water International* 33(1): 19–32.

Davis, T. (2008) 'Cleanup starting at lake', *Arizona Daily Star*, 15 September, www.azstarnet.com/metro/257567 [accessed 9 June 2009].

Deere, C. D. and M. León (2001) *Empowering Women: Land and Property Rights in Latin America*, Pittsburgh, PA: University of Pittsburgh Press.

Denton, F. (2002) 'Climate change vulnerability, impacts and adaptation: why does gender matter?', *Gender and Development*. 10(2): 10–20.

Diaz, H. and B. Morehouse (2003) 'Climate and water in transboundary contexts: an introduction', in H. Diaz and B. Morehouse (eds.), *Climate and*

Water Transboundary Challenges in the Americas, Boston, MA: Kluwer Academic Publishers.

FAO (Food and Agriculture Organization) (2007) 'People-Centered Climate Change Adaptation: Integrating Gender Issues', Policy Brief, Rome: FAO.

FAO (Food and Agriculture Organization), IFAD (International Fund for Agricultural Development), and WFP (World Food Program) (2008) 'High Food Prices: Impacts and Recommendations', paper prepared for the Chief Executives Board for Coordination on 28–29 April, Berne, Switzerland.

Eakin, H. and M.C. Lemos (2006) 'Adaptation and the state: Latin America and the challenge of capacity-building under globalization', *Global Environmental Change* 16(1): 7–18.

INEGI (Instituto Nacional de Estadísticas, Geografía e Informática) (2006) 'Conteo de Población y Vivienda 2005. Resultados Definitivos.Tabulados Básicos', www.inegi.gob.mx/est/contenidos/espanol/sistemas/conteo2005/Default.ap [last accessed February 2008].

Ingram, H., J.M. Whiteley, and R.W. Perry (2008) 'The importance of equity and the limits of efficiency in water resources', in J.M.Whiteley, H.M. Ingram, and R.W. Perry (eds.), *Water, Place and Equity*, Cambridge, MA: The MIT Press.

IPCC (Inter-governmental Panel on Climate Change) (2008) 'Climate Change and Water', Technical paper VI, World Meterological Association (WMO) and United Nations Environment Programme (UNEP).

Klopatek, J.M., R.C. Balling Jr., A.W. Brazel, J. Franklin, and C.J. Watts (1997) 'Changing land use patterns along the United States–Mexican border: effects on ecosystems structure and climate feedbacks', Proceedings of the 12th Annual Meeting of the International Association of Landscape Ecology East Lansing, Michigan.

Lambrou, Y. and G. Piana (2006) 'Gender: The Missing Component of the Response to Climate Change', Rome: Food and Agriculture Organization, Gender and Population Division, Sustainable Development Department.

Lemos, M.C., E. Boyd, E.L. Tompkins, H. Osbahr, and D. Liverman (2007) 'Developing adaptation and adapting development', *Ecology and Society* 12(2): 26.

Maganda, C. (2005) 'Collateral damage: how the San Diego-Imperial Water Agreement affects the Mexican side of the border', *Journal of Environment and Development* 14: 486–506.

Magaña, V.O. and C. Conde (2003) 'Climate variability and climate change, and their impacts on the freshwater resources in the border region: a case study for Sonora, Mexico', in H. Diaz and B. Morehouse (eds.), *Climate and Water Transboundary Challenges in the Americas*, Boston, MA: Kluwer Academic Publishers.

McMichael, A.J., R.E. Woodruff, and S. Hales (2006) 'Climate change and human health: present and future risks', *The Lancet* 368 (9538): 859–869.

Nash, J. (2005) 'Women in between: globalization and the New Enlightenment', *Signs: Journal of Women in Culture and Society* 31(1): 145–67.

Nelson, V., K. Meadows, T. Cannon, J. Morton, and A. Martin (2002) Uncertain predictions, invisible impacts, and the need to mainstream gender in climate change adaptations', *Gender and Development* 10(2): 51–9.

Rea, D. (2008) 'Ven organizaciones desdén al agro; pero creen que diputados avalarán aumentos', *La Reforma*, 9 September, www.reforma.com/nacional/articulo/460/919887/[last accessed November 2008].

Reider, R. (2006) 'Voices of the North and South: finding common ground', in A. Cohn, J. Cook, M. Fernández, R. Reider, and C. Steward (eds.), *Agroecology and the Struggle for Food Sovereignty in the Americas*, International Institute for Environment and Development (IIED), the IUCN Commission on Environment, Economic and Social Policy (CEES), and the Yale School of Forestry and Environmental Studies, 55–9.

Reyes, R. R. (2002) 'Gendering responses to El Niño in Peru', *Gender and Development* 10(2): 61–9.

Robles, R. (2000) 'El Ajuste Invisible', in J. Aranda, C. Botey, and R. Robles (eds.), *Tiempo de Crisis, Tiempo de Mujeres*, Centro de Estudios de la Cuestión Agraria Mexicana A.C., Universidad Autónoma Benito Juárez de Oaxaca: Oaxaca, Mexico.

Robles, R., J.Aranda, and C. Botey (1993) 'La mujer campesina en la Epoca de la Modernidad', *El Cotidiano* 53: 25–32.

Rodriguez, M. and J. Silva (1988) 'Love, Women and Flowers – the cut flower industry in Colombia', documentary film, produced in Colombia, available from Women Make Movies.

Sachs, C. (1996) *Gendered Fields: Rural Women, Agriculture and Environment*, Boulder, CO: Westview Press.

Shiva, V. (2005) *Earth Democracy: Justice, Sustainability and Peace*, Cambridge, MA: South End Press.

Sprigg, W.A. and T. Hinckley (2000) 'Preparing for a Changing Climate: the Potential Consequences of Climate Variability and Change', report of the Southwest Regional Assessment Group for the U.S. Global Change Research Program, Institute for the Study of Planet Earth, University of Arizona, Tucson, Arizona.

Stoleson, S.H., R.S. Felger, G. Ceballos, C. Ratsh, M.F. Wilson, and A. Búrques (2005) 'Recent history of natural resource use and population growth in northern Mexico', in J.-L. E. Cartron, G. Ceballos, and R. S. Felger (eds.), *Biodiversity, Ecosystems and Conservation in Northern Mexico*, Oxford: Oxford University Press.

Vázquez-León, M. and Á. Bracamonte (2005) 'Indicadores Ambientales para la Agricultura Sustentable : Un Estudio del Noreste de Sonora', report for CONAHEC, El Colegio de Sonora, Sonora, Mexico and the University of Arizona Bureau of Applied Research in Anthropology, Tucson.

WEDO (Women, Environment and Development Organization) (2008) 'Women: Essential to Climate Change Solutions', WEDO Media Fact Sheet, New York: WEDO.

Working Group on Climate Change and Development in Latin America (2006) 'Up in Smoke? Latin America and the Caribbean. The threat from climate change to the environment and human development', the third report from the Working Group on Climate Change and Development in Latin America, 48.

Wright, C. and G. Madrid (2007) 'Contesting ethical trade in Colombia's cut-flower industry: a case of cultural and economic injustice', *Cultural Sociology* 1: 255–75.

About the author

Dr Stephanie Buechler is a Research Associate and Lecturer, School of Geography and Regional Development, University of Arizona, Tucson, Arizona, USA.

CHAPTER 8

Building gendered approaches to adaptation in the Pacific

Ruth Lane and Rebecca McNaught

This chapter first appeared in *Gender and Development* 17(1), pp. 67–80, March 2009.

This chapter reflects upon how gendered approaches to climate-change adaptation can be strengthened in the Pacific region. The chapter looks at what has been learnt in the region, surveys some examples of best practice in gender-responsive program-ming, identifies the challenges we face on our journey, and suggests future directions. It is a collaborative effort, comprising input from a number of agencies who have been proactive in the areas of gender, climate change, and disaster risk-reduction in the Pacific Region, including: the Red Cross/Red Crescent Movement in the Pacific region; the UNDP Pacific Centre; and World Wildlife Fund's (WWF) Fiji Country Programme.

The Pacific context

It is only recently that gender and climate change has become a blip on the ra-dar of many Pacific island governments, donors, and development partners in the region. In February 2008 at the 52nd Commission on the Status of Women, during the Interactive Expert Panel on the theme 'gender and climate change', a delegation of leaders from Pacific island governments and civil society made an intervention. In it, they recognized that despite the significant contribu-tion made by Pacific island women to the informal economy, particularly in agriculture, fisheries, and micro-enterprises, the nexus between gender and climate change in the Pacific has not gained much traction. During the in-tervention, Hon. Amberoti Nikora, Minister for Internal and Social Affairs in Kiribati asserted:

> *Adaptation efforts should address the gender specific impacts of climate change in the areas of energy, water, food security, agriculture and fisheries, biodiversity and eco-system services, health, industry, human settlements, disaster manage-ment and conflict and security. It is also important to take into account women's specific priorities and needs and to make full use of their traditional knowledge and practices in the development of new technology to address climate change.*

There are, in fact, already a number of agencies working in the Pacific to do just this. Nonetheless, the intervention at the Panel represents a considerable step forward in demonstrating high-level commitment to addressing these issues in the Pacific. It has created an opportunity for climate-change practitioners to work with practitioners from a range of sectors, including disaster risk-management, environment, agriculture, fisheries, health, and poverty reduction, to raise awareness of the cross-cutting nature of climate change, and to build further momentum in the development of policy to guide practice in climate-change adaptation in these sectors.

Climate vulnerability in the Pacific region

The Pacific region is a vast area, consisting of clusters of small islands and atolls. The 26 independent states and territories within these 30 million square kilometres of ocean are geographically and ethnically diverse, with very varied ecosystems and animal and plant species. The Pacific region has limited land. Its relatively small population of 8.5 million lives mostly in coastal areas, where its infrastructure and developing industries can mainly be found. Agriculture and fishing are the largest sources of national income in the region, followed by mineral mining, timber, and tourism. In the region, subsistence economies still predominate, but monetary economies exist by their side. Protecting and managing natural resources in the region is, therefore, crucial (ADB 2004). Notably, all of these characteristics make the Pacific islands and their cultures extremely vulnerable to the impacts of disasters and climate change (*ibid.*; Mimura *et al.* 2007; UNDP and AusAID 2008).

The Fourth Assessment Report released by the Inter-governmental Panel on Climate Change predicts that climate change is likely to have a number of different forms of impact for the islands of the Pacific. These include a rise in sea level; soil and groundwater salinization; increasing sea-surface temperature; more extreme rainfall patterns; and higher temperature trends. Climate risk profiles generated by the Asian Development Bank for the Federated States of Micronesia and the Cook Islands predict that rare extreme weather conditions or events will become relatively common as a result of global warming (Hay *et al.* 2004).

Many of these phenomena are already evident in the Pacific. Increased frequency of El Niño events is resulting in drought, flood, and an increase in the frequency and intensity of cyclone activity in some parts of the Pacific (Bettencourt *et al.* 2003; Mimura *et al.* 2007). In addition, some countries are already experiencing changes in rainfall patterns. For example, the Tuvalu Meteorological office has recorded a decline in rainfall over the past 30 years. Sea gauges located in the Pacific are recording high sea level more frequently, and the actual levels recorded are getting higher, in countries such as Tuvalu, Solomon Islands, Tonga, and the Cook Islands (Hall 2008). In the Cook Islands, the Meteorological Service has found that drought is becoming more common, and temperatures are rising in the country. There are also more cyclones in recent seasons compared with past periods (Cook Islands Red Cross 2008). In the Republic of the Marshal Islands, some outlying islands in Vanuatu, and parts of Papua New Guinea, salt-water intrusion into fertile soil as a result of storm surges has threatened the agricultural subsistence of communities, making them more dependent on imported foods, and significantly reducing the variety of food available to them (IFRC 2002). Despite the best efforts to reduce greenhouse-gas emissions globally it is clear that we are locked into further changes and impacts in the region over the coming decades. These impacts ultimately affect the livelihoods of communities, households, and individuals and their ability to cope with and adapt to the impacts of climate change and disaster events.

Recognizing the value of gendered local knowledge

Despite the vulnerability of Pacific islands to disaster, research shows that men and women of Pacific island communities have been successfully using their knowledge of their environments to mitigate disasters for generations. They have done this through a variety of traditional practices that have been maintained through informal education across generations. These include food preservation, housing construction, traditional systems of exchange, and most importantly the management of their natural resource base (Campbell 2006). For example, Anderson (2002) notes that during a drought on the island of Yap in the Federated States of Micronesia, local women who knew about hydrology as a result of working the land found potable water by digging a new well that reached fresh water. Gendered divisions of labour in non-disaster or normal times inform the way and extent to which communities can adapt to extreme climatic events. Local gender-specific knowledge must be recognized; it can contribute much to furthering the existing body of knowledge on climate change, as many communities across the Pacific are already witnessing and adapting to changes that are affecting their livelihoods.

Drawing from field experiences and recognizing the strong links between the community on Kabara Island and their natural resources, staff from WWF's Fiji office describe the value of utilizing participatory processes to draw out local knowledge:

Mapping exercises are a versatile and powerful tool for representing information and spatial distribution of community knowledge, including traditional boundaries, agricultural areas and fishing grounds. Maps are also a useful tool in aiding the community to develop, record, organize and present spatial information about their surroundings. In this context, women seem to describe better, subtle details regarding the timeline of noticeable changes on the reef including coral bleaching, the spawning period of certain fish species, algal blooms and related ciguatera fish poisoning incidences and the extent of the dry and rainy periods. While men are better at contributing to outlining the larger features of the mapping such as boundaries and physical features that are of direct significance to their planting and fishing on the outer slope of the reef fringing Kabara Island. In contrast to the women, men were unable to provide details of subtle changes to the reef. In addition,the women's group were more involved as a group in determining and agreeing on the extent of the last rainy period.

As part of WWF Fiji's climate-change awareness community outreach, the information derived from the mapping exercises has been used as baseline data. They can use it to explore further the significance of changes in the local environment, and relate these to climate change. In collaboration with the Fiji Meteorological Service, which has provided valuable information on air temperature and rainfall trends for Kabara (Lau region), WWF has been able to show that changes identified by the community coincide with a long dry period. In addition, the organization has been able to determine that the Kabara community can expect even less rain and longer dry periods, making it necessary for community members to identify suitable adaptation options as a matter of priority.

Responding to the impact of climate change

Local knowledge about climate change, and ways of adapting to it, are not static. Rather, people's knowledge and responses can change over time. In some cases, particular ways of adapting can diminish in effectiveness, as a result of development processes, movement of people to urban areas, and the worsening pressures of environmental degradation and climate change (Anderson 2008).

For example, in the Solomon Islands where the role of the community or village priest is traditionally a male role, the Solomon Islands Red Cross (2008) reports that a traditional priest from the Sogabiri tribe of Simbo in the Solomon Islands used to be able to predict when, and for how long, a strong wind would occur in the tribe's area. This wind, known locally as *komburu*, normally occurred from December to May each year. The priest used to be able to determine when the winds would start by observing whether or not the nuts from *ngali* trees had all fallen to the ground. When they had, the winds would begin. He would also determine the intensity and duration of the winds, by observing the fallen leaves of the native *rarapo* tree. When and where the leaves of the tree fell in relation to the tree and the village would help determine how long the winds were likely to last. Today, as a result of the changing climate, the priest has difficulty trying to determine when *komburu* will come, and how long it will last.

Local warning systems, such as this one, based on local and often gender-specific knowledge of the environment, have enabled Pacific island communities to prepare for extreme weather events for generations. In February 2008, the UNDP Pacific Centre and AusAID jointly sponsored a regional forum on the 'Gendered Dimensions of Climate Change and Disaster Risk Reduction in the Pacific'. The forum, which was held in Suva, brought together practitioners from the fields of natural resource management, disaster risk-management, and climate change, to explore and share gender issues in relation to these fields, to identify gaps in practice and research, best practices, and lessons learned, and to initiate an ongoing dialogue among stakeholders.

During the forum, there were many discussions about the fact that traditional systems for early warning are becoming less effective, as a result of climate change. Participants at the Suva forum agreed that while the verification of local knowledge through climate forecasting is important, work also needs be done on making technical weather-related information relevant to the different roles that men and women play in their communities (UNDP and AusAID 2008). For example, the Samoa Red Cross has been proactive in working in partnership with the Samoan Meteorological Office and local communities, turning climate forecasts in technical language into easy-to-understand messages in the local language (Wolf 2008). Other initiatives have included work undertaken by the Red Cross/Red Crescent Centre on Climate Change and Disaster Preparedness in co-operation with the South Pacific Regional Environment Programme (SPREP). A series of posters has been designed for Fiji, Tonga, the Solomon Islands, Samoa, Vanuatu, Kiribati, and Papua New Guinea, which convey messages about the connections between climate change and human development processes, due to changes to the natural resources on which communities depend. These posters have been specifically designed with the input of communities, in order to make them really useful to target communities. They provide practical examples of what communities can do to address the different effects of climate change. By their existence, they demonstrate the opportunities which exist for 'community to community' communication. Community-awareness initiatives of this sort can enhance popular understanding of the implications of future climate change for the everyday activities of men and women, and this in turn can inform the way people prepare for, adapt to, and cope with these changes.

Learning from gender roles in community-based disaster management

Understanding gendered divisions of labour within Pacific island communities can assist in providing a more in-depth understanding of changes to climate and environment. It can also provide a useful entry point for harnessing the specialized knowledge held by men and women in developing strategies for adapting to climate change. Given the linkages between climate change and increased instance of disaster in the Pacific region, adaptation practitioners can also learn much from research undertaken by practitioners in disaster risk-management in the Pacific. A regional study undertaken in four Pacific island countries by the South Pacific Disaster Risk Program in 2002 found that men and women in Fiji, Samoa, the Solomon Islands, and Kiribati play distinct roles in preparing for disasters. In all four countries, women were more likely to be responsible for the practical preparation of households, including informing family members, storing food and water, and protecting family belongings, while men were found to be responsible for liaising with government administrators, preparing the outside of buildings, making decisions about evacuation sites and timing, managing water sources, distributing emergency relief, and receiving and disseminating early warnings to the wider community (SPDRP 2002).

In a more recent case study undertaken in two communities on Ambae Island, Vanuatu, women's focus-group discussions, undertaken separately from those with men, raised concerns about the fact that the bulk of decision-making in relation to resource allocation following disasters was being carried out by men. Further, there was concern that decisions made by men at the household and community level were not always fair, and most commonly did not involve women (Cronin *et al.* 2004). Concerns were also expressed by the women's focus groups that men were not very efficient in warning women in time for them to prepare adequately, and this made households more vulnerable to loss in the face of disaster (*ibid.*). Similar preliminary findings came from a Vulnerability and Capacity Assessment conducted by Fiji Red Cross, and UNDP's Pacific Centre in the Navua region, on the island of Viti Levu, Fiji. Stephanie Zoll (2008), a United Nations Volunteer working with the UNDP Pacific Centre, says focus-group discussions with women revealed that while there are active women's groups in the region, they have very little role in decision-making processes regarding development. Stephanie notes that this also reflects the employment patterns in the community in many ways. Women are largely confined to the village, while men travel to peri-urban areas to work: this influences the kinds of information that women and men are able to access. Stephanie also found that, during the floods which occur regularly in the region, women, who were less likely to know how to swim than men, sometimes remained in their houses to circulate flood waters, in order to prevent mud from settling into their houses. Finally, women were most likely to be solely responsible for child care during flooding. As Stephanie notes, the gendered roles of these women have obvious implications for both their own safety and that of their children.

The above examples clearly show that gender roles in disasters lead to gendered effects. These are both shaped by, and shape, relationships of power and influence between men and women in Pacific island communities (SPDRP 2002). The examples also clearly demonstrate the dangers of assuming that distinct and separate gender roles are always beneficial to all sectors of the community. While gender roles may be complementary, and may allow communities to adapt more efficiently to climate risk, there are also instances where gender roles may foster inequality, including inequality in access to early warning information and vital resources, and unequal decision-making.

These examples build a clear case for practitioners to undertake further analysis of gender roles, to facilitate better understandings of how inequalities between men and women can contribute to gendered vulnerabilities and ultimately impact upon a community's ability to become more resilient to the impacts of climate change.

Community-based risk reduction

Gender analysis requires development practitioners to work closely with both men and women, to gain understanding of existing gender relations and social systems, in order to address gendered vulnerabilities and inequalities.

One way of achieving this is by using research methods in which women and men participate. Examples are WWF's Climate Witness Community Toolbox, and the International Federation of Red Cross and Red Crescent Societies' Vulnerability Capacity Assessment Toolbox.[1]These toolboxes promote a variety of participatory activities, such as hazard mapping, seasonal calendars, event timelines, and transect walks, aiming to assist communities in identifying the climate risks to which they are exposed. In the context of its work with the community in Kabara, WWF found that community participatory learning and action techniques can be very useful for identifying specialized knowledge held by the men and women regarding the impacts of climate change on their community; collecting gender-disaggregated data that captures how men and women are affected differently by extreme climatic events, and have different perceptions of risk (Patt *et al.* forthcoming); and planning ways in which natural resources can best be used. Furthermore, WWF has noted that use of some techniques, such as community resource mapping, assisted in drawing out the different knowledge held by men, women, and young people of each sex, on Kabara Island.

However, donors and practitioners should be wary of imposing mainstreaming agendas upon communities, and of trying to address perceived gender inequalities in a top-down way. As participatory processes are tools which enable practitioners to let communities drive issues and processes, they will be less effective if practitioners have predetermined the outcomes they wish to achieve.

Even though a particular participatory method may not have been designed for use in a gender-sensitive way, this does not stop it being adapted for this purpose. Shortly after conducting a vulnerability and capacity assessment (VCA) in the Navua Region of Fiji recently, Stephanie Zoll from the UNDP Pacific Centre reflected that the timing of a VCA needs to suit the schedules of both the men and women you wish to target, so it doesn't become a burden (Zoll 2008). This way, men and women can participate freely without pressure of competing priorities. She also noted that it might be useful to have separate focus groups for men and women, particularly if you are looking at gender impacts and differences, as men and women have different perceptions of risk, resources, and needs. Cultural norms might prevent men and women from speaking freely in each other's presence, so you might miss these if everyone is in the same group. It's also important to give people the space to talk.

'Gender-sensitising' participatory approaches in this way may give practitioners a better understanding of existing gender relations and social systems. Using these as entry points is more likely to result in sustainable and positive changes to behaviour and attitudes, which will reduce women's vulnerabilities to climate change, over time. Such an approach can underpin disaster-preparedness programmes, to ensure that these do not inadvertently discriminate against some groups by dispensing resources and information in ways which are harder for them to access.

Human health and security

There are many different ways in which rising temperatures, more intense heat waves, droughts, increased rainfall, floods, and cyclones affect human health in the Pacific region. Floods and cyclones damage vital buildings, such as hospitals and clinics, and injuries and illness caused by extreme weather place pressure on health systems which are already under-resourced. Other effects come about indirectly: for example, the availability and quality of water is affected by a warming and more variable climate, and this not only affects sanitation, but also agricultural production and ultimately nutrition, as well as increasing the risk of transmission by insects and water (McMichael *et al.* 2002; McNaught and Morse 2007). For example, between 1975 and 1995 the annual number of dengue epidemics in the South Pacific rose in correlation with warmer and wetter weather in many countries, as a result of La Niña (WHO 2008).

So disasters can affect human health and security indirectly, and this may in turn hamper the ability of communities to cope with – and recover from – the effects of climate change. For example, it is well-documented globally that women and children are at more risk of sexual abuse during disaster times when compared with non-disaster periods (Weist *et al.* 1994; Byrne and Baden 1995). A study undertaken by the Fiji Red Cross on the relationship between HIV and disaster supports this finding. In addition, the study also made some interesting findings on possible links between exposure to disasters and increased incidence of HIV, AIDS, and sexually transmitted infections (STIs). Results from the study revealed that 83 per cent of respondents had lived through a disaster in the past five years. In addition, the study found that condom use during a disaster was significantly lower than at other times, leading to a raised risk of HIV and STIs. Respondents had less access to condoms during a disaster, and there was a sharp increase in risk-taking behaviour immediately following a disaster. In order to address these issues, the Fiji Red Cross has integrated them into a holistic response package that includes addressing community safety in shelters as well as disseminating condoms and safe-sex messages during and immediately after disasters in a culturally appropriate way (Fiji Red Cross 2004).

Is it really all just about climate change? Men and women as agents of change

The relationship between climate and society is dynamic. Variations in climatic conditions and climate change may have multiple, simultaneous effects. Their effects on women, men, and their households are determined by the ways in which they interact with a range of other factors, such as environmental degradation, development, and urbanization. All these combine in their effect on communities.

For example, Tikina Wai district is on the dry leeward side of Viti Levi, a volcanic island in Fiji. There is a high level of development for tourism in Tikina Wai. A significant proportion of the area's population lives in low-lying areas, and it is here that most of the physical infrastructure, and the prime agricultural land, can be found. All of these factors make Tikina Wai vulnerable to various effects of climate change, including prolonged rainfall, drought, storm surges, and rises in sea level (WWF 2004). During WWF Fiji's initial engagement with the community six years ago, it was found that mangroves along the coastline of Tikina Wai had been significantly depleted because of people's need to make a livelihood, and to follow traditional cultural practices. Mangroves had been cut down for firewood (generally by men), and bark had been stripped off others (generally by women) to produce *tapa*, a local paper cloth used regularly in Fijian traditional ceremonies. Women also fished in the mangrove swamps, mainly for food for the family. Since the major ecological function of mangroves is to provide a nursery for juvenile fish, the unsustainable use of mangroves by the community was slowly causing changes to the ecosystem that would eventually cause a general decline in the availability of fish. In addition, as mangroves provide natural protection against coastal flooding, storm surges, and cyclones, the decline in the number of mangroves that line the coast exposed the outlying coastal villages to a big risk from the elements, and the effects of climate change. The mangroves are the only natural barrier protecting the area and the people who live in it from the risk of coastal inundation and potential rises in sea level.

In order to address this, WWF has worked with the coastal communities to raise awareness of the importance of the mangroves in providing communities with protection from the impacts of climate change. Using participatory approaches, WWF continues to engage with the district community (a total of six villages) to identify ways of protecting the mangroves, and ways of integrating mangrove conservation into development for the areas. Initially, three mangrove areas making up 20 per cent of the communities' fishing area were identified and reserved for protection. This included fishing being banned within these areas. These protected areas were chosen in close consultation with the community on the basis of key biological information such as the location of fish-spawning sites, and giving consideration to the community's need to be able to continue fishing for income and subsistence. Currently, boundaries around the mangroves are being marked, in recognition both of their ecological value, and more importantly the livelihood value of the area as the district's fishing ground. Parallel to this activity, a community-initiated eco-tour of their mangrove areas is being established as part of the overall district development plans. These government-led plans, which include considerable community input, will guide the district representative and council in strategically expressing the community's needs to the provincial and national levels. Simultaneously, WWF Fiji worked with the women of the district to identify debarking techniques that are less harmful to the mangroves, so that the community can continue to use the mangroves to make *tapa*.

This case study demonstrates a multi-faceted approach to reducing risk that includes building community resilience to the adverse impacts of climate change, as well as addressing food security and economic development by capitalizing on the district's location and cultural/aesthetic value for sustainable tourism.

WWF note that while the majority of the decision-making is conducted by the male elders during the open community sessions, it is women and male and female youth who most actively work with WWF in the field to conduct coral-reef or seagrass habitat surveys. In addition, WWF note that women generally use other opportunities to voice their concerns, such as while out in the field or while at the communal cooking area.

WWF's project in Tikina Wai demonstrates that the nexus between gender and climate change is complex, and that gendered vulnerabilities should not be oversimplified by assuming a simple two-way relationship. In Tikina Wai, the entire community is not just vulnerable because of the impacts of climate change; it is also vulnerable as a result of the adoption of patterns of natural resource use arising from gendered roles in the community. WWF's work with the Tikina Wai community demonstrates that the development and implementation of successful strategies to address community vulnerability often depend upon the complementary roles of men and women that require them to work together in partnership to ensure sustainability. It also demonstrates that strategies are more likely to be successful when there is an understanding of gendered roles prior to determining natural resource usage, as this can greatly assist in securing and improving livelihoods and food security. Therefore, gendered vulnerabilities and capacities must be contextualized and analysed in relation to a broad range of factors. This will assist practitioners in working with communities to identify appropriate strategies for adaptation that do not victimize the people who they hope will benefit from the project, but rather place them at the centre of change.

Ways forward

Experiences from the Pacific clearly show that efforts to work with communities to generate gender-sensitive responses to and strategies for addressing climate change are more successful when they involve a number of responses from a number of partners. It is also vital that these multi-stakeholder responses be well co-ordinated. Success also depends on recognition that climate change is a dynamic process, and that the men and women of the Pacific are not victims of climate change, but active agents. Through their own gendered knowledge and actions, individuals, households, and communities can exacerbate or minimize the likely impact of extreme weather. Development practitioners therefore need to understand this fact themselves and develop the confidence of people at community level to meet the challenges that climate change represents. In cases where people's efforts to earn a living are aggravating the negative effects of climate change, development practitioners can assist communities to identify and develop alternative approaches. Adaptation strategies will only be sustainable if men and women are able to provide for their everyday needs. Participatory methods and gender analysis are both empowering tools that can help communities identify their own capacities, as well as suitable adaptation strategies that respond to the needs of men, women, boys and girls. It may also be achieved by strengthening existing partnerships between communities, meteorological services, development practitioners who specialize in the areas of climate change and disaster risk-reduction, and the wider development community. This would have the dual advantage of enhancing shared understanding of the risks posed by climate change, and widening the spectrum of adaptation options available to address vulnerabilities.

In the Pacific region, there are already a number of gender-responsive programmes that fit under the broad agenda of climate-change adaptation, in fields such as coastal protection, agriculture, and fisheries. It is vital that practitioners from the fields of climate-change adaptation and disaster risk-reduction who are committed to developing gender-responsive programmes make these linkages explicit for all development practitioners through advocacy, awareness, and action. It is also essential that best practice, and lessons learned on gender-responsive programming, are widely shared across relevant sectors. Climate change and gender inequality are both currently receiving unprecedented attention both globally and in our own backyard, and it is vital we seize this moment.

Note

1. Further information regarding these tool boxes may be found at www.ifrc.org/what/disasters/resources/publications.asp and www.wwfpacific.org.fj/what_we_do/climate_change/index.cfm, respectively (last accessed November 2008).

References

Anderson, C. (2002) 'Gender matters: implications for climate variability and climate change and disaster management in the Pacific islands', *Intercoast*

Network 41: 24–5, www.crc.uri.edu/download/2002_41_CRC_GenderPopu-lationEnvironment.pdf [accessed 9 June 2009].

Anderson, C. (2008) 'Background Paper: Forum on the Gendered Dimensions of Disaster Risk Management and Adaptation to Climate Change', paper presented at a forum on the Gendered Dimensions of Climate Change and Disaster Risk Reduction in the Pacific, Suva, Fiji, 20–21 February.

Asian Development Bank (2004) *Pacific Region Environmental Strategy 2005 – 2009 Volume I: Strategy Document*, Manila: ADB.

Bettencourt, S., R. Croad, P. Freeman, J. Hay, R. Jones, P. King, P. Lal, G. Miller, I. Pswarayan-Riddihough, A. Simpson, N. Teuatabo, U. Trotz, M. Van Aalst (2006) 'Not If But When: Adapting to Natural Hazards in the Pacific Islands Region – A Policy Note', Washington, DC: World Bank.

Byrne, B. and S. Baden (1995) 'Gender, Emergencies and Humanitarian Assistance', *Bridge development-gender*, Report No. 33, Brighton: Institute of Development Studies.

Campbell, J.R. (2006) 'Traditional disaster reduction in Pacific island communities', *GNS Science Report*, University of Waikato, www.gns.cri.nz/services/hazardsplanning/downloads/SR2006-038trad_mitigation_pacific.pdf (last accessed November 2008).

Cook Islands Red Cross (2008) 'Preparedness for Climate Change: Background Document on Climate Change and Disaster Risk Reduction', Cook Islands: Cook Islands Red Cross.

Cronin, S.J., D.R Gaylord, D. Charley, B.V. Alloway, S. Wallez, and J.W Esau (2004) 'Participatory methods of incorporating scientific with traditional knowledge for volcanic hazard management on Ambae Island, Vanuatu', *Bulletin of Volcanology* 66(7).

Fiji Red Cross Society (2004) 'STI, HIV/AIDS and Disaster Response Package to World Health Organization South Pacific Office', Fiji: Fiji Red Cross Society.

Hall, P. (2008) 'Climate Change and Low Lying Pacific Islands – a Plain Person's Guide to Global Warming, Sea Level Rise and the Threat to the Pacific Islands', Faerber Hall, www.faerberhall.com/topics_enviro.htm [accessed 9 June 2009].

Hay, J. R. Warrick, C. Cheatham, T. Manarangi-Trott, J. Konno, and P. Hartley (2004) 'Climate proofing: a risk based approach to adaptation', Philippines: Asian Development Bank.

IFRC (International Federation of the Red Cross and Red Crescent Societies) (2002) *World Disasters Report: Focus on Reducing Risk*, Bloomfield, CT: Kumarian Press.

McMichael, A., R. Woodruff, P. Whetton, K. Hennessy, N. Nicholls, S.Hales, A. Woodward, and T. Kjellstrom (2003) 'Human Health and Climate Change in Oceania: A Risk Assessment 2002', Commonwealth Department of Health and Ageing, www.health.gov.au/internet/main/publishing.nsf/content/health-pubhlth-publicat-document-metadata-env_climate.htm http://un-fccc.int/resource/docs/napa/tza01.pdf

McNaught, R. and Z. Morse (2007) 'Red Cross Movement: working towards reducing the impacts of climate change on health and poverty in the Pacific region', *Fiji Medical Journal* 26(2): 6–12.

Mimura, N.L., L. Nurse, R.F. McLean, J. Agard, L. Briguglio, P. Lefale, R. Payet, and G. Sem (2007) 'Small islands', in M.L. Parry, O.F. Canziani, J.P. Palautikof, P.J. van der Linden, and C.E. Hanson (eds.), *Climate Change 2007: Impacts, Adaptation and Vulnerability. Contribution of Working Group II to the Fourth Assessment Report of the Intergovernmental Panel on Climate Change*, Cambridge: Cambridge University Press, 687–716.

Patt, A.G., A. Daze, and P. Suarez (forthcoming) 'Gender and climate change vulnerability: what's the problem, what's the solution?', in M. Ruth and M.E. Ibarraran (eds.), *Distributional Impacts of Climate Change and Disasters: Concepts and Cases*, Cheltenham: Edward Elgar.

Solomon Islands Red Cross (2008) 'Preparedness for Climate Change Background Document: Consequences of Climate Change to Humanitarian Work through the Eyes of Solomon Islands Red Cross', Solomon Islands: Solomon Islands Red Cross.

SPDRP (South Pacific Disaster Reduction Program) (2002) 'Gender, households, communities and disaster management: case studies from the Pacific islands', *SOPAC Technical Report*, www.sopac.org/tiki/tiki-sopac_download. php?path=/data/virlib/TR/TR0282.pdf&file=TR0282.pdf&loc=TR [last accessed August 2008].

UNDP and AusAID (2008) 'Workshop Report: Forum on the Gendered Dimensions of Disaster Risk Management and Adaptation to Climate Change', http://regionalcentrepacific.undp.org.fj/HTML%20docs/Workshops %20and%20Seminars/workshop%20and%20seminars%20index.html [last accessed August 2008].

Weist, R.E., J.S.P Mocellin, and D.T. Motsui (1994) *The Needs of Women in Disasters and Emergencies*, Manitoba: Disaster Research Institute.

WHO (2008) 'Health Impacts of Climate Extremes', www.who.int/global-change/climate/summary/en/index4.html [accessed 9 June 2009]..

Wulf, G. (2008) correspondence with author.

WWF (2004) 'Tikina Wai Climate Change, Community Vulnerability and Adaptation Assessment Report', www.wwfpacific.org.fj/climate change/publications.asp [last accessed September 2008].

Zoll, S. (2008) correspondence with author.

About the authors

Ruth Lane has been working in the Pacific on disaster risk-reduction issues for over three years. Currently she holds the position of Pacific Regional Disaster Risk Reduction Delegate for the International Federation of the Red Cross and Red Crescent Societies, based in Suva, Fiji. In this capacity Ruth provides support to 15 national societies in the Pacific region on disaster risk-reduction (including adaptation to climate change) initiatives.

Rebecca McNaught is a Senior Programme Office for the Red Cross/Red Crescent Climate Centre. In this capacity Rebecca provides support to the Federation and Red Cross National Societies in the Asia/Pacific Region by raising awareness of and advocating for Red Cross work on climate change at the regional and global levels and by providing advice on the development and implementation of initiatives focusing on adaptation to climate change. Rebecca has over three years experience working in the Pacific on adaptation to climate change and disaster risk-reduction.

CHAPTER 9

The Noel Kempff project in Bolivia: gender, power, and decision-making in climate mitigation

Emily Boyd

This chapter first appeared in *Gender and Development* 10(2), pp. 70–77, 2002.

A focus on land-use and forests as a means to reduce carbon dioxide levels in the global atmosphere has been at the heart of the international climate change debate since the United Nations Kyoto Protocol was agreed in 1997. This environmental management practice is a process technically referred to as mitigation. These largely technical projects have aimed to provide sustainable development benefits to forest-dependent people, as well as to reduce greenhouse gas emissions. However, these projects have had limited success in achieving these local development objectives. This chapter argues that this is due in part to the patriarchal underpinnings of the sustainable development and climate-change policy agendas. The author explores this theory by considering how a climate mitigation project in Bolivia has resulted in different outcomes for women and men, and makes links between the global decision-making process and local effects.

By and large, climate mitigation projects have been informed by Western ideas of science and development, and predominantly driven by the 'masculine' interests of forestry, accounting, agriculture, and policy-making. This chapter aims to articulate some of the concerns arising from this agenda, and demonstrates how a patriarchal system of decision-making exists at all levels, from global decision-making frameworks to the local implementation of climate mitigation projects. The predominant decision-makers at all levels of decision-making are men: bureaucrats negotiating on behalf of their governments; NGO representatives; extension workers; and decision-makers in local organizations. Concern about the lack of a gender discourse within debates about climate change debate has been raised by writers such as Vandana Shiva (1988). When we discuss global carbon-trading by planting or conserving trees, we are engaging in a debate driven by men, who are biased towards providing technical solutions to the climate-change problem, and who have little understanding of, or regard for, the concerns or interests of women.

This chapter is based on my doctoral research, which was undertaken on one of the world's largest UN carbon sequestration pilot projects: the Noel

Kempff Climate Action Project in the Bolivian Amazon. The research took place between March and September 2001. I used a qualitative approach, drawing on informal interviews, participant observation, rapid rural appraisal, participation in meetings, and an evaluation workshop. The key research objective was to establish how carbon sequestration projects contribute to local sustainable development, and to assess the compatibility of local institutional arrangements with the highly politicised goals and rules of external interventions. The research focused predominantly on the social, institutional, and development contexts within which the project was established, i.e. the framework within which the project took place.

In the process of the research, it became clear that the project was weaker in some areas than others. These weaknesses can be understood within a framework of practical and strategic gender needs (Moser 1993), and have been highlighted as important across a range of projects and programmes (Regmi and Fawcett 1999; Sardenberg *et al.* 1999). 'Practical gender needs' refer to the immediate necessities that women perceive themselves as lacking in a specific context, which would enable them to perform the activities expected of them: for example, a health post, vegetable gardens, or a water pump. 'Strategic gender needs', in contrast, refer to that which is necessary for women to change their status in society. These might include: access to and ownership of land or other property, control over one's body, equal wages, or freedom from domestic violence.

The Noel Kempff project has been operating for five years. During this time, opportunities have been provided for the participation of both men and women. It would be fair to say that women have successfully participated in some aspects of the project, fulfilling practical gender needs such as trying new varieties of legume crops or accessing credit, but that they have predominantly been recipients of charity. Addressing strategic needs has not been a key factor in the project design and implementation. It was evident during the research process that a gender perspective was lacking. In particular, a perspective was needed which recognizes the difference between practical and strategic gender needs, and the existence of gendered institutions, power structures, and hierarchies. I consider these concepts in more detail in the following section.

Embedded patriarchy: the absence of a feminist perspective in existing climate change frameworks

Mitigation through forest management

Growing international concern about climate change has resulted in a number of United Nations agreements, including the United Nations Convention on Climate Change, and the Kyoto Protocol, which came out of it. The Protocol was created in 1997, with the aim that it should be ratified by 2002. It is the first legally binding global commitment to tackling developed countries' greenhouse gas emissions. A key greenhouse gas is carbon dioxide (CO_2), which is chiefly emitted into the global atmosphere through the burning of fossil fuels (industrial emissions are estimated to account for five billion tonnes of carbon emissions, and deforestation 1.6 billion tonnes).

Tropical forests absorb carbon dioxide through the process of photosynthesis. This knowledge led to the inclusion of forest 'sinks'[1] within the policy debate, and initiated a project pilot phase that would test the possibility of mitigating (offsetting) CO_2 emissions through sustainable forest management, conservation of forests (avoided deforestation), or planting trees (afforestation and reforestation). These projects aim to reduce pressure on forests by improving the management of land and forests. The Protocol formally establishes the possibility of reducing carbon emissions through the *flexibility mechanisms*, which allow trading of carbon dioxide on an international market through developed country investments (primarily industry) in carbon mitigation projects in developing countries, such as clean energy substitution in China or forest projects in Brazil. There are also informal discussions ongoing about an alternative carbon market, which would trade carbon from a wide variety of forestry projects. Forest-based CO_2 mitigation projects were established to provide 'win-win' solutions under the umbrella of sustainable development.

'Masculine' bias of mitigation approaches

The new and emerging field of climate change mitigation through project activities in developing countries is based on modern scientific concepts. According to Vandana Shiva, the approach is based on a worldview that supports, and is supported by, the socio-economic and political systems of Western capitalist patriarchy, which dominate and exploit nature, women, and the poor (Shiva 1988). This section gives a feminist perspective on the climate change debate at global and local levels, and uses a 'feminine', human-centred, and rights based approach. If we look at the rules, norms, and aspirations of the institutions which are involved in the debate through a *feminine* framework, we can understand the inequalities which exist in global decision making and power structures, and see how the legacies of colonialism still shape the main institutions in developing countries today.

Historically, the Western mode of development has reinforced a patriarchal style of decision-making. This is reflected in the predominantly technical approach of employees of conservation and sustainable development projects. Denton (2001, 1) notes that, 'The climate change debate is an indicator of how gender issues tend to be omitted, leaving room for complex market driven notions equated in terms of emissions reductions, fungibility, and flexible mechanisms.' These highly technical terms reflect the extent to which complex issues are glossed over and simplified within global responses to climate change. Solutions to the problem might instead be found through focusing resources on understanding how climate change will affect women and men differently, and what measures are necessary to ensure adaptation. The UN, a key decision-making body in climate change issues, has a male-dominated, hierarchical structure. Denton observes how an overall assessment of the climate change debate to date shows that women are absent from decision-making processes, and that decision-making and policy formulation at environmental levels, within conservation, protection, rehabilitation, and environmental management, follow predominantly male agendas (Denton 2001, 1). Not only are the bureaucrats representing their nations predominantly men, but more importantly, the underpinning approach is 'masculine'. The power of an alternative 'feminine' approach to environmental governance and management should not be underestimated. Increased gender awareness within global decision-making on climate change should allow for inclusion of different socio-economic groups, rather than professionals only, and should encourage the participation and representation of those women most vulnerable to climate change (*ibid.*). In her foreword to *Staying Alive* (Shiva 1988), Rajna Kothari suggests how such an approach might look. 'The struggle for femininity is a struggle for a certain basic principle of perceiving life, a philosophy of being. It is a principle and a philosophy that can serve not just women but all human beings. Femininity by definition cannot and should not be a limiting value but an expanding one – holistic, eclectic, trans-specific and encompassing of diverse stirrings.' (Kothari 1988, xiii)

A key characteristic of international-level interventions is the exclusion of social groups, such as indigenous groups and women, from decision-making. At international climate negotiations, we still see disparities between rich and poor nations, women and men, NGOs and government policy-makers. The balance of women and men directly taking part in the decision making remains an issue to contend with, as exemplified at a recent UN climate meeting, when the numbers of male to female professionals elected to the executive board to oversee future forestry and energy projects had a ratio of 11:1(2) This balance is replicated down the chain, from policy to project.

Within carbon mitigation projects, the inclusion of a feminist analysis would assist in the pursuit of the 'win-win' situation that scientists, policy-makers, and NGOs consider forest mitigation projects to have the potential to exemplify. In addition, matters of participation, access to information, and control over decision-making are also important.

Case study: the Noel Kempff Climate Action Project

The Noel Kempff Climate Action Project was established in 1996 in Bolivia, in the region of San Ignacio de Velasco, Santa Cruz. The project's primary objectives were to purchase logging concessions from companies and thereby expand the Noel Kempff National Park to 1.5 million hectares (almost double its original size) to meet conservation aims and earn carbon credits. The project also aimed to contribute to local development benefits through improved local agricultural and forest management practices, to stimulate employment, and to obtain 400,000 hectares of communal land for three key communities

(Florida, Porvenir, and Piso Firme). These are predominantly Chiquitano indigenous communities,[3] of approximately 2000 inhabitants. Funding was obtained primarily from an electrical utility company in the USA, with some financial support from the Nature Conservancy (an international NGO), and Fundación Amigos de la Naturaleza (a local NGO). The government of Bolivia was also closely involved as a broker and partner with the private sector for the carbon credits accrued from the project.

The project has a four-component structure, comprising forestry, agriculture, conservation, and community development. Forestry activities entail monitoring CO_2 fluctuations inside and outside the park, establishing a forest management plan, and ensuring community participation in its implementation. Agricultural activities include land-use planning, testing new crop varieties, and establishing model agro-forestry farms. Conservation activities predominantly involve eco-tourism in one community, and some minor sales of handicrafts to tourists. These activities overlap with the community development programme, *Apoyo Comunitario* (APOCOM).

To summarise, the key characteristics of the project are:

- a primary focus on land-use, land-use change, and forestry;
- the aim of reducing CO_2 emissions with additional biodiversity benefits;
- sustainable development objectives, manifested through locally-focused project activities.

Assessing the project's impact on gender relations

Gender-based inequalities in employment opportunities

The forestry programme provided short-term employment for between 30 and 50 men from the local communities, to establish forest inventories and plant nurseries. They received a salary of up to US$6 per day for their efforts. A small number of women were employed to cook for the forestry workers. The men received a salary for acting as community technicians and providing technical training, and were part of the technical team that managed and drove the community forest concessions in the land titling process (which is still ongoing). There was some effort to encourage the presence of women in the forestry team, but this did not succeed. Women are rarely present at forestry programme meetings and workshops (personal observation).

As part of the conservation activities, approximately 30 men were employed annually for a number of weeks to clear the roads into the national park, and two women from one village were employed as cooks when tourists came to the main park camp. The park also employed six or seven local men as park guards. These men earned up to US$100 per month, which was a very reasonable local salary.

Aside from the female cooks, one female forestry consultant involved in training the forestry team, and the female co-ordinator of the eco-tourism activities, all the technical staff directly involved in the project were male.

Although the work provided much-needed income and status to these community members, the majority of women were not able to benefit directly from this.

Gender inequalities in power and decision-making

The NGO and National Park directors were both men, and were overseen by government technicians based in La Paz, who were all men. At the local level, the project has successfully reinforced the power of traditional councils (*cabildo*) by entrusting them with the land titling process. These are all-male councils consisting of a headman (*cacique*) and a council of 11 men, each with a different task. An attempt was made in one community to encourage the participation of two women in the *cabildo*, but they didn't stay for long, saying, 'We got fed up with the meetings, and you know what men are like – we didn't enjoy it.' The project has also assisted the creation of the region's own indigenous organization CIBAPA (*Central Indigena de Bajo Paragua*), with a male president and his male assistant.

At the community level, power lay with community members who had influence, financial resources, or ties to the old patron and the headman. The other key groups in the community were the fishing and cattle committees. There was a woman mayor in the village, whom project staff said had done a lot for women. Her political appointment by the municipality, however, had created a divide between political factions in the community, so there was little identification with her as a role model (personal observation).

There was a clear distinction between project activities associated with women and those associated with men. Women primarily associated themselves with activities linked to meeting practical gender needs, which had been designed by planners with women in mind. Women generally spent their time in the fields harvesting maize or rice, collecting firewood and medicinal plants, and growing fruit trees and vegetables in their homesteads. They did not work in the sawmills, extract timber, or hunt, and rarely fished. All these are activities typically associated with men.

Neither in the context of the project, nor at community meetings, was there any evidence of a focus on the socio-political and economic roles of women in decision-making, or their relationship with their environment. For example, there are no women on the national park management committee, which is an important forum for participation in decisions on the future of the park, land title, and other related activities. Public meetings were often dominated by a small number of men. During a discussion on the communal water pump in one village, a problem that women had voiced informally about livestock dirtying the water source was not voiced in the general discussion. Instead, there was a male-led discussion about credit for cattle and a boat, and the issue raised by the women was pushed down the list of priorities.

Observations such as this raise concerns about the prioritization of issues, the action subsequently taken, and the invisibility of women and their interests within these prioritization processes. Women would often comment, 'My husband knows about these issues – he attends meetings.' Lack of voice was something that more marginalized men in the communities also experienced. In the smaller communities, women spoke more openly in public, yet still required a great deal of encouragement to speak openly about what they wanted from the project and in their lives more broadly.

Meeting women's needs but not advancing their interests

The project, like many development projects, focused on women's practical gender needs, such as health, education, income-generation, and food production, and neglected the strategic gender needs that could empower women, challenge the existing gender division of labour, and bring about greater gender equality (Momsen 1991).

One of the most appreciated project activities, according to many women, was the presence of a doctor, and the access to flying doctors in an emergency. However, they recognized that the emergency flights were unsustainable, and that the doctor was a temporary presence, which would last only as long as the funds were provided by the charity. Across the communities, I observed that project activities focused on infrastructure provision, such as a health post and an improved school building. Medicines were scarce: women generally obtained credit to purchase medicines, and had difficulty repaying.

At the time of the research, national economic crises were hitting these remote communities hard, and their usual employment opportunities with the sawmills in the region were scarce. The wet season proved a difficult time for communities in finding income and resources, such as fish, and the poor conditions of the roads isolated the communities for several months of the year. Alcohol consumption and drunkenness among men were a common sight within the communities (personal observation).

The main communal activity that women tried to engage in was working on the vegetable plots in each community. The NGO brought seeds for the women to use communally in their 'mothers' clubs' (*clubes de madres*), but they were not successful. Women commented that, 'The communal gardens have failed because we don't like working in groups, we fell out over who was taking gains from the garden and now people plant seeds in their individual gardens.' Or that, 'People stole from the communal garden, that is why it failed.'

The agroforestry farming initiative was only taken up by a small number of families. Many young men remained convinced that large-scale cattle ranching was the solution to their poverty. There were no female-headed households involved in the establishment of a model farm, although they would have benefited from the credit of a bull or cow for the production of milk for their children. Although this initiative was open to all community members, the model plots were very labour-intensive and would have required female-headed households to pay labourers or rely on charity from other male family members to clear plots of land. Some women took up small income generating activities, such as manufacturing chicken coops, and bread making. Those involved expressed pride and satisfaction at having their own activities, but the management of funds and repayment rates was less successful. In one community a large number of women were involved in a palm-canning factory, which received indirect contributions from the project.

A lost opportunity for women's participation and empowerment

If we are to ensure sustainable development associated with the interventions of these multi-component projects, they must address the strategic interests of women. Townsend *et al.* (1999) suggest that these interests include political strengthening, ensuring gender equity in access to education, ending gender violence, decreasing maternal mortality and morbidity, and ending the economic inequalities between women and men that leave women bearing the brunt of poverty.

The project's enforcement of existing social structures and wide reliance on traditional norms of decision-making has weakened women's ability to participate within or influence it. The project could have benefited from strengthening women's groups and addressing women's strategic interests. For example, discussion groups around the issues of women's social and political participation might have created a new dynamic. This idea is inspired by a one-day trial workshop on sexual education for young people, which attracted almost all of the adults in two communities. This demonstrates the widespread interest that exists in a subject that is commonly considered to be 'taboo' in the communities (personal observation).

In the final participatory evaluation of the project, few women were involved from each community, despite efforts to timetable the sessions around women's household duties. Education was high on women's list of priorities, and the project provided small grants (US$100) per family for school tuition for boys and girls. However, concerns were raised about 'girls going away to the city and coming back with a swelling belly'.

Improving women's access to information

Access to information, and what people do with that information, is an important aspect of empowering marginalized sectors within communities. In one community, many women living in the poorer areas noted that they did not attend the technical or other meetings, but that their sons or husbands might have. However, information is not consistently disseminated within the household or at the community level. A number of women pointed to the fact that their husband knew about the project but that they were not told about what went on at meetings. In this community, men were also called upon to help answer questions about the types of project activities going on in the community. In the smallest of the three communities, women noted that they attended all types of meetings, and 'learned a lot from them'. Where the women participated more in the meetings and took a greater interest, they were also the most outspoken in public meetings. The results suggest that although there are differences in the levels of information flow between different communities, across the board it is fair to say that the flow of information between the project, the park, the higher-level decision-makers, the CIBAPA, and the women in the communities could be significantly improved.

Conclusions

In conclusion, if there are to be 'win–win' solutions linking the poverty, deforestation, and climate crises in climate mitigation projects, these projects will have to take into account cross-cutting issues, such as the fact that the current framework is predominantly managed and implemented by men at all levels; that male-dominated social organization is reinforced by Western scientific and development approaches; and that project activities are predominantly targeted towards men, or towards women's practical rather than strategic gender needs.

We can begin to 'bundle' these issues together. One bundle is concerned with equity (including the realization of women's strategic needs), and another with the strengthening of women's role in local governance, participation, and institutions. The technical and top-down nature of projects can be problematic, preventing the development of participatory and inclusive structures. Therefore, design, implementation, and monitoring should be considered from a gender perspective to include men's and women's needs and interests. Challenges ahead include the questions of how local institutions and organizations can ensure that women are incorporated into the decision-making framework and consider strategic gender needs, and, at the higher decision-making level, of how to incorporate a gender analysis within climate change frameworks.

At the community level, we need to consider how to raise the issues of strategic needs through gender workshops. In the example cited in this chapter, the local organization CIBAPA has an important role in ensuring that it encourages women onto its committee. At the technical level, female foresters and extension workers should be encouraged to work with the communities. At the international policy-making level, gender perspectives should be incorporated into the culture of decision-making, which should include a broad and inclusive perspective on the one hand, and mechanisms for the inclusion of women in decision-making on the other.

Notes

1. Terrestrial 'sinks' refer to carbon absorption outside of intentional human action. In particular, carbon uptake from non-managed terrestrial areas is thought to be the result of three processes – increased CO_2 fertilization,

increased nitrogen deposition, and impacts attributed to a changing climate. http://www.wri.org/climate/sinks.html
2. Personal observation from the Seventh Conference of Parties (COP7) meeting in Marrakech, November 2001.
3. For more information about Chiquitano culture and livelihood strategies, see G. Birk (2000) *Owners of the Forest: Natural Resource Management by the-Bolivian Chiquitano Indigenous People*, Santa Cruz, Bolivia: APCOB/CICOL

References

Denton F. (2001) 'Climate change, gender and poverty – academic babble or realpolitik?', *Point de Vue*, 14, Dakar: ENDA.
Kothari, R. (1988) 'Foreword', in V. Shiva (1988).
Momsen, J .H. (1991) *Women and Development in the Third World*, London: Routledge.
Moser, C. (1993) *Gender Planning and Development,* London: Routledge.
Regmi, S.C. and B. Fawcett (1999) 'Integrating gender needs into drinking-water projects in Nepal', *Gender and Development* 7(3): 62–72.
Shiva, V. (1988) *Staying Alive: Women Ecology and Development*, London: Zed Books.
Sardenberg, C., A.A. Costa, and E. Passos (1999) 'Rural development in Brazil: Are we practising feminism or gender?', *Gender and Development* 7(3): 28–38.
Townsend, J. *et al.* (1999) *Women and Power: Fighting Patriarchies and Poverty*, London and Oxford: Zed Books and Oxfam.

About the author

Emily Boyd is a Lecturer at the University of Leeds and a senior research fellow at the Stockholm Resilience Centre. She is working on the interface between climate and development, researching governance and consequences of carbon markets for development and resilient-to-climate adaptations.

CHAPTER 10

Climate change and sustainable technology: re-linking poverty, gender, and governance

Sam Wong

This chapter first appeared in *Gender and Development* 17(2), pp. 95–108, March 2009.

This chapter examines the role of sustainable technology in tackling climate change in developing countries. Drawing on solar home systems in Bangladesh as an example, it argues that increasing women's visibility in technology committees is not necessarily effective in challenging gender stereotypes. Crafting new rules may fail to confront power inequalities. Sustainable technology can exert additional workloads on women. This chapter proposes a gender-sensitive framework for technological interventions, suggesting that extra resources are needed to strengthen institutions at the post-project stage, and that developing alternative livelihood strategies with poor people is crucial to reduce their reliance on local elites for survival.

Introduction

'Climate change and plans for new technology'
(*Times*, 18 December 2007)

'Carbon capture stations must not be delayed'
(*Financial Times*, 15 September 2008)

'Geo-engineering: the radical ideas to combat global warming'
(*Guardian*, 1 September 2008)

This sort of newspaper headline appears often, and epitomises the relationship which is widely believed to exist between climate change and technology: the threats of climate change are imminent, and technology can offer quick-fix solutions. A sense of urgency, embedded in the discourse of climate change, has therefore given the notion of technology a new meaning. A high level of optimism about the power of technology is shared by international development agencies, such as the World Bank, which place technological interventions high on their climate-change and poverty-reduction agendas (World Bank 2000).

There is a growing consensus that climate change will cause more harm to developing countries, because poor people rely more heavily on natural resources for survival (Paavola and Adger 2002). Climate change makes floods and drought more frequent. This is likely to destroy poor people's livelihoods and deepen poverty.

Some evidence has shown technology to be useful in mitigating the impact of climate change, and helping poor countries adapt to changing rainfall and agricultural patterns (Richards 2005). Sceptics, however, argue that the celebratory account of technology in tackling climate change is misplaced. First, while many new technologies claim to be green, doubts about whether they meet the principles of sustainability, in terms of financial viability, social and political acceptability, and long-term environmental impact, have been raised (Stirling 2005). Second, there are also questions as to whether long-term planning about repair, maintenance, and capacity building is adequate and ready to support new technologies (Roy and Venema 2002). Third, concerns have been shown about whether the technological interventions help address the various structural constraints which deny people access to technology, in terms of caste, class, age, and generation (Feenberg 1999).

Gendering sustainable technology

Some scholars have questioned whether the notion of sustainable technology is gender-sensitive enough. Fatma Denton (2002) highlights the uneven distribution of costs and benefits, and different gender perceptions of risks associated with new innovations. Mercy Dikito-Wachtmeister (2000) also argues that powerful men often control technology, and make decisions for their community members.

In this chapter, I want to build on these critiques, and underline the role of governance in mediating the relationships between climate change and technology. I will draw on Joseph Murphy's 'technology-governance-people' nexus to make the analysis.[1] The introduction of new technology always goes hand in hand with changing governance structures. New committees are set up to manage the technology; new sets of rules and roles are defined to resolve conflicts over payment and ownership. Technological interventions, therefore, are more than technical issues. They re-engineer social relationships, and create new patterns of authority. All these changes have far-reaching implications for gender relations.

The chapter draws on research into the impact of solar lighting in homes in a community in Bangladesh. Solar home systems play a significant role in the current renewable-energy technology policies and match the objectives of the Clean Development Mechanism (Wamukonya 2005). In Bangladesh alone, 180,000 solar photovoltaic systems, subsidised by the World Bank, had already been sold to households in 2007 (IDCOL 2007). Solar energy is regarded as abundant and 'free' in many developing countries. The systems offer clean energy, and help reduce the reliance on fossil fuels and the demands for cutting trees for firewood. They can improve people's health by avoiding respiratory diseases from burning charcoal and cow dung in enclosed spaces. Furthermore, solar lighting has been identified as having significant implications for women and gender relations: women feel more secure about moving around and travelling in places which are well-lit after dark, and this has implications for their freedom and mobility. The recent launch of the World Bank's 'Lighting Africa' campaigns has demonstrated the Bank's faith in this technology.

The chapter is based on my research in August 2007 in a Hindu rural community in Chokoria, South Bangladesh. It starts by offering more details about the objectives of the solar home system project. It then goes on to discuss different implications for women, men, and gender power relations, with regard to the newly crafted institutional arrangements to manage the technology. I will make three arguments to illustrate the complex relationships between technology, gender, governance, and climate change. First, I argue that women's participation in community-level committees focusing on technology is not necessarily effective in breaking gender stereotypes. Second, increasing women's representation in public space is not always successful in challenging unequal power structures. Third, technology may have a positive, as well as negative, impact on different aspects of women's lives and gender relations. I argue that solar lighting enables women to continue working on income-generation activities until nearly midnight, but this creates a sense of competition among villagers and puts additional workloads on women. The chapter will conclude by offering insights into building a gender-sensitive framework for future technological interventions in developing countries.

The case study

A community-based solar home system was built for approximately 70 households (that is, for a population of around 700) living in a poor Hindu fishing village in the Cox's Bazer district. This village was one of 37 fishing communities targeted by the United Nations Development Programme (UNDP) and the Department of Fisheries in Bangladesh. These organizations carried out an 'Empowerment of Coastal Fishing Community for Livelihood Security' project (2002–2006), which aimed to mobilize communities to improve the management of coastal fisheries resources and disaster preparedness. They also offered micro-credit financing to promote alternative income-generating activities.

The fishing communities were targeted since the gradual depletion of fish stocks in the sea has threatened their livelihoods. The sponsoring organizations also conducted participatory appraisal exercises which revealed that one of the key causes of poverty lies in an over-concentration of power in the hands of a few indigenous leaders, known as *sardars*. One government official explained: 'There are some local conflicts, (they) arise from local leadership' (interview, 23 August 2007). *Sardars* control most of the boats and fishing nets, and they exploit local fishermen by charging them high fees. *Sardars* are rich and powerful because 'they have more sons, more manpower, they can get more fish...their sons receive better education, they start to loan money to people' (interview with government official, 17 August 2007). In order to address these problems, the organizations recruited a Dhaka-based NGO to run the project and to democratise the village management in an attempt to give power back to local people and to undermine *sardars'* power.

In 2004, the Local Government Engineering Department (LGED) in Bangladesh approached UNDP and the Department of Fisheries, and asked if they were interested in trying out communal solar home systems in one of their 37 communities. The LGED officials, in interview, suggested that they needed a demonstration site to show that it was possible to provide an alternative energy supply to villages, which were not covered by the national grid-based electrification systems (interview, 21 August 2007). The Hindu community in Cox's Bazer was selected because it was the poorest among the 37 communities, and the Hindu fishermen have long suffered from direct competition from their Muslim counterparts, as the latter are more organized and better-equipped (interview with politician, 22 August 2007).

Figure 10.1 shows how institutions were formed, built up, and linked to each other. Any man and woman above 18 years old from each household was encouraged to join the Village Organizations, one for men and another for

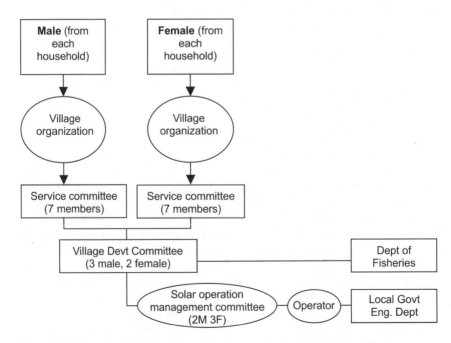

Figure 10.1 Governing structures of the solar home system in Chokoria, Bangladesh

women. The separation of women from men was intended to enable women to express themselves without worrying about men's interference. From each Village Organization, seven members were elected to form a Service Committee. One of the key roles of the Committee was to manage the micro-credit financing. During the construction of the solar home system, a Village Development Committee (VDC) was set up. It comprised three male and two female members, all elected by local villagers. It worked with the Department of Fisheries to deal with local and financial affairs. Under this Committee, a Solar Operation Management Committee (SOMC) was formed to take control of the solar home system. This Committee comprised another five members (two male and three female), also elected by the public. If villagers faced any technical problems related to the solar home system, they were encouraged to meet the members of SOMC. If more serious issues, such as disputes over the payment, arose, villagers should go to see the VDC. If problems persisted, they could seek help from the LGED government officials.

Sardars were not invited to join these committees. The project organizers blamed *sardars*, the indigenous leaders, for causing poverty, since they exploited local fishermen by charging high fees for hiring boats. They were not democratically elected, and thus not accountable to their people. The leadership was male-dominant: 'This is a system...If I am the leader, my son will be the next leader' (interview with politician, 22 August 2007). Therefore, working with *sardars* to improve local governance was not an option. Instead, the sponsoring organizations and the NGO decided to challenge the *sardars'* authority by mobilizing villagers to set up new committees to govern the new technology, to encourage more direct involvement of women, and to exclude *sardars* from participation. All these policies carried a significant meaning in confronting the patriarchical culture and aiming towards power sharing and gender equality.

Despite good intentions, the project remained top-down in nature. The involvement of the community members at the initial stages of the project, such as choosing the technology and planning, was minimal. In interview, the LGED officials regarded the process of choosing technology as 'purely a technical matter'. Since the villagers were not 'good at technology', they felt that they should make the decisions on their behalf (interview, 21 August 2007). They suggested that they preferred the communal solar system to the individual system because it would promote a sense of sharing and create a 'binding force to social integration' (interview, 21 August 2007).

Each household was required to pay 40 taka per month for the maintenance of the system.[2] The payment was based on their monthly expenditure on kerosene used for lighting. The SOMC was responsible for collecting fees on a monthly basis. Villagers received two bulbs, and lighting was switched on from 6pm to 11pm. Five households were also able to afford extra electricity for televisions.

Under the new governance structures, a 20-year-old male villager was trained as an operator to look after the system, and he earned 1,500 taka a month for this. In his words, as a college student, he could earn more by offering private tuitions than this, but he felt that his contributions to his village were more important (interview, 24 August 2007).

The impact of the project was considerable. Before the implementation of the solar home system, villagers had relied on kerosene and firewood for lighting, but this provided light that was so dim that they were forced to stop working and reading before 8pm. Now, the solar lighting enabled people to pursue activities into the evenings. Women could engage in income-generation activities, such as net-making and repair, in the evening at home. Men did not get involved wtih net-making or repair since these activities were considered 'women's work' and men were not 'skilled enough' (interviews with female villagers, 22 August 2007). While some men made use of the new source of lighting to read religious books at home or watch television in their neighbours' home, others still went to bed early because they said they were tired after a whole day's work of boat-repairing and fish-selling (interview with male villagers, 22 August 2007). In this Hindu community, parents were keen on their children's education. Their children could read and write more easily, and later into the night.

The initial success of the project led LGED to think they could use the project as a model – a 'demonstration site'. However, at the end of the project in 2006, it was found that 56 out of 70 households had failed to pay the monthly fees for more than eight months. Eventually, LGED decided to stop providing lighting to those who failed to pay. This suggested that there was a significant problem in terms of the long-term financial sustainability of the system. In addition, when the project was over in 2006, the Dhaka-based NGO left the community, and there was no more support from the NGO in addressing some contentious issues, such as disconnection.

My research

What went wrong with the project? To find out about the impact of the project on women, men, their households, and wider gender relations, I talked to my Bangladeshi NGO friend and asked him to introduce me to the Dhaka-based NGO which was responsible for the project. I obtained a grant from the UK's British Council to conduct this research. My NGO friend worked as my interpreter, and we visited the village in August 2007. We adopted a semi-structured interview approach, and talked to various social groups, including village leaders, local politicians, women, children, religious leaders, and government officers. We taped, transcribed, and coded the interviews and used secondary data to make our analysis. We interviewed eight men and nine women.

We aimed to explore how the project and the technological interventions interacted with the livelihoods of men and women, as well as the gender power relations within the households. We were also interested to examine how far the new institutional arrangements which formed part of the project

– such as establishing new committees, increasing women's representation, democratising decision-making processes, and enhancing transparency and accountability – were effective in promoting gender equality and challenging power inequalities.

Institutionalizing women's participation

The sponsoring organizations stated that they had a strong commitment towards women's empowerment: 'it is not easy to empower women, but I will try…If women are empowered, everything is fine' (interview, 18 August 2007). All female villagers had been invited to form the Service Committee; two women joined the VDC; three became members of the SOMC. Such inclusion helped enhance women's visibility in the public space.

Despite good intentions, my research suggested that the project organizers had not paid sufficient attention to the particular dynamics of empowerment – in which power must be claimed from below, by women themselves. Empowerment cannot be delegated or imposed by project planners, but project organizers did not seem clear about these issues.

Women were included in the committees largely for practical reasons. Men were out at sea, fishing, for six months between August and January every year. The project organizers needed the women to make decisions about the daily functioning of the community. As a local politician explained: 'Men are working outside. Women are living for 24 hours in the community, so they are nominated' (interview, 22 August 2007). Worse still, decisions made by women were considered provisional. When men returned, they could challenge the decisions and make amendments (interview with female committee members, 22 August 2007).

Evidence also shows that the working committees helped reinforce, rather than challenge, gender stereotypes. From the project organizers' perspective, women possessed better social skills, so they, rather than men, were seen as more suitable to collect the fees (although there was no evidence to prove that community members found it harder to say no to a man collecting fees than to a woman). In contrast, the LGED officials felt that the post of operator should be taken up by men only, because women, from their perspective, were perceived as either technically incompetent, or lacking interest in mechanical things (interview, 21 August 2007). Therefore, when they looked for a suitable local villager to train as an operator, they only targeted young adult males, and this reinforced the fixation with gender stereotypes.

An unanticipated consequence of this was that it offered the 20-year-old male operator an opportunity to become powerful and influential within the community, since he controlled the times at which the electricity supplies were switched on and off (although in principle, LGED had fixed the time). He managed to extend the electricity supplies till midnight during the Pujah festivals. In interviews, he admitted that villagers attempted to bribe him in order to extend the opening hours of the electricity supplies during their wedding celebrations (interview, 24 August 2007). On a few occasions when he was late home, he asked his brothers to operate the solar home system on his behalf. Although this violated LGED regulations, local villagers did not think it was a big deal as long as the lighting was provided on time. Furthermore, a community member told me that she did not want to upset her good relationships with him because she said she never knew when she might need his help, such as mending the bulbs (interview, 23 August, 2007).

.   A close examination of the division of labour within the committees also indicates that the female committee members did not challenge gender inequality and stereotyping. While taking up most of the administrative tasks, they were happy to let their male counterparts deal with external communications. They explained that women were 'less educated, (and have) less vocabularies than men', so it was better for men to represent the community and to liaise with the government officials (interview, 22 August 2008). This self-exclusion had constrained women from building wider social networks. Asked who controlled the solar lighting, a female committee member suggested her husband because he 'earns, who makes money' (interview, 20 August 2007). These examples showed the extent to which women rationalize their own subordinate roles in society, making it unlikely that they will challenge and change gender power relations and take on traditionally 'male' tasks.

Other questions, as to who these women are and what interests they represent, need to be carefully considered. In interviews, villagers thought that the women chosen for the committees should possess certain characteristics: they had time to serve; they were educated and had relevant skills, such as accounting; they were honest. Our investigation suggested that women with these attributes were not the poorest in their village. The women on the committees had already been active in local affairs. In contrast, the very poor women, such as the widowed and the disabled, were not included in the committees. Women without sons were also discriminated against (interview with poor female villager, 24 August 2007).

To summarise, the case study showed very clearly that raising women's visibility in the newly formed committees did not necessarily enhance their decision-making power or challenge gender inequality.

Confronting power inequalities between villagers and elites

To what extent were these new institutional arrangements effective in democratising local management and challenging unequal power structures? The answer hinges on how *sardars* and local villagers responded. According to a government official, *sardars* were 'not happy' about the changes (interview, 23 August 2007). Rather than making direct confrontation, *sardars* exerted their influence in the new committees through their control of the finance. Many committee members relied on *sardars* for boat-hire and loans, so they felt the need to appease *sardars* in return for stable livelihoods. As a result, they invited *sardars* to play an 'advisory' role in the committees. A female committee member justified their action: 'people respect them' (interview, 26 August 2007).

Apart from silencing opposition by ensuring some committee members were 'not to say anything' (interview with government official, 23 August 2007), *sardars* discredited the new governance structures in order to erode the villagers' confidence. On one occasion, *sardars* applied for 40,000 taka of micro-credit funding from the VDC for investment. The committee members believed that this would help create employment opportunities for the village, so they approved the application. To their surprise, *sardars* refused to pay back on the due date. Other community members followed suit, and refused to pay back. A villager explained: 'this creates a situation that, oh, actually, *sardars* don't need to pay, therefore we don't need to pay' (interview, 26 August 2007). Although some villagers made formal complaints to LGED, and the government officials intervened and tried to pressurise *sardars*, their interventions proved ineffective, because of their limited political influence at the local level. As a result, the micro-credit system collapsed. In the short term, some poor community members might benefit from the collapse of the micro-credit system since they did not need to repay, but an NGO worker suggested that in the long term, the poorest villagers ended up suffering the most because the micro-credit system was intended to help them obtain cash and develop small business in order to escape the poverty trap (interview, 25 August 2007).

The new conflict-resolution mechanisms discussed earlier, which had been designed by the organizations who funded the project, proved unpopular in the village. In interviews, villagers explained their preferred method of conflict resolution. They would first visit their neighbours if disagreements arose. If the problems could not be addressed, they would go to see *sardars* to seek justice. They also expected the religious leaders to intervene. From the perspective of villagers, going to the government officials was not an option, as they were considered outsiders, who did not know much about the community. The villagers did not go to the committee members either, because they were worried that their personal matters would become public if the committees discussed their problems in the meetings (interview with female villager, 25 August 2007).

Crafting institutions to shape people's interactions is never straightforward (Ostrom 2005), and this example shows that villagers' preferences for conflict management were mediated by social practices and cultural norms. The new rules might have offered new possibilities, but villagers did not follow them because they did not consider the new institutions as the 'right' way to do things, and the prevailing conflict-resolution mechanisms helped *sardars* consolidate their authority.

Complexity of gender dynamics

Sylvia Chant and Matthew Gutmann (2000) warn that conducting gender research can easily become 'women's studies', because researchers are pre-occupied with women's lives, without taking a wider perspective of how social structures shape gender relations. There is also a danger of portraying all women as victims and all men as perpetrators, and of considering women, as well as men, as a homogenous group. Cecile Jackson (2000) suggests that power is both context- and culture-dependent, and while not all women are powerless, not all men are powerful. She underlines the paradoxes that some women possessing power may exploit other women, and these women become the agents who help reproduce marginalization.

My case study shows some of these gender dynamics. In interviews, the less-poor female committee members saw themselves as being different from other women. They explained that they had better time-management skills and felt more willing to take risks, such as starting a new business. One member stated: 'Yes, sometimes I feel it, because I'm spending my time for the well-being of the community. So many households all love me. Yeah? And sometimes I feel happy and proud' (interview, 22 August 2007). By the end of the project, the less-poor women did not show sympathy for their poorer counterparts whose lightbulbs had been taken away. Instead, they considered it as a personal failure and blamed them for a lack of savings culture: 'Those people (who) have saved their money get the facilities. Those who have not deposited their money, they're suffering' (interview, 21 August 2007).

Unintended consequences of institutional reforms

Frances Cleaver (2003) indicates that increasing women's participation, without considering their multiple obligations and workloads, can cause more harm to women. This case study raises similar concerns. Before the installation of the solar home system, villagers relied on kerosene for lighting. Yet the light was so dim that they had to stop working before 8pm. Now, the solar lighting extended women's working hours till 11pm, when the solar home system went off. In interviews, women felt that they needed to seize this opportunity to work hard in the evening, in order to make more money for their families. The system also created a sense of competition among female villagers who felt they lagged behind their neighbours. As a result, the new technological intervention has, unwittingly, increased women's working hours and exerted an extra burden on their already-tired bodies.

Men made use of the solar lighting to pursue leisure activities in the evening, such as watching television, reading religious books, or gathering together for a chat. That said, many men went to bed long before the solar systems were turned off at 11pm. They said that they were tired after working so hard on repairing boats or selling fish in the markets in the day. They supported their wives to carry out income-generating activities because they thought women could combine their domestic duties and income generation at home (interview with male villagers, 22 August 2007).

Financial sustainability and seasonal work

During my research, I found out that 56 out of 70 households could not afford the payment, and consequently their light bulbs were taken away. The reasons for failure to pay for the lighting were to do with the way in which villagers earned their living. Villagers explained that fishing was a seasonal business, and the method of paying for the new form of lighting was incompatible with their income patterns. While using kerosene had suited them as it could be bought in bulk as and when they had money, they needed to pay a regular monthly amount for the solar lighting. If they failed to pay, debt accumulated (interview, 26 August 2007).

The fee collection caused friction in the village. The SOMC went out to collect fees monthly, but the committee members told us that the experience was not pleasant. Owing to seasonal fluctuations of the fishing industry, many poor households had problems in paying the fees punctually. Quarrels easily arose about delayed payment. On one occasion, a SOMC member felt she was pushed by a villager, and she decided to quit the post. Other members followed. As a result, the SOMC was disbanded in December 2006.

After the intervention of LGED, it was re-established and new committee members were elected. In order to avoid conflict, LGED passed a new rule, stressing that no more late payment would be tolerated; otherwise, the Committee would disconnect the electricity supplies. The unintended consequence of this measure, as stated earlier, was that 56 out of 70 households were disconnected when we visited the village in August 2007 since most poor villagers had failed to pay the fees promptly.

As a consequence, the high disconnection rate has also created a big gap between the haves and the have-nots. Lighting has become a visible symbol of status and wealth. This impact was more obvious in night time because only a few households could enjoy lighting and TVs. In interviews, those mothers whose electricity supplies were disconnected felt guilty because their children were deprived of the opportunity that the lighting could bring. Some children also felt inferior, because they could no longer study after 8pm. A child told us: 'Television will not write your future! But reading will write your future... Yes, sometimes I feel inferior' (interview, 26 August 2007). As a consequence, the solar home system has undermined the norms of co-operation among community members. It has also widened, rather than narrowed, the gap of inequality.

Conclusions

The sense of urgency embedded in the discourse of climate change has given technologists a sense of optimism (Moser and Dilling 2004). The perceived global scale of the 'crisis' has also offered an opportunity to put large-scale, expert-led technological interventions on trial. Using sustainable technologies to help developing countries mitigate the impact of climate change and adapt to new weather and agricultural patterns may be well-intended. But the blind faith in technology is worrying, since the current development contradicts the principles derived from the 'Small is Beautiful' campaigns which stressed that any technological interventions should be culturally sensitive, context-specific, and legitimate (Bortman 2005).

Another worrying sign is that policy makers and politicians are tempted to try out the new innovations in order to demonstrate their leadership, and/or to reduce the pressure from the media and lobbying from the pro-technology groups. As a consequence, too much attention has been given to the macro technical systems, but too little to the links between technology and the micro process of people's everyday life (Shove 2003).

This chapter has focused on the issues around governance and institution building. It has analysed the impact of the solar home systems on a small Bangladeshi village, from a gender perspective. It has demonstrated that technological interventions and institution restructuring work closely together – some institutions were imposed newly by the project, and other existing institutions, such as the role of *sardars*, were deliberately sidelined. It has also shown that the installation of the solar home system does not simply involve building physical infrastructure, but it also aims to achieve good governance – to challenge unequal power structures, to advocate women's empowerment, and to promote transparency and accountability.

This case study adds to the considerable body of research which shows that increasing women's visibility in the community by promoting their participation on committees is not necessarily effective in challenging gender stereotypes. Female committee members have been socialized into an acceptance of gender inequality and they cannot just step outside this once they are on committees. In this case, women claimed that men, rather than women, were better at communicating with government officials. Crafting new rules was also proved ineffective in challenging their authority. Villagers' preferences for conflict resolution, for instance, were strongly embedded in social practice and cultural norms. The newly formed institutions, however, were not considered to be the right way to do things.

The project organizers' decision not to work with the local leaders might appear to be the right thing to do because *sardars* were identified as the cause of poverty. That said, a lack of detailed understanding of the complexity of people's livelihoods (such as the dependence of poor people's livelihoods on local elites), and a lack of public participation at the initial stages of the project (such as the choice of technological interventions and the approach to governance restructuring), made this top-down project fail to challenge the power inequalities between the funders and local communities in the first place (Cornwall and Coelho 2007).

Policy implications

In order to develop a gender-sensitive framework for technological interventions, I propose four points. First, sponsoring organizations should avoid imposing technological interventions and governance restructuring on communities. Women and men themselves have to be responsible for designing and building institutions which appear appropriate and useful to them. Institution building takes time, and it requires strong political will and resources to support local people even after the end of the project (Wong 2008). Second, donors should consider preparing additional funds for post-project development in order to build resilient and robust institutions. Third, the success of challenging power inequalities lies in developing sustainable alternative livelihood strategies with local people. This will reduce poor people's over-reliance on the rich and the powerful. Fourth, literature has shown that NGOs can work closely with local communities to challenge power inequalities in community development (Cornwall and Coelho 2007), but the choice of NGOs matters. My case study has shown that the Dhaka-based NGO could not offer continual support to the village when the project was over because of the distance involved. Selecting neighbouring NGOs may help develop trust and bonding between development workers and local people.

Notes

1. Murphy's analytical framework explains how social practices mediate the effectiveness of technological systems. The first component of the framework is technology. Murphy argues that technology can be seen as a means to achieve sustainability, but the process of selecting technology is not apolitical. He challenges technological determinism, and underlines the fact that technologies are socially constructed, shaped by people's perceptions and cultural contexts. He suggests that there has been a paradigm shift, moving away from the top-down, hierarchical, and expert-driven approach to a more local, decentralized, and participatory direction (although there are many obstacles in achieving this). The second component is governance. He defines governance as the relationships between the state and people. The shifting emphasis from government to governance marks the changing roles of the state, market, NGOs, and community in managing technology. The institutional arrangements, he argues, shape, and are shaped by, how people and technology interact. The third component is people. He argues for a deeper understanding of the multiple identities of people and the complexity of their motivation in adopting sustainable innovations. He criticises the rational choice model for over-simplifying human actions. He suggests that most of our decisions are not made consciously, and that we tend to follow routines, habits, and social conventions in our everyday lives.
2. The gross national income per capita in Bangladesh was $1,230.00 in 2006, equivalent to 581 taka per month. Asking each household to contribute 40 taka per month for the solar lighting seemed reasonable, since

the payment was less than 7 per cent of their total incomes. However, these statistics could be misleading. My research suggested that this Hindu community was much poorer than its Muslim counterparts. People living in rural areas also tended to be poorer than those living in urban areas. Furthermore, the failure to pay monthly contributions led to the accumulation of debts, and this is why the payment systems collapsed.

References

Bortman, J.(2005) 'Small is beautiful – technology as if people mattered', *Journal of Technology Transfer* 2(1): 77–82.

Chant, S. and M. Gutmann (2000) 'Mainstreaming Men into Gender and Development: Debates, Reflections and Experiences', Oxfam Working Papers, Oxfam GB, Oxford.

Cleaver, F. (2003) 'Men and masculinities: new directions in gender and development', in F. Cleaver (ed.) *Masculinities Matter!*, London: Zed Books.

Cornwall, A. and V. Coelho (2007) *Spaces for Change? The Politics of Citizen Participation in New Democratic Arenas*, London: Zed Books.

Denton, F. (2002) 'Climate change vulnerability, impacts, and adaptation: why does gender matter?', *Gender and Development* 10(2): 10–20.

Dikito-Wachtmeister, M. (2000) 'Women's participation in decision-making processes in rural water projects, Makoni District, Zimbabwe', unpublished Ph.D Thesis, University of Bradford, UK.

Feenberg, A. (1999) *Questioning Technology*, London: Routledge.

IDCOL (Infrastructure Development Company Limited) (2007) 'Annual Report 2006–2007', Dhaka: IDCOL.

Jackson, C. (2000) 'Men at work', *European Journal of Development Research* 12(2): 1–21.

Letherby, G. (2003) *Feminist Research in Theory and Practice*, Buckingham: Open University Press.

Moser, S. and L. Dilling (2004) 'Making climate hot: communicating the urgency and challenge of global climate change', *Environment* 46: 32–46.

Murphy, J. (2006) *Governing Technology for Sustainability*, London: Earthscan.

Ostrom, E. (2005) *Understanding Institutional Diversity*, Princeton: Princeton University Press.

Paavola, J. and N. Adger (2002) 'Justice and Adaptation to Climate Change', Working Paper 23, Tyndall Centre for Climate Change Research.

Richards, P. (2005) 'Plant biotechnology and the rights of the poor: a technographic approach', in M. Leach, I. Scoones, and B. Wynne (eds.), *Science and Citizens*, London: Zed Books, 199–214.

Roy, M. and H. Venema (2002) 'Reducing risk and vulnerability to climate change in India: the capabilities approach', *Gender and Development* 10(2): 78–83.

Shove, E. (2003) 'Converging conventions of comfort, cleanliness and convenience', *Journal of Consumer Policy* 26: 395–418.

Stirling, A. (2005) 'Opening up or closing down? Analysis, participation and power in the social appraisal of technology', in M. Leach, I. Scoones, and B. Wynne (eds.), *Science and Citizens*, London: Zed Books, 218–231.

Wamukonya, N. (2005) 'Solar home system electrification as a viable technology option for Africa's development', *Energy Policy* 35(1): 6–14.

Wong, S. (2008) 'Building social capital by institutionalising participation: potential and limitations', *Urban Studies* 45(7): 1413–37.

World Bank (2000) *Energy and Development Report*, Washington, DC: World Bank.

About the author

Sam Wong is Lecturer in the Division of Archaeological, Geographical and Environmental Sciences at the University of Bradford.

CHAPTER 11

The bio-fuel frenzy: what options for rural women? A case of rural development schizophrenia

Nidhi Tandon

This chapter first appeared in *Gender and Development* 17(1), pp. 109–124, March 2009.

Schizophrenia, from the Greek roots schizein ('to split') and phrēn ('mind'), is a psychiatric diagnosis that describes a mental illness characterized by impairments in the perception or expression of reality. The key message of this chapter is that mainstream agricultural policy is at odds with what needs to happen on the ground, and is being further entrenched by the bio-fuel industry. It presents a strong case for locally owned food and fuel sources. The movement demanding these is a critical movement that women need to lead, in the face of mega-trends that continue to remain outside their remit and influence. It may be that the only way for women to effect real changes to policy is to lead change in the fields, and at grassroots and communal levels. In other words, self-sufficient communities should promote their ways of life in all their diversity, to present a viable counter-movement to today's global and monolithic agricultural structures, standards, and markets. It is local people who feel most strongly about local livelihoods, and they can take responsibility for action around local issues.

Bio-fuels: where we are today[1]

With financial support from the Asian Development Bank, the Philippines has set aside a million hectares for *jatropha* (palm oil) plantations. A native Latin American plant, *jatropha* is a wild shrub, easy to establish, quick-growing and hardy, and not browsed easily by cattle or goats. Its seeds contain up to 40 per cent oil, and the plant is now cultivated on a massive scale for bio-diesel, in several countries including India, Malawi, Swaziland, and Indonesia.

In Mindanao, an island in southern Philippines, where the plant's local name is *tuba-tuba*, whole tracts of arable land used for food crops, like rice, are gradually being turned into agro-industrial plantations for bio-fuels. For Erlinda Garcia, and other village women, the rush to plant *jatropha* has meant losing the patches of *cogon* grass that they harvested for roofing, and the freshwater snails which lived in ponds, now drained for plantations. The women used to sell the snails and *cogon* grass, and were employed as seasonal weeders, gleaners, and harvesters on the rice fields. Without these livelihood sources, Erlinda is learning about *odig* – organic, diversified gardening: 'I can plant squash, string beans and other vegetables using organic fertilizers and pesticides' (Reyes 2007).

In the village of Kugwe in north-west Cameroon, where palm oil is already the main cash crop, increased international demand for palm oil has put further pressure on women. Here, the palm-tree farms are the property of the head of the family. Food crops grown in these farms belong to women to feed the family and sell in local markets. Processing farm produce is also women's work, no matter what the crop. Using their legs and feet, women smash the oil-palm nuts to produce oil, which represents about 75 per cent of the community's earnings. When it comes to income-sharing, however, proceeds from the sale of harvested palm oil belong to the head of the family. If the head of the family hires a professional harvester, the latter would still draw on the labour of women and children from the household. For every 40 litres of first-grade oil, the women receive seven litres for household use. The remaining oil is shared equally between harvester and owner. Often women and children gather fibre and squeeze out low-grade oil to add to their remuneration. Apart from being the main labour force in oil production, the women are also the main conveyors of the finished product, taking it from farms to the main market, some eight kilometres away. This involves carrying 20 to 40 litres of the finished product (at times, with a baby as well) on the back, over rugged stony roads and steep hills. This weight and the arduous journey put further stress on women's physical health and well-being (Yitamben 2008).

On the other side of the continent in Swaziland, 200 kilometres south of Mbabane, a 400-hectare farm in Hluthi is a hive of activity for 250 workers planting and harvesting *jatropha* seeds. A five-metre tall plant can be expected to yield around five kilogrammes of seeds: enough to produce one litre of oil. But for all the hope invested in the plant, Thuli Makama, director of the Swaziland environmental group Yonge Nawe, thinks things could turn sour. 'How long will it be before rural people are being moved off their land to make way for these plantations? We agree that they have a potential to give a badly needed boost to agriculture, to earn foreign exchange and reduce dependency on oil...but the potential for environmental and social damage are just as great' (AFP 2007).

As with many things left unregulated and unmonitored, development initiatives can exacerbate existing inequities. The rapid expansion of the bio-fuel sector is no different, and rural women are once again suffering the consequences of development policies that are driven by national policies, government subsidies, profit opportunities for agribusiness and energy companies, and the ever-growing fuel consumption in international markets.

Despite the fact that bio-fuels will only ever be one small element in a worldwide future energy mix,[2] the immediate impact on women's land-use options, on their income and livelihoods, on food affordability and related costs of living, and, ultimately, on the price of farmland, is enormous. In combination, these factors threaten the already narrow confines within which rural women operate.

The impacts of first-generation bio-fuel crops based on intensive mono-culture cropping are already having systemic local and global effects. At the global level, the most visible and immediate impact is the huge increase in the prices of staple foods, including wheat, rice, and corn – the *tortilla* riots in Mexico and rice queues in Thailand are testament to this.[3]

What is the impact?

This section outlines local-level impacts of these trends (while noting that there are also, obviously, global implications).

The shifting of cash-crop production from food to fuel use has negative effects on local food access. Palm oil and soybean oil are two important calorie sources for peoples living in Asia, Melanesia, and parts of the Middle East. Demand for these oils is now competing with demand for palm oil to fuel cars in Europe. Shifting from growing food and fibres to bio-fuel requires new (and costly) inputs. Many bio-fuel initiatives follow a mono-cropping system which intensifies soil and land degradation and water pollution through intense use of fertilizer and pesticides, and introduces more new and potentially invasive crop species to natural ecosystems (such as eucalyptus, pine, and acacia).

This shift has not resulted in any improvement in the low rural employment levels associated with mechanised farming of cash food crops. In the tropics, 100 hectares dedicated to family farming generates 35 jobs. Oil palm and sugarcane provide just ten jobs per 100 hectares, and eucalyptus just two. Soybean plantations provide just half a job for the same area of land (Holt-Gimenez 2007).

There is increased competition for farmland. Land for bio-fuels is often in direct competition with all other land use, including food and fibre crops. If one looks at rural development through a land-use lens, the trends point towards farmland converting to bio-fuel, and grazing land edging ever closer into forests and nature reserves, or onto marginal lands. According to Sawit Watch,[4] the number of land conflicts in Indonesia has risen sharply, as demand for palm oil has increased. Over 400 villages have already suffered as a result (Rettet den Regenwald e.V. 2007). Women are increasingly facing fewer choices about land use, and in many cases, are forced onto marginal lands.

The trend towards bio-fuels is also resulting in previously uncultivated land being stripped for cultivation – leading to deforestation and habitat fragmentation. In Malaysia and Indonesia, the development of new land to meet the demand for palm oil is contributing to a 1.5 per cent annual rate of deforestation of tropical rainforests.[5] Many women source forest bio-diversity products for their livelihoods.

If land-tenure systems are weak, there is risk of appropriation of land by large private entities interested in lucrative bio-fuels markets. The sale value of farmland is increasing. It is only a matter of time before prices for farmland will increase across the board in developing and developed countries alike.[6] Yet poor people, who often farm under difficult conditions and who generally have little negotiating power, may have no option but to sell their land at low prices. Where land is legally owned by the state, which is typical in most African countries, small farmers may find that their land has been allocated to large, outside investors (Raswan *et al.* 2008).

The ripple effect of price hikes for farmland in developing countries may have further negative implications for women. Lone women farmers are usually leasees, rather than owners, of the land they farm, while married women are dependent on male relatives for access to land in patriarchal systems. Only a few women may have some means to invest in land. Women are not involved in the decisions around land use. They only become involved in decisions around land use (and by extension, natural resource use) as a last resort, when things have already got out of hand.

By extension, women are typically not participants in the discussions and decisions around monetary aspects of land use and value. What keeps them from being persuasive and forceful advocates on behalf of securing communal revenues from carbon sequestration of their forest lands is their lack of information, insights, and engagement in the evolving carbon market and the emerging economic value proposition of ecosystems and bio-diversity.

Cultivation of bio-fuels is leading to higher prices for food. Jacques Diouf, Director General of the Food and Agriculture Organization (FAO), singled out bio-fuel programmes as one of the major contributing factors to the global price rise of food linked to the diversion of farmland from food to fuel crops.[7] According to IFPRI (the International Food Policy Research Institute), for every percentage increase in food prices, an additional 16 million people are threatened with hunger, with rural and urban poor people worst hit. Food-price increases accelerated in 2008, on top of a 181 per cent increase in global wheat prices over the 36 months leading up to February 2008, and an 83 per cent increase in overall global food prices over that period (World Bank 2008). Progress in reducing poverty and hunger has been limited in recent years. Excluding data for China, the absolute number of hungry people has increased from 823 to 830 million between 1992 and 2004 (FAO 2006).

In the face of seemingly overwhelming negative impacts of commercial bio-fuel farming, what can women farmers and peasants realistically do to ensure that their livelihoods, food sources, and land uses are protected? A women's entrepreneurial support organization in Cameroon, ASAFE, is promoting the domestication of indigenous forest crops around Kugwe which can be sustainably harvested by women and children to supplement their livelihoods. Will they be able to retain control over this additional income, and for how long, before its profitability is claimed by the men of the village? In Erlinda's case, an arguably positive outcome may be emerging from her search for new sources of livelihood. But this begs another question, why is it that women are primarily only *reacting* to these changing circumstances, and are not able to *proactively* take steps to influence policy or adapt to change before 'things turn sour'?

Bio-politics of trade-offs between food and fuel

Decisions about land use and crop choice are heavily influenced (if not imposed) by business and global trade and aid decisions that are taken outside the realm of the farm, on the international trading floors of agri-commodities, and in the board rooms of development banks and aid institutions. The 2008 food-price crisis was evidence of a series of trade policies and domestic subsidies that fed into even more market speculation, which in turn drove world prices on agri-commodities ever higher (this was before the financial crisis towards the end of 2008).

In the developing world, especially those countries where there is not much collateral with which to negotiate, farmers and landowners are being influenced, or have little alternative choice other than, to take short-term risky decisions involving cash-crop farming and a reliance on external inputs. These decisions have long-term implications for farmers' livelihoods and global food supply, at a time of uncertainty and lack of understanding of the opportunities and risks of bio-fuels for ecosystems and livelihoods.

High stakes and profit motives

Early ventures into the bio-fuel markets were assured of high returns on investments. A 2006 report (Goldman Sachs 2006) on bio-diesel estimated that the first shipments of palm bio-diesel to Europe were priced at about $700 per ton.[8] It went on to advise that 'palm bio-diesel manufacturers can realize profit margins of US$170/ton (about 25 per cent of sales). Taking into account capacity costs of about US$11 million for a facility of 60,000 tons per year implies a gross return on investment of 90 per cent, or a payback period of 1.1 years' (*ibid.*, p. 4).

Investors in the commodity-market capitals of the world forecast that the bio-fuel industry could help to ease world hunger. The commonly held perception is that more fertilizer, more mechanization, and more pesticide use would increase agricultural productivity in developing countries. With this perception, governments are encouraged to adopt bio-fuel production policies to attract further investment that would support agricultural improvements, which would 'benefit food production, accelerate rural economic development, and alleviate poverty and migration to the cities. Higher world crop prices will support farm income' (*ibid.*, p. 4).

Big business, however, is buffered from irregular harvests, because ultimately the consumers pay a higher price. Small farmers are *not* buffered in this way. The US-based National Oceanic and Atmospheric Administration recently declared the return of El Niño, a global weather phenomenon that investors recognize as being adverse for agricultural production, but positive for prices (and profits). Plantation companies are usually net beneficiaries from El Niño; any production shortfall is more than made up for by higher selling prices. What does this imply in terms of agro-industrial responses to climate change and plantation systems? Is there really an incentive to change farming methods to cope better with climate change, when the market and price speculation make up for any shortfall in quantity?

The 'wealth creation' driving investment motivation is clear, and is in stark contrast to the driving forces behind the acquisition of knowledge, which brings value to agricultural systems as a whole. Lester Brown, president of the Earth Policy Institute, describes this as the beginning of a great tragedy: 'The United States, in a misguided effort to reduce its oil insecurity by converting grain into fuel for cars, is generating global food insecurity on a scale never seen before'.[9]

A rural backbone with no support

One might expect that rural-based subsistence farmers would be spared the vagaries of international markets by growing what they need to eat and heat with. But most of the time, this is not the case. More commonly, when crisis strikes, rural households are faced with narrower options, have fewer reserves to draw on, must do more with less, and are left to their own devices to manage risk – often with adverse consequences. In some rural locations, migration to cities means some households are initially protected in times of economic crisis. Eventually however, family members may lose urban jobs and return to rural areas, remittances from family members may decline or stop altogether, and changes in the relative prices of basic household necessities put further stress on the rural household. While this may be the year in which urban populations exceed rural populations globally, the rural sector is, *de facto*, the social security net for most people and should be treated thus by policy makers.[10]

History shows that when small-scale farming systems are intact, rural areas are better able to absorb shocks than urban areas. One of the reasons why rural people were able to survive the long civil war in Uganda (1971–1986) was the resilience of subsistence agriculture – a sector very much run and led by women. The sector that contracted most severely during that period was construction and manufacturing (the asset-producing sector, employing mostly men). However, relative to gross domestic product (GDP), subsistence agriculture grew during the war, and only contracted to its pre-war status after peace was restored.

It is precisely for this reason that much more needs to be done to enable land owners, farmers, and rural populations to support their communities in times of the shifting priorities brought about by climate change. While it may be premature for countries to have a clear road map, more research and analysis is needed to enable us to better manage the trade-offs between energy and food security, and the implications for the economy and society of the bio-fuel and climate-change investments in rural areas. This research and analysis must take account of the perceptions, interests, and needs of women farmers and rural workers.

In 1980, 30 per cent of annual World Bank lending went to agricultural projects. This declined to 12 per cent in 2007, while the current overall proportion of all official development assistance to agriculture is only 4 per cent.[11] Of equal concern is that now the World Bank is seeking to double its lending for agriculture in Africa, and there is a real possibility that most of this increase will go to the bio-fuel and bio-technology arenas, and not to small-scale self-sufficient farming.

This is echoed in a recent report prepared for the Canadian Food Security Policy Group:

> *Like other donor countries, prior to 1990, Canada recognized the importance of agriculture in developing countries by directing approximately 20 per cent of its aid towards agricultural development. But, also like other donors, it cut its aid for agricultural development dramatically during the 1990s, falling by 34 per cent between 1990 and 2000. The 57 per cent drop in aid for agriculture to sub-Saharan Africa was particularly steep and difficult to understand.*
> (Canadian Food Security Policy Group 2007, p. 2).

Schizophrenic rural development

The current agricultural industrial complex, the trade and subsidy regime, and its transport and processing systems, are clearly unwilling and unable to address the poverty and food issues that were the focus of attention at the Club of Rome 30 years ago.[12] Monsanto's Chief Executive, Robert Shapiro, told a Greenpeace Business Conference recently: 'the commercial industrial technologies that are used in agriculture today to feed the world…are not inherently sustainable. They have not worked well to promote either self-sufficiency or food security in developing countries' (Vasilikiotis 2000, p. 2).

Quite to the contrary, import and export policies have further deepened the crisis, and have set the world up for an international food system that is inherently at odds with itself, and on the verge of triggering the worst global food crisis in two generations.

What we are witnessing now is the coupling of two complex systems, one for food and the other for energy, into which new global linkages are being introduced, in the form of 'renewable fuels', new financing systems,[13] and greater uncertainties in the weather due to climate change. The convergence of these factors is increasing pressures on land use in a multitude of ways, and policy makers are unable to make clear decisions based on available information. In the agricultural arena, the traditional tensions around using land for food, feed (pasture), fibre, and forest now have a fifth factor to contend with: land for bio-energy.[14] Experiments with bio-fuels and bio-technology are compounding the problem, as farmers shift from monoculture cash-crop plantations to mono-culture forest and bio-fuel plantations, whose long-term effects on soil and wa-ter are still unquantifiable and unknown. It is as though no lessons have been learned from the exacting toll taken on farmers by so-called high-yield crops, which increased farmers' dependence on external inputs for irrigation, fertil-izers, and pesticides, in order to achieve those high yields.

At the same time, we are witnessing increased urgency and understanding of the importance of bio-diversity, and of small-scale subsistence farming, as the critical solutions on which to pin our hopes for successful adaptation to climate change. It is generally recognized that the agri-food sector plays a criti-cal role in preserving rural landscapes, and contributing to sustainable rural development. The European Union (EU), for instance, has introduced regula-tions which require farmers to 'apply usual good farming practice' in order to qualify for certain EU funds. Good farming practice involves nutrient manage-ment planning, protection of water, good grassland management, compliance with animal welfare and hygiene standards, proper use, handling, and storage of pesticides and chemicals, and the protection of wildlife habitats. The Inter-governmental Panel on Climate Change (IPCC) affirms that 'sustainable de-velopment can reduce vulnerability to climate change by enhancing adaptive capacity and increasing resilience. At present, however, few plans for promot-ing sustainability have explicitly included either adapting to climate change impacts or promoting adaptive capacity' (IPCC 2007, 18).

We are witnessing two farming systems that are at odds with each other. In most developing countries, there are two conflicting models. One is large monoculture plantations (eucalyptus, soybeans, rice, sugar cane), on lands held by a few large companies which promise to make agriculture a predict-able process – when in fact nature is *not* predictable, and even less so with climate change. At the other end of the spectrum, there are small-scale farmers – and especially organic farmers – who work very carefully alongside nature. They comprise peasant, indigenous, and landless communities, coming to-gether to form collectives, producing together and demanding agrarian re-form, emphasizing the role that small-scale family farms play in revitalizing rural areas and their economies.

Women mobilize in protest

As highlighted above, women subsistence farmers are excluded from deci-sions on resource management and crop choices. Furthermore, they have no insurance against the direct consequences of these same decisions, including high costs of food in an era of high-cost fuel, and disaster and risk manage-ment in the face of climate changes and climate disasters. More often than not, women do not have access to comprehensive information about the implications or impacts of their choices or actions, but are, perversely, at the front line of activities which inform the decisions which affect them. For decades now, women have been bearing the brunt of experiments with

farming livelihoods, including the fall-out from experiments into genetically modified organisms and toxic pesticide use, and coping with the loss of
male earners due to high suicide rates in India, due to indebtedness associated with input-intensive agriculture.[15]

Typically, the only changes that women have orchestrated involved protracted – and sometimes violent – protests, through mobilizing collective action locally and internationally. In some instances, women's groups have been
successful in preventing further damage to their local eco-systems and livelihoods. Niger Delta Women for Justice, for instance, brought together international activists, in solidarity with Nigerian peasant women, and numerous
grassroots organizations, to stop the gas-flaring activities of five oil companies
in the country – AGIP, Chevron, Mobil, Shell, and Texaco. In January 2006,
Nigerian courts ordered Shell to stop the flaring of natural gas. Since the late
1990s, there have been repeated efforts to stop gas flaring, oil spillages, and
blowouts in the oil-rich Niger Delta.[16]

More recently, on 8 March 2008, peasant women mobilized against agribusiness, and in favour of the Brazilian people's food sovereignty. Nine
hundred women, members of Via Campesina in Rio Grande do Sul, occu-
pied 2,100 hectares of monoculture eucalyptus plantations belonging to the
Swedish–Finnish transnational company, Stora Enso. The occupation of this
ranch by the women of Via Campesina had various objectives:

- to demand that these lands illegally acquired by Stora Enso be expropri-
  ated in favour of the Agrarian Reform;
- to demand that projects proposing a reduction of the frontier strip be
  withdrawn from the Senate and the Federal Chamber, as they will only
  lead to greater land concentration in benefit of foreign companies, while
  involving a threat to the ecosystems and to Brazil's sovereignty, causing
  greater environmental destruction and more poverty for the people;
- to denounce the impacts of monoculture eucalyptus plantations – depletion of water sources, elimination of flora and fauna due to agro-
  chemicals applied in the plantations – that end up affecting peasant
  farming, as can be testified by the rural population of the Municipality
  of Encruzilhada do Sul, where Aracruz Celulose has an enormous green
  desert (*World Rainforest Movement Bulletin*, April 2008).

In an era of industrial agriculture, the decisions about what is grown, where,
by whom, and for what price, are no longer made by those who are doing the
growing. The only public recourse that women have is to resort to protracted
protest.

Urgent issues for women to address

In today's increasingly complex and interdependent rural settings, we need to
ask some critical questions that will enable women to be more proactive.

- What are the ways in which women's needs, priorities, and decision-making can be supported in favour of positive decisions for their livelihoods as well as for the long-term stability of the planet's health?
- How can women reclaim autonomy over their farming and land-use choices, and make both food and fuel considerations central to their farming?
- Is there an argument in favour of women farmers focusing on growing for local subsistence, local community, and local bio-diversity, rather than export markets?
- How should women participate in the discussions and decisions around the new bio-fuel agro-economies that could divert their livelihoods (or even physically displace them) away from food production and/or farming land?
- If women continue to be left out of investment and international aid targets, how can they combine forces to secure income and funds independently for their fuel and food objectives?
- At the same time, as climate patterns shift, farming knowledge (which is never static) needs to evolve with interaction with natural resources, production systems, intelligent technologies, and livelihoods to ensure that women who are in the front line of dealing with climate disasters, can manage and plan for climate change. How can this be done?

Women for food and fuel self-sufficiency, diversity and conservation[17]

Few internationally agreed plans for promoting sustainability have explicitly examined the strengths, versatility, and resilience of subsistence organic farming, and even fewer have considered the critical roles that women are playing in managing communal food and fuel sources. For all the lip service that institutions like the World Bank[18] pay to gender and women's empowerment, the fact remains that mere crumbs of support are offered to rural women, and then only when there is some return on investment, or some novel pilot initiative to be promoted.

In order to support women in leading change at the grassroots level, there needs to be focused attention, organizational capacity, and resources systematically dedicated and packaged to support rural women's needs. Women who both secure household energy and produce crops could benefit from 'food-fuel' intercropping to meet their community's food and energy needs. Using and renewing biomass resources in a way that complements organic farming practices could make fuel as central a component to the farm plan as food and fodder. At the crux of all this, naturally, is women's access to farmland.

Resources, information, and know-how need to be designed with groups of women to enable them to take a decisive and concerted stand for more knowledge-intensive, bio-diversity-rich, conservationist, and health-conscious farming methods. Women need information on the newest developments in the bio-fuel and other bio-technology sectors.

They need to understand that bio-fuels are not a green solution, but are rather a trade-off in terms of land and water use and ultimately ecosystems and livelihoods. Women need to consider efficient ways of using traditional biomass fuels, which offer a clean and sustainable energy source. They need to develop collective negotiating power to ensure that small-scale biomass cultivation and processing production is established for local use. They need to learn about policies and incentive models such as those within Brazil's Social Fuel Seal programme that help smallholders to receive fair prices when they sell biomass to large processors.

Organic agriculture provides a concrete and promising alternative to vulnerable societies to manage production in today's risky climates.[19] By its very nature, organic farming comprises highly diverse farming systems, and by extension increases the diversity of a household's income sources, and hence its capacity to absorb adverse effects of climate change. Organic farming is also a low-risk farming strategy with low input costs and a much lower likelihood of crop failure and loss due to pest or disease attack.[20]

In an interview for *Mother Earth News*, an organic farmer in the USA said:

> First, organic pioneers were ridiculed. Then, as evidence of the benefits of organic farming became more obvious…mainstream chemical agriculture actively condemned organic ideas as not feasible. Now that the…public has become enthusiastic about organically grown foods, the food industry wants to take over. Toward that end, the US Department of Agriculture-controlled national definition of 'organic' is tailored to meet the marketing needs of organizations that have no connection to the agricultural integrity 'organic' once represented.
> (Coleman 2001, p.1)

He went on to emphasize, 'The decision to farm organically was a statement of faith in the wisdom of the natural world, to the quality of the crops and livestock, and to the nutritional benefits of properly cultivated food. [Organic] farmers' goals were to grow the most nutritious food possible, while protecting the soil for future generations. Responsible growers need to identify not only that our food is grown to higher more considered standards, but also that it is much fresher because it is *grown right where it is sold*' (*ibid.*).

The organic and eco-agriculture movements are gathering pace in farming communities across the world. Women's groups combined forces in Andhra Pradesh, India to turn away from pesticide use, and are managing diversified agro-ecological farms (Kavitha 2004).

A network of small-scale farmers in the Caribbean island states, the Knowing and Growing network, has been working with women farmers and producers since 2004, providing training workshops on organic farming and information and communication technologies. During one workshop women farmers visited an organic chocolate farm in Grenada and saw for themselves how cocoa trees grown under the shade of mango trees were protected from the devastation of the hurricanes that hit the island in 2005 (NID/JOAM 2006).

In Bangladesh, ten 'rules' of ecological agriculture provide the basis for development of the Nayakrishi Andolon (New Agriculture Movement), a community-based farmer movement now numbering more than 170,000 farm families in 15 different districts. Several local governments have declared their territories pesticide-free zones, joining forces with Nayakrishi farmers to stop the sale and use of pesticide within their boundaries (Mazar *et al.* 2007).

These examples highlight the critical importance of local knowledge, local systems, and local decision-making.

Concluding note

Climate change will bring with it a disaster divide, where once again those with the means and the power will continue to profit from bio-fuel production in developing countries, and promote technological innovations over lifestyle changes. Experience so far from the management of other public goods and common resources is that it is powerful and rich people who tend to benefit during periods of resource mismanagement and who are least affected by subsequent regulation, while poor and disenfranchised people regularly lose out on both counts.

Protest is an action only of last resort. Where women have control over resources and land-use choices, they are liable to be proactive about making food and fuel decisions that benefit their immediate communities.

Notes

1. Bio-fuels are liquid fuels derived from biomass (plant and animal matter). First-generation bio-fuels are produced from the edible parts of crops. Second-generation bio-fuels can be produced from cellulose biomass such as straw, agricultural waste, woods, and grasses. Next-generation bio-fuels will be developed from algae and genetically modified plants that are the subject of much research and investment.
2. According to the International Energy Agency, bio-fuels will represent only 4 to 7 per cent of the world's road-fuel use by 2030, compared with 1 per cent in 2005.
3. In 2008, US wheat export prices rose from $375 per ton in January to $440 per ton in March, and Thai rice exports increased from $365 per ton to $562 per ton.
4. Sawit Watch is an Indonesian network campaigning against industrial oil-palm plantations, founded in 1998 by Indonesian NGOs.
5. Fargione *et al.* 2008, p.1. In November 2007 a team from RAINS (Regional Advisory and Information Network Systems) discovered massive destruction of vegetation cover over a large stretch of land near a village called Alipe within the White Volta River Basin in the northern region of Ghana. Heavy agricultural machinery were systematically pulling down trees and decimating the area. Enquiry revealed that the site was to be the beginning of a large *jatropha* plantation developed by a Norwegian bio-fuel

company called BioFuel Africa – a subsidiary of BioFuel Norway (*World Rainforest Movement Bulletin* 129, April 2008).

6. Prices had already risen right across Europe and more than doubled in the UK in the 18 months from January 2007(Commodities boom drives up land values, *Financial Times*, 24 April 2008).

7. Jacques Diouf, speaking at a conference in India, 9 April 2008.

8. While bio-diesel is made from edible oil feed-stocks, bio-ethanol is made from sugar-based feed-stocks like sugar cane or corn starch. Both are bio-fuels and have lower emissions, but the key difference is that bio-ethanol is a substitute for gasoline, while bio-diesel is a substitute for petroleum diesel. Diesel engines are common in Europe, which is one reason for the success of bio-diesel.

9. See www.casavaria.com/cafesentido/2008/02/06/282/why-ethanol-pro-duction-will-drive-world-food-prices-even-higher-in-2008/ (last accessed November 2008).

10. The latest United Nations population figures suggest that in 2008, humans shifted from being a rural species to being an urban species, with more than half the world's population living in urban areas

11. Official development assistance (ODA) is defined as those flows to countries on Part I of the DAC (Development Assistance Committee) List of Aid Recipients (developing countries) and to multilateral institutions for flows to Part I aid recipients which are: i. provided by official agencies, including state and local governments, or by their executing agencies; and ii. each transaction of which: a) is administered with the promotion of the economic development and welfare of developing countries as its main objective; and b) is concessional in character and conveys a grant element of at least 25% (calculated at a discount rate of 10 per cent), www.oecd.org/dataoecd/26/14/26415658.pdf (last accessed November 2008).

12. The Club of Rome is a not-for-profit organization, independent of any political, ideological, or religious interests. Its essential mission is 'to act as a global catalyst for change through the identification and analysis of the crucial problems facing humanity and the communication of such problems to the most important public and private decision makers as well as to the general public.' Its activities should: 'adopt a global perspective with awareness of the increasing interdependence of nations. They should, through holistic thinking, achieve a deeper understanding of the complexity of contemporary problems and adopt a trans-disciplinary and long-term perspective focusing on the choices and policies determining the destiny of future generations', www.clubofrome.org/ (last accessed November 2008).

13. There are new financial instruments in place in the form of taxes, levies, bonds, and concessional loans and grants, loans and grants from the International Bank for Reconstruction and Development and the International Development Association, as well as various carbon schemes, to mention a few.

14. Bio-energy includes fuel sources that have been used for millennia, such as fuelwood, cow dung, and charcoal. Today bio-fuel production is on a steep curve upwards. Global ethanol fuel production, which accounts for over 90 per cent of total bio-fuel production, more than doubled between

2000 and 2005. Global bio-diesel production nearly quadrupled between 2000 and 2005 (Worldwatch Institute 2006).

15. The agrarian crisis in India has resulted in large scale suicides of farmers estimated to be over 100,000 in the last decade. The system has not addressed the needs of small farmers, the rising costs of farm inputs and the inequalities and increasing burdens placed on rural communities

16. See www.ndwj.kabissa.org/ (last accessed November 2008).

17. The Organic Agriculture community is aware of the potential of OA for climate-change adaptation. See IFOAM 2007 or the International Trade Centre's report 'Organic Farming and Climate Change'. This publication concludes that organic agriculture has much to offer in mitigation of climate change through its emphasis on closed nutrient cycles, and is a particularly resilient and productive system for adaptation strategies. It also raises the issue of whether organic agriculture should be eligible for carbon credits under voluntary carbon offsetting markets and the Clean Development Mechanism.

18. The World Bank Group president announced increased support to improve the economic conditions of women in developing countries, including rural areas where they face rising food prices and discrimination: '....gender equality is also smart economics' said Zoellick, World Bank Spring Meetings, 11 April 2008, Washington DC.

19. In contrast to the industrial/monoculture approach advocated by the biotech industry, organic agriculture is described by the FAO as 'a holistic production management system which promotes and enhances agro-ecosystem health, including bio-diversity, biological cycles and soil biological activity'.

20. Evidence from farming practice, monitoring and research – Networked Intelligence for Development and Rowan's Royale organic coffee farm, Blue Mountain, Jamaica.

References

AFP (2007) 'Swaziland spots seeds of recovery in bio-fuel plant', www.raw-story.com/news/afp/Swaziland_spots_seeds_of_recovery_i_07292007.html [accessed 9 June 2009].

Brown, L.R. (2008) 'Why ethanol production will drive world food prices even higher in 2008', Earth Policy Institute, 24 January, www.earth-policy.org/Updates/2008/Update69.htm [accessed 9 June 2009].

Canadian Food Security Policy Group (2007) 'Effective aid for small farmers in Sub-Saharan Africa: Southern civil society perspectives case studies in Ethiopia, Ghana and Mozambique', Ottawa: Canadian Food Security Policy Group.

Coleman, E. (2001) 'Beyond organic', *Mother Earth News*, the Original Guide to Living Wisely, December/January.

Dar, W. (2007) 'Research needed to cut risks to bio-fuel farmers', Science and Development Network, http://www.scidev.net/en/opinions/research-needed-to-cut-risks-to-biofuel-farmers.html [accessed 9 June 2009].

FAO (Food and Agriculture Organization) (2006) 'The State of Food and Agriculture: Food Aid for Food Security?', Rome: FAO, ftp://ftp.fao.org/docrep/fao/009/a0800e/a0800e.pdf, [last accessed November 2008].

Fargione, J., J. Hill, D. Tilman, S. Polasky, and P. Hawthorne (2008) 'Land clearing and the bio-fuel carbon debt', *Science* 319(5867): 1235–8.

Goldman Sachs (2006) Global Investment Research, ASEAN: Agriculture: Plantations: Bullish on Bio-Diesel.

Holt-Gimenez, E. (2007) 'The Bio-fuel Myth', *International Herald Tribune*, 10 July.

IFOAM (2007) 'OA's role in countering CC', www.ifoam.organic_facts/benefits/pdfs/climate_change_english.pdf [last accessed November 2008].

IPCC (Inter-governmental panel on climate change) (2007) 'WMO/UNEP Climate Change 2007: Impacts, Adaptation and Vulnerability', Summary for Policy Makers, 18

Kavitha Kuruganti (2004) 'Success Story: An Indian village says "no" to pesticides', www.peopleandplanet.net/doc.php?id=2342 [accessed 9 June 2009].

Mazhar, F., D. Buckles, P.V. Satheesh, and F. Akhter (2007) 'Food Sovereignty and Uncultivated Bio-diversity in South Asia: Essays on the Poverty of Food Policy and the Wealth of the Social Landscape', Ottawa: IDRC.

NID/JOAM (Networked Intelligence for Development and Jamaica Organic Agriculture Movement) (2006) 'Information Technologies in Support of Organic Agriculture, Knowing and Growing: Regional Training Workshop for Women Entrepreneurs', 24–29 May 2006, Grenada Workshop Report, www.networkedintelligence.com [accessed 9 June 2009].

Raswant, V., N. Hart, and M. Romano (2008) 'Bio-fuel Expansion: Challenges, Risks and Opportunities for Rural Poor People. How the poor can benefit from this emerging opportunity', paper prepared for the round-table organized during the thirty-first session of IFAD's Governing Council.

Rettet den Regenwald, e.V. (2007) 'Orang-Utans sterben fur nachwachsende Rohstoffe', www.regenwald.org/ [accessed 9 June 2009].

Reyes, L. S. (2007) 'Bio-fuels gain, but food farms, forests lose', Mindanao Bureau.

Vasilikiotis, C. (2000) 'Can organic farming "feed the world"?', University of California, Berkeley, CA.

World Bank (2008) 'Rising Food Prices: Policy Options and World Bank Response', internal briefing note for Development Committee meeting, http://siteresources.worldbank.org/NEWS/Resources/risingfoodprices_backgroundnote_apr08.pdf [accessed 9 June 2009].

World Rainforest Movement Bulletin (2008) 'Communities and tree monocultures – The Brazil of Stora Enso: Violence against women and made-to-measure legislation'.

Worldwatch Institute (2006) 'Biofuels for Transportation: Global Potential and Implications for Sustainable Agriculture and Energy in the 21st Century', Washington, DC: Worldwatch Institute.

Yitamben, G. (2008) Extract from interview with President of ASAFE, Mme. Gisele Yitamben, 28 April, www.asafe.org [last accessed November 2008].

About the author

Nidhi Tandon is a social activist working with women's groups in developing countries, director of Networked Intelligence for Development, and an independent gender and development consultant. She is from East Africa and is currently based in Toronto.

CHAPTER 12

Women's rights in climate change: using video as a tool for empowerment in Nepal

Marion Khamis, Tamara Plush, and Carmen Sepúlveda Zelaya

This chapter first appeared in *Gender and Development* 17(1), pp. 125–135, March 2009.

An innovative project in Nepal has seen women's empowerment make rapid progress through the use of video discussions about climate change. In this exploration of the project, we ask what we can learn from the use of such technology, and consider the implications for international development agencies and their efforts to support women's rights.

Introduction

Let's all sit together and discuss
When we discuss things, let's do it sensibly.
First of all let's save the trees and plants.
Let's keep the village environment clean.
If we do this, we will be happy.
Let's unite and move forward and be aware of the situation.

(A song by the women of Bageshwori, Nepal, about their needs in regards to climate change)

In January 2008, a joint action research project was launched by the Institute of Development Studies (IDS) and ActionAid Nepal. Taking place in Bageshwori and Matehiya communities in the west of the country, the aim was to explore how the use of participatory video could help poor and marginalized women secure their rights in the face of the effects of climate change.

The project is the latest step in a wide-ranging process undertaken by ActionAid to explore the impact of climate change on poor communities worldwide, and their responses to the challenge. This process began in 2006 with the development of an agenda to bring the voices of poor communities to the global climate-change debate, in order to put pressure on governments to support communities in adapting to climate change.

The project was based on research into the experience of communities using ActionAid's system of Participatory Vulnerability Analysis (PVA),[1] which allows communities to identify the most common hazards that threaten their lives, assets, and livelihoods and organize themselves to take action. The research provided strong evidence of communities increasingly affected by flooding, storms, and droughts, exhausting their ability to cope. It also highlighted their need for information, resources, and technical knowledge.

In 2007, a further research project explored the adaptation priorities of poor and vulnerable women in climate-change hotspots in south Asia, in order to find out how adaptation funding should be spent in order to make a difference to poor women. The intention was to present their perspectives in their own voices, thus bringing them into the international debate on climate change from which they were largely excluded.

The ensuing report, 'We know what we need: south Asian women speak out on climate change adaptation' (Mitchell *et al.* 2007), demonstrated the impact of climate change on women in the Ganges River Basin in Bangladesh, India, and Nepal, and the coping strategies and mechanisms they have adopted in response. It offers guidance on spending finance for climate-change adaptation so that the interests and needs of women are prioritized. It also puts forward a case for ensuring that women participate equally in debates about climate change. The research findings, and lessons from previous projects, led to a wave of innovation in ActionAid, as the organization considered how women can be supported locally in their advocacy efforts.

Power, rights, and change: the path to women's empowerment

It is ActionAid's firm belief that poverty is more than the deprivation of material resources. It is often the result of unequal and unjust power relations, including gender inequality, which leads to the denial of people's most fundamental human rights.

It follows that, in order to be effective in promoting women's rights, it was necessary for ActionAid to look for a formal way to allow women to take control over their engagement in national and international climate-change policy processes. In doing so, ActionAid would be living up to its own commitment to promote genuine processes of awareness and empowerment by allowing women in particular to determine the changes they want to see, and to analyse their situation from their own personal experience through a power and rights lens. This work would focus on poverty in all its dimensions, and enable us to reflect on how the rights of people are shaped by immediate needs, as well as their access to political spaces and power.

The mechanics of participatory video

The participatory video project arose as an opportunity for IDS and ActionAid to continue to build on previous research, while contributing both to the empowerment of women in Nepal and to wider social change.[2]

The project was rolled out in April 2008 with a workshop held in Nepalgunj, Nepal, for staff from the Bheri Environmental Excellence (BEE) Group, ActionAid's local partner organization, and community members from the Bageshwori and Matehiya Village Development Committees (VDCs) where the project would be implemented.[3] The workshop was organized and facilitated by an IDS researcher with the assistance of ActionAid Nepal and attended by 12 participants, four of whom were women from the research locations.[4]

The workshop provided staff and community members with the skills to conduct their own video interviews with local women about the changes to the weather as they have been experiencing them, how they are coping, and what could be done to adapt. After watching and discussing these interviews as a group, the women of the community then chose their most pressing adaptation issue on which to make a video.

The factors that would determine the success of the project, such as affordable, easy-to-use video technology, and the low level of literacy of some of the project participants, had been carefully considered before it started.[5]

The women went on to develop a story about their main concern regarding climate-change impacts through the creation of a storyboard (that is, a series of drawings that represent the final video), and participated in making a video about the issue. ActionAid's local partner organization then edited the video according to the storyboard created by the women. Finally, the video was shown to the community for discussion, and to local government, NGOs, and international NGOs to build awareness on the issues and generate support.

Beyond the initial training, the role of the IDS researcher and ActionAid Nepal was constrained to providing advice and support to the organizations co-ordinating the project, and helping build the links between the different organizations involved. These would be instrumental in making the project effective for local, national, and international advocacy.

As of November 2008, BEE Group and the women from Matehiya and Bageshwori had completed all phases of the research, up to the point at which they would begin to show the finished video to the communities, and start advocacy with local decision-makers by showing them the footage. Although the videos and films were complete by July, the monsoon rains, flooding, and the annual festival season delayed community and local government showings.

In the next sections we will look in more detail at how the project evolved in the two different villages, and the changes observed.

The experience in Bageshwori

The organization Heifer International had been working in Bageshwori and had helped establish five women's groups with members from various ethnic and social classes in 2006. The video project built on these already established groups. In an introductory meeting of the video project attended by more than 100 women from these groups, each group nominated three women to be part of the core group involved in the project. Trained BEE Group staff and community members operated the video camera and asked questions relating to how the weather has changed over the last ten years, the impact on their lives, and what solutions they would prioritize to help them adapt.

After the interviews, the Bageshwori women decided to share what they learned with the broader community. They helped organize a singing competition with songs performed by the women and children on climate change and disasters. Song lyrics talked about the destruction of the jungle and how that has led to floods and landslides. Many of the singing groups called for deforestation to be prevented, so that floods could be reduced.

A group of women calling themselves the Hariyali group identified themselves as women who felt they could, and would, take collective action on some of the issues:

What can we say to those who destroy the jungle?
What can we say as women?
We have to save ourselves if there is an outbreak.
What can we say as women?
The men also have to fight by our side.

Let's all sit together and discuss
When we discuss things, let's do it sensibly. First of all let's save the trees and plants.
Let's keep the village environment clean.
If we do this, we will be happy.
Let's unite and move forward and be aware of the situation.

(Extract from a song written and performed by the women of Bageshwori, 10 June 2008)

The Bageshwori women then made their final video drama in which they elaborated on the impact of drought on their livelihoods and made a call for increased training in new farming techniques, plus resources – including small loans – to develop off-farm activities such as goat and chicken rearing. In the film, the women dramatize the success of their lives after training:

We did not even have a rupee to our names before but now at every women's group meeting we see that we have been able to save money. We have been able to send our children to school with the money we earn by selling vegetables.

The experience in Matehiya

Matehiya is one of the most remote communities in Banke district. Due to inaccessibility and a decade-long conflict in the area, the provision of basic services such as electricity is very limited.

As in Bageshwori, the Matehiya project is taking place within an existing ActionAid project, Disaster Risk Reduction through Schools (DRRS). That project had already brought women together and engaged them in discussions with the rest of the community – a standard element in ActionAid programme interventions. According to the Matehiya Disaster Management Committee Chairman, until that project started it was not part of local culture for women to be involved in community decision-making meetings. Slowly, women are becoming more involved through disaster training classes, but their voice in decision-making is still limited.

For our new video project, the two female community members who had participated in the video workshop organized 15 women for the study, making sure to include women from the *Tharu* ethnic group, who are often excluded in this region.

The interview video footage they produced showed that most of the women were concerned about decreased crop production due to weather extremes of excessive or little rain, as well as irregular weather patterns compared with the past. In common with the women in Bageshwori, the women in Matehiya are facing deforestation problems that add to their burden of gathering fodder and firewood, as well as increasing the risk of flood.

The women said they are facing many more problems because of their multiple roles, as one testimony, from Rati Rokai, shows:

> *Now no matter how hard we work in planting the crops, they are destroyed. Even if the men do one job, then it is considered important. But if we do ten different things, we are still not valued. What can we do? This is in our fate. This is the situation of women. We have to work hard to feed ourselves.*
> (10 May 2008).

Along with the problems discussed in the interviews, the women of Matehiya prioritized what they needed to do in their final video, which took the form of a drama. In the video drama, the women are visited by a man from a local NGO who hears their concerns and takes the women to the District Agriculture Office to ask for resources, training, and small loans. That meeting enables the women to get training in knitting, tailoring, and goat rearing, and to obtain small loans for livestock. The final two scenes show a woman able to send her three children to school on her sewing income, and a woman who is now self-sufficient from goat rearing.

Building women's sense of power

At the time of writing there were signs in both Bageshwori and Matehiya that the process of making the videos and the spin-off activities had led to women becoming much more conscious not only of the challenges facing them, but of their own potential power to respond.

Building 'power within'

A sense of 'power within' is essential for women to realize their rights – since this is the dimension of power that gives them a sense of their own potential to change their lives and destinies, and enables them to have the confidence to analyse the problems they are facing. Women in these communities need to feel that they are able to secure their rights to the basics of life in the face of climate change.

The project did seem to help women build a sense of their own potential. For instance, after the experience, Basanti Sunar, from Bageshwori, commented:

> *The video encouraged us to identify the problems and gave us the means to solve them with more impact. Now we are able to distinguish the past and present of weather change and the challenges it brings to our life. Before, we had difficulty to speak. But when we use the video and see the pictures of ourselves, we have more confidence. We see we can share experiences. It makes us ambitious to know new things.*
> (International DRRS Peer Review, interview by researcher, 2 August 2008)

In Matehiya, there are early indications that the video study is helping empower women in this community. One participant, Birma Budhathoki, who is illiterate, stated:

> *The first time, when we interviewed, we did not believe that illiterate women could do anything. But now, I am encouraged. I see that we can do things. I see that even illiterate women have power if given the proper channels. When we see ourselves on the video, we see how we express ourselves. We see that we are able to express our ideas.*
> (ibid., 3 August 2008)

Birma Budhathoki reported she had found her involvement in the process very empowering. She was originally a key informant in Nepal's country case study for the 'We know what we need' report, and subsequently became a participatory video training facilitator, helping lead the women's climate study in her community.

Power with and power to: from analysis to action

Participatory video has helped generate knowledge about climate vulnerabilities for women in these two communities, built the women's capacity to express their concerns, and generated video dramas that convey messages about the action they most need and want from different organizations that might enable them to adapt better to changing climatic conditions.

Women have come together to communicate their concerns to the wider community. The process of making the videos has catalysed a process whereby they have strengthened themselves as a group – an 'us' – with legitimate, shared concerns and demands that they are able to identify and express. For example, in Matehiya, the film production was one of the first projects in the community led by the women themselves.

Women wanted their concerns taken to local government, NGOs, international NGOs, national government, and international bodies. As expressed by Basanti Sunar from Bageshwori, 'We hope our voices will go to bigger places'.

In this context, Basanti Sunar understood the need to take things to district-level and higher decision-makers. Due to the ten-year conflict in Nepal, many local governments were not able to solve community problems, so many communities have a strong desire to share their message as widely as possible.

Climate change may be just the start: the Bageshwori women indicated that they also want to use video to send messages to the men in the community not to go abroad for work, to encourage the use of compost fertilizer over chemical fertilizer, and to promote the use of improved seeds (information from focus group by ActionAid Nepal/IDS research team, September 2008).

We have also started to observe greater ties between the ActionAid partner BEE Group, and women in the communities. For example, PVA is a process involving the larger community to identify and try to solve their own problems. When the community ran its PVA in 2006 in Bageshwori, it involved only six women from the community. When using the community-led video research with the women of Bageshwori, more than 100 women were involved in discussions and the singing competition (interview, Ram Raj Kathayat, BEE Group Project Co-ordinator, August 2008).

As evidence of continued support, BEE Group submitted a 2009 project proposal to ActionAid in the hope of continuing its advocacy efforts.

Power over: overcoming challenges to enable women's voices to travel and influence

The greatest challenge now is ensuring that BEE Group and ActionAid can easily use the video footage for advocacy.

The potential for sharing the women's concerns at a national level is great, as Nepal is currently defining its National Adaptation Programme of Action (NAPA) to respond to climate change. The NAPA is to be completed in 2009, and ActionAid Nepal is already part of national and international platforms that are engaged in the process.

Most importantly, as an organization committed to a rights-based approach, ActionAid is accountable to women in the communities, and to our funding affiliates, to demonstrate that this work genuinely helps women in rural areas claim their rights. Of course, the primary obligation in regards to account-ability is between ActionAid, our local partners, and the women themselves. The task ahead is to provide the necessary resources, linkages, and guidance to BEE Group for advocacy that allows the women to forge relationships with the institutions that make important decisions and shape their realities. They need that direct contact and outreach.

Lessons from women in the climate-change adaptation study

From the individual to the community, it appears that participatory video is allowing women to see themselves as part of their wider community – and one with a legitimate voice. The empowerment process with women is about both individuals and their communities.

Women are showing that they have the ability to come up with serious and long-term solutions, benefiting the community at large. The interviews brought forth many suggestions – for example, a strong need to plant trees and strengthen community forests as a means to help with climate-change adaptation. In Nepal, forests are often controlled by communities. They use them for firewood, fodder, flood barriers, etc. In some areas of Nepal, community forests are run by women's groups, but not in Matehiya or Bageshwori. By strengthening their power within the forests, women will have better access to the natural resources they need for their livelihoods. The final video dramas focused on more individual needs for better cropping techniques and income-generating activities.

The findings of the original 'We know what we need' report are similar to the views expressed in the videos: women need information, resources, and technical knowledge to help them adjust to climate-change impacts. Women have clear needs, such as the desire to boost off-farm income. The difference with the video process is that women now feel they are involved in the re-search and action process, and are not just providing information to external researchers. There is a sense of empowerment and self-confidence in being actors, and not mere recipients: 'I felt proud watching the video. Now I know that making a video is not the work of only men. We can also make it as good as they can', says Laxmi Bohora from Matehiya (focus group by ActionAid Nepal/IDS research team, September 2008).

However, there are challenges and lessons to be learned. An important one concerns the ability of a single video drama to be used at different 'levels' of decision-making. Since the videos produced by the women are in Nepali, they have the advantage of being easily accessible, culturally relevant, and personal to the community and local government officials. However, there is an obvi-ous challenge in that the final films are less suitable for advocacy at levels involving non-Nepali speakers and at both national and international levels. The women's concerns may also be focused at the micro-level, without mak-ing links to the changes needed at national or international level.

The interview process is one tactic to try and counter this challenge, in that the footage may be used for national and international advocacy videos while the final video dramas remain in the community and district level, or are edited for a broader audience. Another tactic to make local films more useful for advocacy might be for ActionAid and our local partners to support a feedback process from policy makers to the communities, which could then help women build their understanding about the preferences of different audiences.

Another lesson concerns the need for such video research projects to be accompanied by 'hard' data to complement the information generated, in order to allow an accurate interpretation of the information collected. For example, the video footage shows a trend whereby women tend to provide community solutions for adaptation in their one-on-one interviews, but focus more on individual problems and solutions in the final group-produced film.

The process of making a video presents a unique opportunity for women to research their concerns for action, while providing valuable information that could be further analysed by others and that analysis shared in turn with the women.

Challenges and lessons for ActionAid

The challenge remains for ActionAid to help women concerned by climate change to get their message heard and validated not only in the power structures of the global policy community, but also within ActionAid itself.

Projects like this one are a result of ActionAid's sustained efforts to make women's rights operational, showing that participatory methods are key to translating rights-based approaches into programme work. Many ActionAid staff, as practitioners elsewhere, are sometimes unsure on how to 'do' women's-rights work, leading to confusion, frustration and often resistance. They are also concerned about the implications for the communities we work with of emphasizing the importance of mobilization and advocacy as part of our understanding of promoting change to claim rights.

Although ActionAid's understanding of a rights-based approach does not imply the suspension of provision of services, people sometimes have a more narrow interpretation of women's rights, one that revolves mostly around political participation and mobilization (the more strategic concerns), rather than the provision of basic services (the more practical needs). As this project shows, however, exploring women's needs does not obstruct the path towards their empowerment. Women often tend to start the consciousness process by diagnosing their most pressing needs, and then move to more strategic thinking when realizing what they need to do to produce change or claim their rights.

An important challenge remaining is the perception that women's rights and the demands of women at the grassroots are 'fluffy'. Often women's demands and requests are perceived as vague or too simple to stand up in the more sophisticated sphere of policy making. Women in their communities who go through the enabling process to come up with their own demands seem not to grasp or focus on more substantial or structural issues that policy makers can address.

However, their voices are part of the empowerment effort and their opinions are valid in that they reflect their experiences at the local level. It is true that in complex and more technical terrains such as trade and aid, where economic arguments and governance concerns are at the forefront, needs-based demands, such as the ones women have as regards adaptation to climate change, may appear difficult to channel. Moreover, demands for more participation at the local level, and for the empowerment of women, are often dismissed as challenges to local cultural norms – or as challenges which cannot be addressed by international policies.

Most issues that affect people at the local level are subject to a similar challenge, but women often face the double discrimination of having to first convince their own communities that they are entitled to come up with their own judgements and demands, and then confronting political spaces that have men as gatekeepers. Their demands will often be dismissed for the simple fact that women are advancing them. This needs to be discussed in international NGOs working with a rights-based approach, since the right to participate remains an important entry point for good governance and the sustainability of policies at the local level, including on climate change. It is the responsibility of international NGOs who have a privileged access at the local, national, and global levels of policy to enable and accompany the process for translating local demands to legitimate understandings within global debates. When climate-change debates focus exclusively on carbon emissions, ignoring the way adaptation-fund resources are allocated for women, it is necessary for organizations such as ActionAid to make sure that women's demands are translated in its own policy messages.

ActionAid's experience confirms that to promote rights – anybody's rights – does not necessarily require doing different things, but it does require doing things differently. Needs and rights-based approaches are part of the same spectrum. In some cases women's rights will be stumbled upon in this journey, rather than explicitly pursued, but this can also be an advantage as it can contribute to overcoming some of the obstacles mentioned. The use of new technologies should not be underestimated, and nor should the need for participation of the most vulnerable and excluded communities of women. The work done on climate change so far internationally and in Nepal are good examples of this, and show that understanding will change and ownership will be generated as the links between power, poverty, and women's rights become clearer.

Notes

1. Participatory Vulnerability Analysis or PVA is an ongoing process of building awareness and understanding of why disasters occur and how they can be reduced. It is done by vulnerable communities themselves, together with their leaders and government, who do a joint analysis on problems, aggravating factors, strengths, and solutions. Mapping local hazards and identifying what makes a group vulnerable allows them to identify key issues and develop plans for follow-up action. The shared analysis and understanding of problems, solutions, and who is responsible allows communities to hold others to account while taking action on their own.
2. The initiative was proposed by Tamara Plush, then an IDS Masters student in International Development: Participation, Power and Social Change, and one of the authors of this chapter. The study was implemented in collaboration with ActionAid Nepal, ActionAid International Emergencies and Conflict Team, IDS, Bheri Environmental Excellence (BEE Group), and the women's groups from Matehiya and Bageshwori.
3. BEE Group works in the Matehiya and Bageshwori VDCs. Participatory video workshop participants included members previously trained in disaster risk and reduction activities through the ActionAid Nepal's Disaster Risk and Reduction through Schools (DRRS) project.
4. Tamara Plush, one of the authors of this chapter, was the lead researcher and workshop facilitator in the participatory video action research project in Nepal. She worked closely with ActionAid to develop and manage the project for her Masters at IDS.
5. In Matehiya VDC, the literacy rate among females is just 11.65 per cent (Gautam *et al.* 2007, 13).

References

Braden, S. (1999) 'Using video for research and representation: basic human needs and critical pedagogy', *Learning, Media and Technology* 24(2): 117–29.

Gautam, D., S. Jnavaly, A. Sharma, and A. Amatya (2007) 'Climate change impact on livelihood of women: Banke and Bardiya District of Nepal', ActionAid Nepal.

Mitchell, T., T. Tanner, and K. Lussier (2007) 'We know what we need! South Asian women speak out on climate change adaptation', ActionAid International and the Institute of Development Studies.

About the authors

Marion Khamis worked in the International Emergencies and Conflict Team at ActionAid International between 2004 and 2008 and is now part of the Climate Change and Development Group at the Institute of Development Studies.

Tamara Plush is a graduate of the Institute of Development Studies (IDS) with a Masters in International Development: Participation, Power and Social

Change. She now works as a participatory video consultant and a CARE International Climate Change Communications Officer.

Carmen Sepúlveda Zelaya works as Women's Rights Policy Officer at ActionAid UK, and is currently pursuing her Ph.D. at the Institute for the Study of the Americas, University of London.

The authors would like to acknowledge the support of Stephanie Ross in writing this chapter.

CHAPTER 13

Engendering the climate-change negotiations: experiences, challenges, and steps forward

Minu Hemmati and Ulrike Röhr

This chapter first appeared in *Gender and Development* 17(1), pp. 19–32, March 2009.

The United Nations is formally committed to gender mainstreaming in all policies and programmes, and that should include policy-making processes relating to climate change. Yet gender aspects are rarely addressed in climate-change policy, either at the national or at the international levels. Reasons include gaps in gender-sensitive data and knowledge about the links between gender justice[1] and climate change; and the lack of participation of women and gender experts in climate-related negotiations. This chapter shares insights and experiences from the international climate-change policy process, recounting the history of women's participation, demonstrating progress achieved, and hoping to inspire women and gender experts to get involved – at the local, national, regional, and international levels.

Climate-change policy – does gender make a difference?

International negotiations about global climate protection have been slow, delivering meagre results. The debate began over 20 years ago, articulating the target of achieving 20 per cent in CO_2 emissions reductions, and ended up in the Kyoto Protocol with a mere 5 per cent – and even this has been questioned time and again. In some European countries, women have been more supportive of their governments' climate-protection policies than men, and would also be more supportive of more ambitious reduction goals, basically expecting their countries and the European Union to take a leadership role. The international climate negotiations are in dire need of such support.

This chapter is written from our perspective as gender experts and civil-society activists working to raise awareness of gender and climate-change issues, and to integrate gender considerations into climate-change policy making, particularly at the international level. We have been active in this area and the broader gender and sustainable development discourse for the past ten plus years, and founded the network GenderCC – Women for

Climate Justice. GenderCC is connecting women and gender experts from around the world, providing information and capacity development on the issues, as well as information on the process of political engagement, in order to achieve gender mainstreaming in climate-change-related policy making through increased knowledge and active participation in decision-making.

Margaret Skutsch (2002), expert in development co-operation, energy, and climate change, offers two arguments for including gender considerations in the process of climate-change policy development: the idea that such gender mainstreaming may increase the *efficiency* of the climate-change process; and the idea that if gender considerations are not included, progress towards gender *equity* may be threatened. In other words, the quality of policy making will remain unacceptably low, if the discourse does not consider the gender issues, including relevant differences between women's and men's experience.

If getting the social impact of climate-protection commitments and targets, mitigation and adaptation policies onto the agenda broadens the debate and changes it into a discussion framed by the principles of sustainability, then this will also provide entry points for gender considerations. Broadening the debate may have the following positive effects for climate protection:

- The debate on climate change has been very narrow, focusing on the economic effects of climate change, efficiency, and technological problems. However, it would be better if policies and measures that aim to mitigate climate change were based on a more holistic understanding of human perception, values, and behavioural choices. That would include considering the specifics for different groups in society, including women and men. If policies are tailored to respond to the interests and needs of both women and men, and to further the goal of gender equality, they will be more effective – for example, campaigning for energy efficiency should involve consideration of who uses which appliances and for which purposes.

- Taking into account a variety of perspectives from different social groups would lead to improved measures and mechanisms – that is, solutions that reflect the interests not only of the powerful, but also of less influential groups whose voices are rarely heard at international conferences.

- If the terms of the debate are broadened to include the social impact of climate change, this would attract representatives from women's organizations to take part in the policy process and influence the debate. We know very well from sustainability-policy processes (e.g. the Rio Earth Summit and United Nations Commission on Sustainable Development[2]) that it does indeed make a difference if women's representatives and gender experts stand up for women's rights and gender considerations – in terms of the development of a just and inclusive policy-making process, which is linked to high-quality analysis, negotiations, and decisions. This applies even more if gender expertise is coupled with in-depth knowledge of the issues under consideration, which is why networks such as the Gender and Disaster Network, ENERGIA, GWA, and WOCAN[3] are working so hard – and with some success – to ensure gender issues are 'mainstreamed' in international agreements.

- Being more inclusive of different voices, and ultimately developing policy which is more appropriate and hence more effective, would also improve the recognition and acceptance of the international policy process by the general public.

Taking a gender perspective on climate change into account in negotiations might also enable us to avoid possible negative effects of climate-change measures and mechanisms on gender equality. For example:

- Market-based instruments can affect women in different ways from men, because of differences in income levels, and in access to markets and services. These policies would need to be very carefully designed, and informed by a full gender analysis, in order to avoid worsening gender inequality.
- Commitments made to reduce the carbon emitted by private households may have an adverse impact on gender equality. The gender division of labour, and stereotypes about women's and men's roles, leads to a disproportionate amount of work in the home being done by women. Requirements that households should use less energy would therefore have most impact on women. In general, private households are the societal institutions with the least influence and representation of their interests in the context of climate negotiations.
- Technological solutions are not always the solutions preferred by women: 'faster, bigger, further' are rather masculine principles, which one may also find in the climate-change policy process. Women tend to believe that technical solutions, such as further development of biofuels, or carbon capture and storage, are not sufficient to meet the requirements of developing a low-carbon economy.
- When flexible mechanisms, such as those in Clean Development Mechanism (CDM) projects, don't explicitly take into account women's energy needs, especially for doing domestic work, and/or for income-generating activities which are often home-based, then women may not benefit from them. In order for energy, produced within CDM projects, to be accessible and affordable, local women must be involved in their development.

In conclusion, climate-protection instruments and measures have potential to exacerbate existing inequalities, if they do not take full account of gender differences, and gender relations. However, when integrating gender considerations, such instruments and measures can indeed contribute to increasing gender equality.

A history of women's participation in UN climate-change negotiations

The UNFCCC was adopted in 1992 in Rio de Janeiro, during the UN Conference on Environment and Development (the 'Rio Earth Summit'). All other outcomes of the conference, like Agenda 21, the Rio Declaration, or the Conventions on Biodiversity and on Desertification and Drought, include a strong focus on women's concerns and recommendations. Only the UNFCCC is lacking a gender perspective. One might have reasonably expected that gender would be brought forward for consideration at subsequent UNFCCC Conferences of the Parties (COPs), particularly in light of the agreement's overall lack of specificity around targets and rules for mitigating climate change.

Some efforts (see below) were made in this direction, e.g. by holding side events, raising awareness of gender issues among COP participants and negotiators, and by networking and discussing positions and statements during the COPs, but they quickly fell by the wayside during negotiations and between the annual meetings. Until today, no gender analyses have been conducted in relation to the instruments and articles of the UNFCCC and the Kyoto Protocol. We can assume that this gap is linked to the lack of participation by gender experts in the negotiations: women are not one of the 'constituencies' included as observers in the UNFCCC process (like the major group 'women' in the Commission on Sustainable Development process). This might be one reason why experts on equal opportunities and women's rights kept away from the negotiations for a long time. We know very well from other UN processes that if women's organizations and gender experts are not involved, gender issues are not addressed.

Women's activities at the UNFCCC Conferences of the Parties (COPs)

COP1: Parallel to the first COP, held in Berlin in 1995, an international women's forum, 'Solidarity in the Greenhouse', was held. It attracted 200 women from 25 countries who discussed their views on climate protection. A list of requests was developed for consideration by the Parties, and a letter written to the chair of the conference (Angela Merkel, the former Minister for Environment and current Chancellor of Germany). In hindsight, this encouraging start can be understood as the result of the drive and euphoria that flowed from the Earth Summit. The international women's movement acted on the assumption that, from Rio onwards, Agenda 21 and all other UN decisions to integrate women/gender perspectives into policies would be incorporated into every future process, at least at the UN level. But history has shown this to be too optimistic: from the states who are party to the agreement and the UNFCCC Secretariat to the scientific community, climate protection has been – and continues to be – presented as a gender-neutral issue.

COP6: After the remarkable beginning in Berlin, it took five years until women's and gender perspectives appeared again in the conference programme. This happened at COP6 in 2000 in The Hague, when a side event,

'The Power of Feminine Values in Climate Change', was held. Banished to the back corner of the exhibition hall outside of the conference centre, there was little opportunity to draw attention to the issues. Notable at this COP were the many statements published in the daily newsletters of the NGO community bemoaning the low participation of women – even through COP6 actually saw the highest percentage of women yet (see Figure 13.1). The articles also highlighted the important role of women in the negotiations. The women who were actually present were portrayed as serving as peace keepers and bridge builders between opposing parties (see below). However, there was no explicit recognition of the different perspectives brought by women.

COP7: The first (and only) official mention of women is contained in the text of a resolution agreed at COP7 in Marrakech in 2001. Decision FCCC/CP/2001/13/add.4 calls for more nominations of women to UNFCCC and Kyoto Protocol bodies. It also tasks the Secretariat with determining the gender composition of these bodies, and with bringing the results to the attention of the Parties.

COP8: At COP8 in New Delhi, in 2002, a workshop was organized by the gender and energy network ENERGIA, in co-operation with the United Nations Development Programme (UNDP). The workshop was entitled 'Is the Gender Dimension of the Climate Debate Forgotten? Engendering the Climate Debate: Vulnerability, Adaptation, Mitigation and Financial Mechanisms' (Parikh and Denton 2002). This workshop received a lot of attention, but focused exclusively on the situation in developing countries.

COP9: ENERGIA, together with LIFE (another women's organization) invited those interested in gender and climate change to attend a meeting at COP9, held in Milan in 2003. Thirty people came together to discuss strategies on how to increase co-operation and improve lobbying efforts to try to achieve a stronger integration of gender perspectives. There was also a side event, 'Promoting Gender Equality, Providing Energy Solutions, Preventing Climate Change', organized by the Swedish Environment Minister and her colleagues from the Network of Women Ministers of the Environment.

COP10: Building on activities at COP9, two side events were organized at COP10 in Buenos Aires, in 2004, by the emerging informal gender and climate change network; one focusing on adaptation in the South, the other on mitigation and women in industrialized countries. During the conference, the network released the statement, 'Mainstreaming gender into the climate change regime'.

COP11 – COP/MOP1: A shift in women's activities was achieved in Montreal in 2005. In preparation for the conference, a strategy paper was drafted by LIFE and Women in Europe for A Common Future (WECF), identifying possible points at which gender issues could enter the climate-change debate. Women activists engaged in a range of complementary activities:

- Raising awareness and disseminating information through an exhibition booth focusing on 'gender – justice – climate', through two web-cast 'climate talk' events, and a statement on the issues in a plenary session;

- Using women's caucus meetings to build participants' capacity to work on gender issues, and jointly working on strategies to do this; and
- Developing a future research agenda and initiating a gender and climate change research network through convening a research workshop.

These activities helped kick-start a new era in women's involvement and gender issues in the UNFCCC process. After almost ten years of discontinuous and unco-ordinated participation by women's organizations, the path from COP1 was finally picked up again.

COP12 – COP/MOP2: This COP, held in Nairobi, Kenya, in 2006, directed the focus to sub-Saharan Africa, which will be strongly affected by climate change. Not only are African women likely to suffer greatly from climate change because of their primary responsibility for providing for their families – drawing on natural resources including water, fuel wood, and subsistence agriculture – but they have enormous abilities, and potential to push forward economic development in their countries. Their support is needed to ensure climate-change adaptation measures succeed. These issues were addressed in a women's plenary session statement. As in previous years, a group of women, co-ordinated by LIFE and 'genanet – focal point gender, environment, sustainability' advocated for social aspects of climate change to be recognized – especially where the interests of women are concerned. An exhibition booth provided information as well as serving as a space for delegates to debate gender issues. There was clearly growing interest in bringing gender into the negotiations. A side event was held to present the initial results of a research review on the topics, undertaken by the authors in co-operation with the Food and Agriculture Organization.

COP13 – COP/MOP3: A major breakthrough was achieved at COP13 in Bali. For the first time in UNFCCC history, a worldwide network of women, GenderCC – women for climate justice, was established. The group published several position papers, articulating the women's-rights and gender-equality perspectives on the most pressing issues under negotiation. For the first time, various organizations and institutions organized a range of activities on women's and gender issues. They were met with interest, increasing awareness, and an increased expression of commitment to gender justice from a number of stakeholders.

Six months before COP13, at the annual meeting of the Subsidiary Bodies in Bonn in May 2007, the Indonesian Ministry for the Environment, preparing to host the COP, had expressed its commitment to support women's involvement in the conference. Later on, the Ministry also expressed the desire to integrate a commitment to gender equality in the deliberations. The president of the conference, Indonesian Minister for the Environment Rachmat Witoelar, expressed his commitment to mainstream gender into the Bali outcomes during a meeting with Indonesian civil-society organizations at the margins of COP13 in Bali in 2007. Although he did not succeed doing this, his statement constitutes a strong message.

Some days after the conference, the *Bangkok Post* published an article refer-ring to Thailand's Minister of the Environment expressing his disappointment with the Bali outcome, and calling on governments to support women's roles in combating global warming. Beyond such statements, there were also a great variety of activities addressing women's and gender concerns going on around the Bali COP, for example:

- Side events run by development organizations, women's and women ministers' networks, and governmental departments. These were among the most visible activities on gender and women's issues. Altogether, six side events – the highest number ever – had women's and/or gender is-sues as their main focus, or integrated them in a broader framework. The events addressed issues like deforestation, adaptation, financing, energy, biodiversity, and future climate regime, among others.
- The Women's Caucus was co-operating closely with the newly estab-lished Climate Justice Caucus. Issues of climate justice are proving to be an excellent entry point for highlighting gender issues (see below).
- Trade unions, traditionally a partner for campaigning on gender equal-ity, were approved as a constituency to the UNFCCC for the first year. They expressed their interest in co-operation and included a paragraph on gender equality and gender mainstreaming in their lobbying docu-ment, as suggested by the Women's Caucus.
- A press briefing by the newly established global network GenderCC – women for climate justice, and media coverage in various countries, generated additional attention beyond the closed conference area.
- Daily Women's Caucus meetings helped to draft positions and state-ments, and to co-ordinate lobbying efforts among participants. The Women's Caucus and GenderCC were also the main node of contact be-tween the women and gender advocates and the UNFCCC Secretariat.

Climate justice – an entry point for gender justice

The notably increased attention paid to climate justice and the need to integrate gender issues into climate-change work is certainly the outcome of many, many conversations with individual delegates, and is due to the increasing presence of women, in addition to other aspects of the multi-track advocacy strategy that a small group of women and gender experts has engaged in at the COPs over the years.

It seems that 'gender equality' is finally beginning to be accepted as one of the core principles of mitigating climate change and adapting to its impacts. This may be forced by the importance of establishing ways of dealing with climate change that are just and equitable – referred to as 'climate justice' or 'climate equity' – in the commitments for a future climate regime, and the increased understanding among at least some of the organizations forming the UNFCCC constituencies that the discourse on climate change needs to be widened beyond its current main focus on technologies and economic instruments. In particular, it is absolutely essential to address equity issues in order to allow developing countries to commit to climate-change mitigation in the future climate-change regime. Root causes of climate change, like consumption patterns in industrialized countries and quickly developing societies, and the current pervasive model of economic growth, must be brought onto the agenda immediately. Women and gender activists have been questioning the dominant perspective focusing mainly on technologies and markets, and want to put caring and justice in the centre of measures and mechanisms.

Some countries, and the UNFCCC Secretariat, also seem to have become more open-minded towards gender concerns. During a side event titled 'Integrating gender into climate change policy: challenges, constraints, perspectives', and in various smaller debates, participants expressed their concerns about the lack of gender considerations in the climate debate, and assured their support for future activities. One of the tasks, and challenges, for the future will be to pay very close attention to the specific ongoing negotiations, and work closely with like-minded parties to ensure appropriate agreements are reached: much of the negotiations are very technical and detailed, and negotiators will only be able to pay attention to advocacy efforts that are indeed immediately relevant to the 'text' that is currently under deliberation. However, such advocacy not only requires significant immersion in the negotiation process, it also often requires compromises in the ways we put forward women's concerns and articulate gender considerations. For example, we can make suggestions on how to mainstream gender into specific market mechanisms by providing particular sentences for the decision text – but we may also want to criticize the way in which 'the market' is being portrayed as the main arena to provide climate-protection mechanisms. GenderCC is committed to engaging closely with ongoing negotiations, yet without compromising the independent, and sometimes radical, stance that the network has developed. Taking gender aspects into account implies a shift away from dominant, market-based mechanisms to people-centred ones. This is a message that is not warmly welcomed in most of the climate-change community. Hence, while there has been a step change at Bali in terms of awareness of and public commitment to gender sensitivity, really integrating gender into climate protection will remain a big challenge.

Participation of women in the UNFCCC negotiations and its impact

Representatives of government

At the UNFCCC, governmental delegations are composed of senior staff from research, industry, and associations, in addition to state ministerial representatives. At the highest level – that of heads of delegations – women are substantially less well-represented. Figure 13.1 shows the development of women's representation in governmental delegations at UNFCCC COPs.

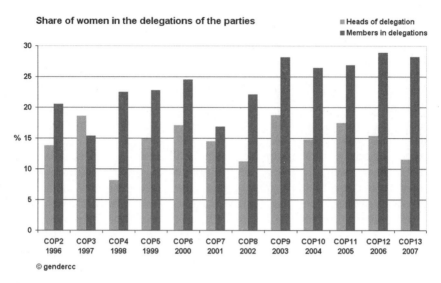

Figure 13.1 Women delegations in the UNFCCC negotiations

Non-government observers

Women are not a distinct constituency among the groups of observers at the UNFCCC. This is reflected in very low participation of women's organizations at the first ten COPs: from 1995 until 2005, there were a total of only 23 persons explicitly representing women's organizations, half of them as members of the larger NGO delegation, and the others as small women's delegations from women's organizations. Since then, the participation of women's organizations' representatives has slightly increased, and six women's organizations (of about 850 NGOs, i.e. 0.7 per cent) are accredited to the UNFCCC as observer organizations today. At most, one or two of them have been regularly taking part in the annual conferences with their own delegations. This unusually low level of participation of women's organizations – compared with other UN processes – may be due to the different structures of participation (there are no 'Major Groups', as at UN Commission on Sustainable Development meetings, for example), but also to the lack of recognition of women and gender aspects in the negotiations.

Apart from the representatives of government, there are six groups of non-governmental observers – called 'constituencies' – in the UNFCCC process: business and industry representatives; environmental organizations; municipal/regional networks and local governments; indigenous peoples; the research community; and, since 2007, trade unions. Among the constituencies, women are generally under-represented in delegations, and most of the leading positions are held by men.[4]

The quality of women's participation

Despite their relatively low numbers, the quality of women's participation at the COPs has been very high. Some commentators assert that women played an extremely important role in shaping the Kyoto Protocol. Delia Villagrasa, who for many years directed the NGOs Climate Action Network-Europe and e5 (European Business Council for a Sustainable Energy Future), has reflected on the role of women in the ongoing negotiations, based on her personal, direct involvement over the years: 'Women were able to play a strong and generally positive role for climate protection based on their networking and interpersonal skills, and their ability to think and plan for the long term, even though they were generally under-represented in the decision-making positions in their respective communities' (Villagrasa 2002, 41).

In the official delegations, the two women who did lead delegations – for Germany and Switzerland – were described by Villagrasa as having acted 'in ways which differentiated them from their male colleagues in a crucial manner: they actively and often went out of their "bunker", interacting strongly with other delegations beyond formal sessions. In particular, they were pro-active in linking with delegations from developing countries' (*ibid.*, 41), and furthering their integration into decision-making processes. As delegations from developing countries were often only one- or two-person strong, they were not able to follow the negotiations which played out over numerous parallel meetings. Although the German and Swiss lead negotiators 'had to represent their countries' interests in the negotiations, their personal integrity and openness earned the respect and trust necessary to "build bridges" between nations. [...] This type of female interaction helped to forge links and mutual understanding' (*ibid.*), allowing them to build the alliance necessary to achieve the adoption of the Kyoto Protocol. Jennifer Morgan, then director of the World Wildlife Fund's international climate programme, described the situation at COP1 as follows: 'Although women are in the vast minority in this male-dominated UN structure, they are [...] the individuals who stand out and say – let's cut the rhetoric, break the gap between the negotiations inside the building and events in the real world and let's move forward' (Women for Peace and Ecology 1996,19). The role and importance of women in the climate negotiations has not been studied since. However, this would be a worthwhile piece of research to do, particularly in the light of the often-maintained argument against pushing for women's participation that it doesn't make any difference if climate negotiators are women or men. It would also be interesting to analyse the role and impact of individual women, like the late Joke Waller-Hunter, previous Executive Director of UNFCCC, and the effects of women's networks within the web of relationships among individual negotiators.

Gender as an issue in climate-change negotiations

During recent UNFCCC Conferences, women and women's organizations have picked up the thread from the first COP, and further developed their work towards integrating a gender perspective into climate policy making. Significant progress has been made that can be built upon during the current negotiations towards a post-Kyoto, or Copenhagen, climate regime.

Yet overall, as stated earlier, the continued absence of gender issues in the climate-change debate is striking, both in negotiations and in the development of mechanisms, instruments, and measures. Margaret Skutsch (2002) asserts that this is due to a demand for rather generalized intended outcomes. She shows, for example, that in shaping the Kyoto Protocol, negotiators needed to focus on universal issues in order to create necessary consensus, and speculates that gender issues might have diverted attention. According to Skutsch, gender aspects simply did not have a place in the crisis atmosphere that surrounded the whole debate around the Kyoto Protocol.

There could also be a link between the profiling of gender/women's issues at the COPs and the importance of state-of-play of issues in the negotiations. When negotiations get stuck, or when they are prolonged and boring, space may open for 'gender' or 'women's participation' topics. Female lobbyists and negotiators sensitive to gender issues have asserted that these issues are being used to fill gaps, rather than as substantive agenda points in the negotiation process, and similar observations have been reported by indigenous people's representatives.[5]

In a successful post-Kyoto regime, gender *must* form an integral part of the whole process and outcomes. From other policy processes we know very well that only if gender aspects are integrated in the documents will there be a chance to refer to them and hold governments accountable to their commitments.

The debate needs to be set firmly into the context of sustainable development and its inclusion of social/equity aspects in environmental issues. The Principles of the Rio Declaration should serve as the overall framework for developing fair and effective policies for mitigation and adaptation. Therefore, the preparations for the second commitment period under the Kyoto Protocol[6] need to draw upon women's experiences, and put forward indicators and other tools to monitor changes in gender relations which have been developed in international and national sustainable development processes and strategies. It is important to draw upon the expertise of women, feminists, and gender-and-development experts, who should be involved in the preparations of positions and drafts and advise, and challenge, negotiators during the process. This would mean linking up with relevant international bodies, national departments, and women's networks, as well as gender-and-development experts; and establishing women as a distinct constituency in the UNFCCC process.

Women's organizations and networks will continue their efforts towards strengthening the involvement of the international women's movement in the climate process, thus also strengthening the demand for gender main-streaming; undertaking general advocacy to support gender equity in the pro-cess of the climate-change decision-making process; and lobbying for women's rights generally. However, equally important is the ability to argue – in detail – why and how gender concerns should and can be integrated into climate-related policy making. This requires expertise from gender and climate-change experts who can help formulate policies that are avoiding putting women at a disadvantage but are rather gender neutral or help to further gender equity. Our organizations and networks will also continue to build alliances with oth-er constituencies, who share concerns about social and economic justice and human-rights issues in the context of climate change, such as trade unions and indigenous peoples.

Climate change is the crucial issue today, a fact that is becoming more ap-parent every year. We will not be able to master the huge challenges associated with climate change without ensuring justice – and there is no true justice without gender justice.

Notes

1. We are using the term 'gender justice' because it is more encompassing than 'gender equity' or 'gender equality'. Gender justice puts a focus on 'what is just?' and 'what kind of justice do we want?' Is it about distribu-tional justice? In the context of climate policy, that would mean that all people have the same emission rights per capita. Or is it about recogniz-ing knowledge and competencies, e.g. of indigenous women in relation to using forest resources? Is it about putting an economic value to such knowledge, or about creating a different economy? The term 'gender jus-tice' articulates a feminist approach that goes beyond seeking an equitable share in the existing power system, which has been causing the current problems. We believe this system needs to be changed. Working towards that goal, we combine strategies of campaigning from the outside with advocacy strategies operating on the inside. The present chapter is focus-ing on the latter.

2. The United Nations Commission on Sustainable Development (UN CSD) is the body mandated to monitor the implementation of the main out-comes of the Rio Earth Summit (1992) and the Johannesburg World Sum-mit on Sustainable Development (2002). Women have been very active and a driving force in the civil-society movement around the Rio Sum-mit and in many years of the UN CSD meetings, achieving access to ne-gotiations for non-government representatives, making statements, and lobbying effectively to influence decisions. One result is that Agenda 21, the main outcome document of the Rio Summit, contains nine chapters on so-called 'Major Groups', the first one being 'Women' (the others are Children and Youth; Trade Unions; Business; Farmers; Indigenous People; Science and Research; NGOs; Local Government). These chapters spell out how non-government groups need to be closely involved in decision-making and implementation of sustainable development.

3. ENERGIA: International Network on Gender and Sustainable Energy. GWA: The Gender and Water Alliance. WOCAN: Women Organizing for Change in Agriculture and Natural Resource Management.
4. Villagrasa (2002) provides more detailed figures on the gender distribution within the NGO and business delegations. (No updated analysis of such data has been published since.) While men dominated among the biggest environmental NGOs, there were strong women leaders in the global network of climate-campaigning organizations, the Climate Action Network. Villagrasa asserts that the good international networking among these NGOs is due to women's leadership (*ibid.*, 42–3).
5. G. Alber, Director of the Climate Alliance of European Cities with Indigenous Rainforest Peoples; personal communication.
6. The Kyoto Protocol is not signed by states for an indefinite period, as it was always seen as a first step and trial period for some of the mechanisms that it includes. The first period of commitment to the regulations in the Protocol ends in 2012. Because nations take considerable time to discuss and ratify international laws, the regulations that shall be included in the Protocol beyond 2012 need to be negotiated by the end of 2009. Hence, the COP planned to take place in Copenhagen in December 2009, will be the crucial event to agree the international climate-protection regime for the foreseeable future. In addition, it is those years between now and, say, 2020, when our emissions will determine how severe the future climatic changes will be – within the upper limits of what humankind can cope with, or beyond.

References

Hemmati, M. and U. Roehr (2007) 'Gender and climate change: Existing research, knowledge gaps, and priorities for the future', report prepared for FAO, unpublished.

Mukhopadhyay, M. (2007) 'Gender justice, citizenship and development: an introduction', in M. Mukhopadhyay and N. Singh (eds.) *Gender Justice, Citizenship, and Development*, New Delhi: Zubaan and Ottawa: IDRC.

Parikh, J. and F. Denton (2002) 'Gender and climate change: Vulnerability, adaptation, mitigation and financial mechanisms', Proceedings and Thematic Paper prepared for COP8.

Roehr, U. (2004) 'Gender relations in international climate change negotiations', published in German in: U. Roehr, I. Schultz, G. Seltman, and I. Stieß, *Klimapolitik und Gender. Einer Sondierung möglicher Gender Impacts des europäischen Emissionshandelssystems*, Frankfurt.

Skutsch, M. (2002) 'Protocols, treaties, and action: the "climate change process" viewed through gender spectacles', *Gender and Development* 10(2): 30–9.

Skutsch, M. (2004) 'CDM and LULUCF: what's in for women?', a note for the Gender and Climate Change Network, Enschede, Netherlands.

Villagrasa, D. (2002) 'Kyoto Protocol negotiations: reflections on the role of women', *Gender and Development* 10(2): 40–4.

Women for Peace and Ecology (1996) 'Solidarity in the Greenhouse', International Women's Forum to the UN Climate Summit, 1–2 April 1995, Berlin.

About the authors

Minu Hemmati is a clinical psychologist with a doctorate in organizational and environmental psychology. Since 1998, she has been working as an independent adviser with international organizations, governments, non-government organizations, women's networks, research institutions, and corporations. Minu has wide experience with international policy making on sustainable development; with stakeholder participation and collaboration processes; and with project implementation and evaluation in developing countries.

Ulrike Röhr, an engineer and sociologist by background, has been working on gender issues in planning, Local Agenda 21, environment, and especially in energy and climate policy for over 20 years. In recent years she was committed to mainstream gender into climate policy at local and national levels as well as into the UN climate-change regime, and to strengthen women's involvement in the negotiations. Ulrike is co-founder of the network GenderCC – Women for Climate Justice. She is head of genanet – focal point gender, environment, sustainability which is aiming to support gender mainstreaming in environmental policy by providing information, organizing a network of gender and environment experts, advising environment organizations, carrying out studies, and developing statements. genanet is part of the German women's organization LIFE, based in Berlin.

CHAPTER 14
Conclusion

Geraldine Terry

Many of the ideas and strategies put forward in the chapters here, such as sup-porting women's empowerment, are key elements of gender and development (GAD) thinking and practice, although you are unlikely to come across them in many other works on climate change. Their very familiarity is encouraging; it means that GAD analysts and women's rights activists need not shy away from working on climate change in the mistaken belief that it is a techni-cal issue we are not equipped for. In fact, it is vital that GAD voices become stronger and more confident in climate debates, because the viewpoints repre-sented in this book are unique and badly needed.

On the other hand, human-induced climate change is a symptom of the unsustainable development processes that the world has pursued to date. With this in mind, many argue that the current policy framework for address-ing climate change is hopelessly narrow; we need to go beyond its confines and address the fundamental issue of what alternative types of development we want. The Rio Declaration on Environment and Development (1992) states in its first principle; 'Human beings are at the centre of concerns for sustain-able development' (UN Department of Economic and Social Affairs n.d.). Yet women have had relatively little influence on official development policies up to now, either in the North or South. And while 'green' organizations are foremost in calling for a radical rethink on future development paths, some such groups have little interest in women's gender concerns and priorities. In fact, some of the policy measures that green groups promote have the po-tential to harm women's gender interests unless we are vocal in raising these issues ourselves. It is all too easy to imagine scenarios where restricted access to fossil fuels in the South, or individual energy consumption quotas in the North, result in increased domestic work for women, unless they go hand-in-hand with changes to the prevailing gender divisions of labour and access to alternative technologies. Think of the implications if women in developing countries were denied access to kerosene for cooking without being offered environment-friendly alternatives, for instance.

In response to this dilemma, some activists are highlighting the need for al-ternative visions of sustainable development that have gender justice at their heart, as well as long-term environmental viability. Emily Boyd and Nidhi Tandon both start to do this in their chapters, in different ways. For Minu

Hemmati and Ulrike Röhr, as well as Rosa Rivero Reyes, addressing climate change as a 'stand-alone' issue, divorced from any meaningful debate about development paths, would be treating the symptom rather than the disease. Röhr et al. (2008) argue that genuinely sustainable development would put the unpaid care economy centre-stage, learning from the insights of feminist economists. For them, it should be about promoting well-being; 'As an alternative to a lifestyle with a large carbon footprint, many people are thinking more about spaces for families and friendships, spaces that make possible sensible, goal-oriented living' (Röhr et al.: 13).

There are academics who maintain that the threat of climate change should be seen as an opportunity to 'take a quantum leap in sustainable development' (Women's Environment and Development Organization 2008). Women's rights activists can make that leap; they have a distinctive contribution to make to an alternative discourse that is growing in strength all the time, but as yet lacks a gender justice perspective. That is the long view. More immediately, we have to get on with the job of drawing attention to the gender dimensions of climate change, making sure that adaptation and mitigation efforts are effective and do not deepen existing gender inequalities, and, more ambitiously, that they promote gender justice.

Vulnerability, adaptation, and empowerment

Gendered vulnerability, either to disasters or long-term climate trends, is not synonymous with gendered poverty, as many of the authors here argue. An Oxfam report on the impact of the tsunami on women (Smyth 2005) points to the complexity of processes involved in the greater number of deaths among women in that disaster. Since Terry Cannon's chapter was originally published, an influential study has confirmed that women tend to die in greater numbers than men during and immediately after disasters. Its authors present compelling statistical evidence to the effect that these relatively higher mortality rates for women are due to their low social status, or, in their words; 'the socially constructed gender-specific vulnerability of females built into everyday socioeconomic patterns' (Neumayer and Plümper 2007:551). The corollary is that women's empowerment is an excellent strategy for more effective and equitable disaster preparedness.

Given that climate change threatens human security in both the short and long terms, it may be artificial and unhelpful to make a distinction between disaster risk reduction and adaptation. There is a strong message in this volume that empowerment strategies are also crucial for enabling women to deal with climate stresses that unfold over long timescales. The emphasis should be on strengthening poor women and men's general ability to react, their flexibility and resilience. However, although adaptive capacity in itself may be generic, interventions designed to strengthen it should be based on analyses of vulnerability that reflect particular contexts. Women's gendered needs and interests will vary, depending on the situation. The authors here, for instance, put forward diverse ideas as to what women need to adapt, after careful consideration of the specific contexts in question. For Nidhi Tandon it is control over land, for Sara Ahmed and Elizabeth Fajber it is underlying systems like transport infrastructure, and for Stephanie Buechler it is access to new livelihoods.

The full involvement of women in decisions around adaptation is, of course, essential from a gender justice point of view, given their general vulnerability. This includes decision-making within households. Otherwise, as a study of smallholders in Tanzania and Kenya found (Eriksen et al. 2005), adaptation strategies may disadvantage women, even though they seem to work well at household and community level. Again, women may have different perceptions of climate risk from men, as Valerie Nelson ad Tanya Stathers point out. Very few studies have been done on gendered perceptions of environmental risk in the global South, although there is a considerable body of research on this in industrialized countries. One study that *has* looked at gendered perceptions in the South found that, overall, women and men in a rural South African community were worried about different climate risks (Thomas et al. 2007). This strengthens the case for women's participation in adaptation policy-making and practice, as it is the only way to make sure their priorities are addressed as well as men's.

Women's involvement in deciding how to respond to a changing climate should also lead to more effective adaptation. Given unequal gendered power relations, strategies might be pursued because they reflect and reinforce gender inequalities, rather than because they represent the best adaptation choices. This is what seems to have happened with farmers in part of Ghana's Central Region. A recent study found that the livelihood diversification strategies they adopted in response to environmental and economic change were not optimal adaptations for the households concerned. Rather, they had been chosen by male household heads because they reflected their gender interests (Carr 2008).

With reference to public policy processes, Rosa Rivero Reyes writes here that Piura's disaster prevention and sustainable development policies have benefited from women's input. Of course, as several of this volume's authors warn, women's participation in public decision making is about more than seats on committees. To begin with, their roles and responsibilities in policy making need to be subjected to gender analysis. Are they merely acting out their existing gender roles, and at the same time having to take on even more unpaid work than before? Or is the nature of women's involvement likely to challenge the gender *status quo*?

Mitigation and gender justice

In their critiques of two very different mitigation projects in developing countries, Emily Boyd and Sam Wong show how they have been conceived and implemented with scant attention to gender issues. Yet, although Boyd suggests that giving women a voice in the Noel Kempff Project might have benefited its activities, nowhere does she suggest that the project failed to meet its own sustainable development objectives. And according to Wong, the failure of a solar lighting project in Bangladesh was due to its top-down approach and neglect of other types of power relations, rather than its inattention to gender issues. Nidhi Tandon's attack on bio-fuels production rams home the message that mainstream approaches to sustainable development can result in organizations promoting 'mitigation' activities that fail to address, or even actively damage, poor women's interests in developing countries. The value and cost of women's time, labour and energy are left out of conventional economic analyses. This reinforces the argument made above that we need to look again at the sustainable development model, with a gender justice perspective.

Meanwhile, what about mitigation efforts in the countries that produce most of the greenhouse gases (GHGs)? Given the significance of climate change and the urgency of its challenge, it is sometimes hard to believe that 'a cluster of world carbon markets today constitutes the major international response to global warming' (Lohmann 2008:20). Both current GHG levels and the international community's grotesquely inadequate policy responses are bound up with gender inequalities in industrialized countries. For one thing, there is evidence that women and men in rich nations contribute differently to carbon emissions (Johnsson-Latham 2007). Granted, the hard evidence is still limited, partly because of the huge scale of emissions. Disaggregating emissions by gender, which would mean analysing energy use within households, would generate new insights into what is causing climate change. In turn, that should help to develop mitigation solutions based on sound social analysis rather than, as now, neo-classical economics (Röhr et al. 2008). Secondly, in developed countries women generally take environmental risks more seriously than men do (Sundblad et al. 2007 and Satterfield et al. 2004). And as Hemmati and Röhr write, in some industrialized countries at least, women are more likely than men to support strong climate protection policies. So the fact that ordinary women's voices are not clearly heard in mitigation debates probably makes it easier for governments to drag their feet, as we see in many industrialized countries today. The overwhelmingly masculine bias in mitigation decisions is a tragedy from many points of view. It is also a GAD issue, because the ultimate consequences of a failure to act include harm to women in developing countries.

Influencing climate policies

We are at a critical stage in history. Efforts to reduce GHGs over the next 20 or 30 years will determine the levels at which they can be stabilized (IPCC 2007). After that, it may be too late. So, while we engage in 'blue skies thinking' to create gender-just visions of sustainable development, we must also urgently reduce the GHGs being belched into those skies. The immediate imperatives for women's rights campaigners must be to influence national and international climate policies such as the post-2012 agreement under the UNFCCC and to actively monitor how they are implemented. The mitigation objectives should be to make sure they result in genuine, substantial emissions cuts, and that both adaptation and mitigation objectives do so in a way that promotes gender justice.

Experience of other international agreements shows how important it is to get gender considerations into the text of international agreements right at the start; only then can governments be held to account later. One useful tactic for international advocacy is to draw attention to the lack of consistency between UN documents such as the Beijing Platform for Action (1995) and the UNFCCC, which pays no attention whatsoever to gender issues. WEDO (2008) provides a comprehensive list of UN commitments concerning gender and the environment. Agenda 21, for instance, calls on governments to 'eliminate all obstacles to women's full involvement in sustainable development and public life', a commitment that was confirmed at the World Summit on Sustainable Development in Johannesburg in 2002. Yet, as Minu Hemmati and Ulrike Röhr write in their chapter, the proportion of women at international climate conferences has been very low indeed, even compared with other UN processes.

Gender and climate change networks are calling for gender issues to be integrated throughout the post-2012 agreement; significant increases in the number of women representatives at climate negotiations; and in addition the inclusion of gender specialists. As outlined by Hemmati and Röhr, the GenderCC Network is also advocating for poor women's interests in key policy areas such as the newly adopted UNFCCC mitigation strategy 'Reducing Emissions from Deforestation and Forest Degradation'. Financing for adaptation is critical, and investing in building women's adaptive capacity would be an effective, holistic approach. As the impact of climate change intensifies, more and more public funding in both industrialized and developing countries will be needed for public adaptation measures. So drawing on gender-budgeting and gender-auditing techniques to compare the gendered costs and benefits of alternative adaptation strategies would also be a useful way to ensure that poor women's interests and priorities are not overlooked. The same applies to funding for mitigation. In fact, the gender-budgeting movement is an excellent example of how existing GAD-related approaches and tools could usefully be applied to the climate change crisis (for information on gender budget techniques, see, for instance, Hofbauer Balmori 2003). Macro-economic and trade policies agreed in other institutional arenas, such as the European Union or the World Trade Organization, will also affect emission levels (IPCC 2007), so advocacy efforts should be directed at these as well as at policy processes that are explicitly about climate protection. Hemmati and Röhr suggest that the emergent 'climate justice' lobby provides a useful advocacy entry point. Since the Conference of the Parties in Bali (2007), there are signs that a gender perspective is being included in climate justice messages, thanks to the influence of women's rights campaigners and gender advocates.

As for policy-making at other levels, several authors here mention the National Adaptation Programmes of Action (NAPAs). Most of the NAPAs produced so far acknowledge the gender dimensions of adaptation, but fail to address them in any meaningful way. However, the chapter by Marion Khamis and others identifies NAPA processes as opportunities to bridge the gap between poor women's priorities and national policies.

Of course, advocacy needs evidence and examples to support its arguments. There is a lot we can draw from the chapters here, but there are some notable gaps in the collection too, highlighting areas where more information is urgently needed. Perhaps the most glaring under-representation is sub-Saharan Africa; we need more studies from that region, which is one of the most vulnerable to climate change. There is also the familiar bias here towards women. Although this is a perennial criticism of GAD, many readers would argue that it merely reflects the severe structural disadvantages that women in developing countries generally experience relative to men. On the other hand, there is some evidence that in certain contexts men may also suffer from gendered vulnerability to climate change effects. So we need to go beyond generalizations about 'men' and 'women' and instead document the whole range of gendered vulnerability.

As several authors in this volume, like Sara Ahmed and Elizabeth Fajber, stress, we need more research on gender-sensitive adaptation, including evaluations of what has been tried so far. Other omissions include studies on gendered climate impacts in urban contexts; information on gendered differences in vulnerability within households; and research on the more indirect ways that climate change is likely to affect gender relations. This last area includes the gendered impacts of conflict, which is predicted to increase as natural resources like water become scarce in some areas (Women's Environment and Development Organization 2008). This is quite a long 'shopping list', but in the meantime the literatures on gender issues in relation to disasters, agriculture, livelihoods, political ecology and so on contain many insights that are relevant to gender and climate change. They can inform our thinking and support advocacy and campaigning.

Advocacy and campaigning to integrate gender justice into official climate policy is critical. But given what is at stake, if we limit ourselves to that we might as well re-arrange the Titanic's deckchairs in a gender-sensitive manner as it steams towards its iceberg. Calling for effective and gender-just climate policies in the short term, and envisioning gender-just models of sustainable development for the future, go together. Women, especially women in the South, need policy makers to hear their adaptation and mitigation concerns right now, even though it can be frustrating to work within the mainstream approach; this engagement in policy could itself help to produce new ideas and debates about development directions. Of course, women's fair numerical representation in debates is not enough in itself to transform the discourse, but it is a necessary first step. As for practical adaptation and mitigation efforts on the ground, women's meaningful participation in deciding what needs to be done could also widen the debate, at the same time as it reduces women's gendered vulnerability.

Notes

1. This point was made by Ulrike Röhr, one of the pioneers in the field of gender and climate change, at the Gender and Climate Change Round-table organized by the UK Gender and Development Network and the UK's Department for International Development at the Institute of Development Studies on 28 May 2008.

References

Carr, E. (2008) 'Between structure and agency: Livelihoods and adaptation in Ghana's Central Region', *Global Environmental Change* 18: 689– 99.

Dankelman, I., K. Alam, W. Bashar Ahmed, Y. Diagne Gueye, N. Fatema, and R. Mensah-Kutin (2008) 'Gender, Climate Change and Human Security: Lessons from Bangladesh,

Ghana and Senegal', WEDO with ABANTU for Development in Ghana, Action-Aid Bangladesh and ENDA Senegal, http://www.wedo.org/learn/library/media-type/pdf/gender-climate-change-human-security [accessed 9 June 2009].

Eriksen, S. H., K. Brown and P.M. Kelly (2005) 'The dynamics of vulnerability: locating coping strategies in Kenya and Tanzania', *Geographical Journal* 171(4): 287–388.

Gustafson, P. (1998) 'Gender differences in risk perception: Theoretical and methodological perspectives', *Risk Analysis* 18 (6): 805–11.

Hofbauer Balmori, H. (2003) 'Gender and Budgets: Overview Report', BRIDGE Cutting Edge Pack, Brighton: BRIDGE, Institute of Development Studies.

Johnsson-Latham, G. (2007) 'A study on gender equality as a prerequisite for sustainable development: What we know about the extent to which women globally live in a more sustainable way than men, leave a smaller ecological footprint and cause less climate dhange', Report to the Environment Advisory Council, Sweden.

Lohmann, L. (2008) 'Climate Crisis – Social Science Crisis' Draft chapter available on http://www.thecornerhouse.org.uk/summary.shtml?x=562064 for the forthcoming publication: M. Voss (ed.), *Der Klimawandel. Sozialwissenschaftliche Perspektiven*. Wiesbaden: VS Verlag für Sozialwissenschaften, im Erscheinen.

Neumayer, E. and T. Plümper (2007) 'The gendered nature of natural disasters: The impact of catastrophic events on the gender gap in life expectancy, 1981–2002', *Social Science Research Network*.

Raworth, K. (2008) 'Coping with climate change: What works for women?' Oxford: Oxfam GB.

Röhr, U, M. Spitzner, E. Stiefel and Uta V. Winterfeld (2008) 'Gender justice as the basis for sustainable climate policies: A feminist background paper', Bonn: Genanet and German NGO Forum on Environment and Development.

Satterfield, T. A., C.K. Mertz and P. Slovic (2004). 'Discrimination, vulnerability, and justice in the face of risk', *Risk Analysis* 24 (1): 115–29.

Smyth, I. (2005) 'The tsunami's impact on women', Oxfam International briefing note, March 2005, www.oxfam.org.uk/resources/policy/conflic_disasters/[accessed 9 June 2009]

Sundblad E-L. Biel, A. and T. Garling (2007) 'Cognitive and affective risk judgements related to climate Change', *Journal of Environmental Psychology* 27:97–106.

Thomas, D., C. Twyman, H. Osbahr and B. Hewitson (2007) 'Adaptation to climate change and variability: farmer responses to intra-seasonal precipitation trends in South Africa', *Climatic Change* 83(3): 301–22.

United Nations Department of Economic and Social Affairs (n.d.) 'Rio Declaration on Environment and Development', www.un.org [accessed 9 June 2009].

Women's Environment and Development Organization (2008) 'Gender, Climate Change and Human Security: Lessons from Bangladesh, Ghana and Senegal', New York: Women's Environment and Development Organization.

Resources

Compiled by Liz Cooke and Geraldine Terry

Gender and climate change

Changing the Climate: Why Women's Perspectives Matter (2007), WEDO, http:// www.wedo.org/files/Changing the Climate why women's perspectives matter 2008.pdf

This short factsheet from the Women's Environment and Development Organization provides an excellent introduction to the subject of gender and climate change, covering the key issues clearly and remarkably concisely. This is a very useful resource for anyone needing to get to grips with the essential points in a hurry.

Gender and Climate Change (2007), Lorena Aguilar, Ariana Araujo and Andrea Quesada-Aguilar, IUCN, http://genderandenvironment.org/admin/admin_ biblioteca/documentos/Factsheet ClimateChange.pdf

This factsheet provides examples of recorded, and possible, gender-differentiated effects of climate change, and gives a list of recommendations, including that the United Nations Framework Convention on Climate Change (UNFCCC) should develop a gender strategy, and that climate change strategies need to build on existing gendered strategies already being practiced, and incorporate lessons learned about agricultural, livestock, water, and coastal management, as well as disaster management. It also provides an interesting table, which sets out the linkages between MDGs, climate change, and gender, showing how the gender-differentiated effects of climate change will affect the areas targeted by the MDGs.

Gender and Development 10(2) (July 2002), http://tiny.cc/2DJRX, www.gender anddevelopment.org

This 2002 issue of *Gender and Development* examines gender and climate change – one of the first publications to do so. It features an editorial by Rachel Masika and the following eleven articles: 'Climate change vulnerability, impacts, and adaptation: why does gender matter?', by Fatma Denton; 'Climate Change: learning from gender analysis and women's experiences of organizing for sustainable development', by Irene Dankelman; 'Protocols, treaties, and action: the 'climate change process' viewed through gender spectacles', by Margaret

M. Skutsch; 'Kyoto Protocol negotiations: reflections on the role of women', by Delia Villagrasa; 'Gender and climate hazards in Bangladesh', by Terry Cannon; 'Uncertain predictions, invisible impacts, and the need to mainstream gender in climate change adaptations', by Nelson et al.; 'Gendering responses to El Niño in rural Peru', by Rosa Rivero Reyes; 'The Noel Kempff project in Bolivia: gender, power, and decision-making in climate mitigation', by Emily Boyd; 'Reducing risk and vulnerability to climate change in India: the capabilities approach', by Marlene Roy and Henry David Venema; 'Promoting the role of women in sustainable energy development in Africa: networking and capacity-building', by Tieho Makhabane; and 'Transforming power relationships: building capacity for ecological security', by Mary Jo Larson. Produced at a time when approaches and policy responses were largely focused on scientific and technological measures to address climate change, this collection explores the relationship between gender, poverty, and climate change. Examined, for example, is the relative importance of gender or poverty in understanding vulnerability to the effects of climate change, with Margaret Skutsch's article suggesting that poverty is the main variable, while Irene Dankelman's piece demonstrates the significant role that gender relations – through their role in influencing which resources women or men can access – play in determining sensitivity to climate change, and their capacity to adapt to the outcomes.

Gender and climate change: mapping the linkages: A scoping study on knowledge and gaps (2008) BRIDGE, IDS, www.bridge.ids.ac.uk/reports_general.htm

This 36-page report from BRIDGE, commissioned by the UK's Department for International Development's Equity and Rights Team, provides an invaluable survey of the existing literature on gender and climate change, illustrating the linkages between climate change and gender inequality, identifying knowledge gaps, and providing recommendations for future areas of research. The report has three sections, followed by key conclusions and recommendations for future research, plus references, and an extremely useful annotated bibliography. The first section – Mapping the gender impacts of climate change and the implications for gender equality – outlines how climate change will exacerbate existing gender inequalities in relation to health; agriculture; water; wage labour; climate-change-related disasters; the aftermath of disasters; migration; and conflict. The second section – Adaptation in the face of climate change: a gendered perspective – explains the particular constraints on women's capacity to adapt to existing and predicted effects of climate change, but also makes the point that women are not passively accepting changing environmental conditions. They are already adapting agricultural practices where possible, and have a great deal of understanding of what kind of interventions need to be made in order to ensure sustainability in future. The third section – Climate change mitigation and gender inequality – makes the point that up until now, work on gender and climate change has mainly focused on impact and adaptation, with mitigation – the reduction of greenhouse gases – receiving little attention, and this section makes the case for gender equitable participation in international negotiations and decision-making on mitigation policies.

Gender and climate change (2006), Ulrike Röhr, in Tiempo: A bulletin on climate and development, Issue 59, www.tiempocyberclimate.org/portal/archive/pdf/tiempo59high.pdf

Arguing that until very recently, gender issues have been neglected in the climate change debate, this article discusses gender and climate change in the South, focusing on adaptation, and gender and climate change in the North, focusing on mitigation. In the South, climate change often affects the areas that are the basis of livelihoods for which women are responsible, for example, nutrition, and water and energy supplies. The author argues that the effects of climate change will lead to women spending more time on traditional reproductive tasks, which will reinforce traditional work roles and work against a change in which women might begin to play other roles. The gender-differentiated effects of climate change, and the often-untapped knowledge of women with regard to adaptation strategies, make it essential that there is equal involvement of men and women in adaptation planning. In the North, it is equally as important that women are involved in planning protection programmes. Energy policy and urban and transport planning are male-dominated sectors. The author asks what the effect on planning is if it is almost exclusively developed from the perspective of one gender, whose experience usually excludes the work involved in caring and providing for others and cites a study which indicates that women in the North perceive climate change as more dangerous than do men, and that they are more willing to alter environmentally harmful behaviour. Recommendations include: more investment in research and production of gender-disaggregated data, the integration of gender into climate change negotiations and policy making, and the participation of women in decision making and negotiations.

Gender: The Missing Component of the Response to Climate Change (2006), Yianna Lambrou and Grazia Piana, FAO, www.fao.org/docrep/010/i0170e/i0170e00.htm

In this extremely thorough 44-page paper from the UN Food and Agriculture Organization, the authors, after setting out the scientific fundamentals of climate change and explaining the international community's response to climate change – the UNFCCC and the Kyoto Protocol – go on to examine issues around the gender-differentiated impacts of climate change. These include emissions of greenhouse gases and mitigation, and women's adaptive capacities, including a discussion of the lessons learned from natural disasters; namely, that interventions to save lives and secure livelihoods are more efficient when gender issues are properly understood and addressed. Arguing that gender aspects have been neglected in climate change negotiations thus far, the authors call for gender to be mainstreamed into the critical issues on the climate change agenda; mitigation, adaptation, capacity building, and the

Clean Development Mechanism (CDM), which aims to incorporate mitigation considerations into development policy. At the end of the paper there
is a useful set of annexes, which as well as a bibliography, include; a table
providing information on the likely regional impacts of climate change and
the associated vulnerabilities and adaptive capacities of affected populations,
and a table setting out the potential impacts of climate change on the MDGs;
a fuller description of the CDM; and the text of a paper authored by women's
environmental groups which was presented to women environment ministers
at the Eleventh Conference of the Parties to the UN Framework Convention
on Climate Change (COP 11), held in Montreal in 2005. The paper stresses
the importance of women continuing to lobby national negotiators for the
full integration of gender issues into climate change policies in the post 2012
stage of international negotiations.

Sisters on the Planet: four inspirational women and the fight against climate
change *(2008), Oxfam GB, www.oxfam.org.uk/sisters*

Available either online, or on dvd (with accompanying handbook), *Sisters
on the Planet* is a useful teaching or campaigning tool. It seeks to get across
the message that while climate change affects us all, it is already having a
disproportionate impact on people in developing countries, hitting women
the hardest by exacerbating existing inequalities. However, it makes clear that
women are also effective agents of positive change. Four short films present
the stories of Sahena, from an increasingly flood-prone Bangladesh, who has
trained as a disaster prevention officer for her community, overcoming preju-
dice along the way; of Muriel, who works to tackle climate change from her
position within the Brazilian Environment Ministry; of Martina, a Ugandan
farmer, battling to feed her family and protect its livelihood in the face of
more and more extreme weather conditions; and of Melissa, a primary-school
teacher in the UK, who teaches her pupils about climate change and more
sustainable ways of living.

Up in Smoke: Asia and the Pacific (2007),www.iied.org/pubs/pdfs/10020IIED.pdf

Up in Smoke – Africa 2 (2006), www.iied.org/pubs/pdfs/10018IIED.pdf

Up in Smoke: Latin America and the Caribbean (2006),
www.iied.org/pubs/pdfs/10017IIED.pdf, also available in Spanish, www.iied.
org/pubs/pdfs/10017SIIED.pdf

*Africa: Up in Smoke – The second report from the Working Group on Climate Change
and Development* (2005),
www.iied.org/pubs/pdfs/9560IIED.pdf , also available in French, www.iied.org/
pubs/pdfs/10005IIED.pdf, Portuguese, www.iied.org/pubs/pdfs/10007IIED.pdf,
and Spanish, www.iied.org/pubs/pdfs/10006IIED.pdf

*Up in Smoke: Threats from, and responses to, the impact of global warming on hu-
man development* (2004),

www.iied.org/pubs/pdfs/9512IIED.pdf, also available in French, www.iied.org/
pubs/pdfs/10008IIED.pdf, Portuguese, www.iied.org/pubs/pdfs/10009IIED.pdf,
and Spanish, www.iied.org/pubs/pdfs/10010IIED.pdf

For those seeking information on the effects of climate change on the environment and human development in a regional context, these reports from
the UK Working Group on Climate Change and Development – a network of
environment and development organizations – provide some accessible, well
illustrated, and well laid out explanations, evidence, and case studies. However, although attention is paid to gender issues, this is not consistent across
the reports, or even within individual reports, and for a full understanding
of the gender-differentiated impacts of climate change in any one region, it
would be necessary to read more widely

Adaptation

Gender Equality and Adaptation (2007), Ariana Araujo and Andrea Quesada-
Aguilar, in collaboration with Lorena Aguilar and Rebecca Pearl, IUCN and
WEDO, http://genderandenvironment.org/admin/admin_biblioteca/documen-
tos/Factsheet Adaptation.pdf

In this factsheet, the authors argue that social, economic, and geographical
characteristics determine the vulnerability of people to climate change, with
poor women being more vulnerable to natural disasters as a result of existing socially-constructed gender roles and behaviours. For example, in gen-
der-inequitable societies, boys are likely to receive preferential treatment in
rescue efforts, and both women and girls suffer more from shortages of food
and economic resources after a natural disaster. The authors make the point,
however, that while women are disproportionately affected by disasters and
rapid environmental changes, their knowledge and responsibilities related to
natural resource management are often critical to the survival of their communities. The paper ends with a list of recommendations, which includes:
that gender considerations must be included in the United Nations Framework Convention on Climate Change's international Adaptation Fund; that
global and national studies should produce gender-differentiated data on
the impacts of climate change and emphasize the capacities of women and
men to adapt to and mitigate climate changes; and that there is an improvement in women's access to, and control over, natural resources in order to
reduce poverty and vulnerability, to manage and conserve natural resources,
and to ensure that women have resources to adapt properly.

*We know what we need: South Asian women speak out on climate change adapta-
tion* (2007), Tom Mitchell, Thomas Tanner, and Kattie Lussier, ActionAid/IDS,
www.actionaid.org/assets/pdf/ActionAid%20%20IDS%20Report%20_We%20
know%20what%20we%20need.pdf

This report presents the findings of research carried out among poor women living in rural communities in the Ganges (or Ganga) river basin, which lies within the borders of Bangladesh, India, and Nepal. This area already suffers from weather-related hazards brought about by climate change, hazards which are predicted to worsen in the future. Participatory research tools were used to explore the impact of changing monsoon and flooding patterns on these women's livelihoods; their existing coping strategies; constraints to adapting to these conditions; and their priorities, in terms of adaptation, for the future. The results showed that despite limited resources, information, and support, these women had already started to adapt to a changing climate, and can clearly articulate what it is they need to secure and sustain their livelihoods more effectively. Their priorities include: a safe place to live and store their harvest and livestock during the monsoon season; better access to services such as agricultural extension; training and information about adaptation strategies and livelihood alternatives; and access to resources to implement effective strategies and overcome constraints. The paper stresses that for funding for adaptation to be effective and efficient, as well as gender equitable, poor women must be fully involved and their experiences and needs reflected and prioritized in both policies and interventions on climate change adaptation.

Mitigation

A study on gender equality as a prerequisite for sustainable development: What we know about the extent to which women globally live in a more sustainable way than men, leave a smaller ecological footprint and cause less climate damage (2007), Gerd Johnsson-Latham, The Environment Advisory Council, Ministry of the Environment, Sweden, www.genderandenvironment.org/admin/admin_biblioteca/documentos/rapport_engelska.pdf

For a global reduction in the level of greenhouse gas emissions to be brought about, development that is sustainable is necessary. With this in mind, this paper examines the gender-specific differences in the lifestyles and consumption patterns of women and men, and thus their environmental impact. With a focus on issues of mobility and access to transport, it describes how men, mainly through their greater mobility and more widespread travel, account for more carbon dioxide emissions than women, in both the North and the South: in Sweden, 10 per cent of all car drivers, primarily men, account for 60 per cent of all car driving in Sweden and thus for the same proportion of emissions and environmental impact. The paper calls for gender equality to be a prerequisite for sustainable development policy: for sustainable and gender-equal transport systems to be developed, through, for example, boosting women's participation in decision-making on community planning, traffic systems, and transportation; investing more resources to improve women's mobility, including public transport, which causes less environmental damage; and considering the introduction of individual emissions rights: and for a strengthening of the social dimensions of sustainability, for example, designing a gender-equal social model that focuses less on goods and more on services that reduce the ill-health, stress and time poverty of people (mostly women).

Reforestation, Afforestation, Deforestation, Climate Change and Gender (2007), Lorena Aguilar, Ariana Araujo and Andrea Quesada-Aguilar, IUCN, http:// genderandenvironment.org/admin/admin_biblioteca/documentos/Factsheet Foretry.pdf

This 6-page factsheet from the World Conservation Union (IUCN) gives a very useful introduction to the subject of gender, forestry, and climate change mitigation. Forest ecosystems play an important part in the global carbon cycle. Reforestation (reestablishment of forest after its removal) and afforestation (the establishment of forest in areas that have not been forested for at least 50 years) have both been integrated as forestry-based mitigation schemes into the Kyoto Protocol. The factsheet describes the often different productive and reproductive roles of women and men with regard to forest resource management and argues that 'mitigation strategies represent a unique opportunity to include women in forestry programmes and acknowledge that gender relations will influence many aspects of forest management and governance proposed for reducing greenhouse gases.'

Biofuels

Gender and Bioenergy (2007), Ariana Araujo and Andrea Quesada-Aguilar, in collaboration with Lorena Aguilar, Andrea Athanas and Nadine McCormick, IUCN, www.genderandenvironment.org/admin/admin_biblioteca/documentos/Factsheet BioEnergy.pdf

This factsheet from the World Conservation Union (IUCN) provides valuable information on gender and bioenergy and biofuels – an understanding of the gendered nature of energy production and consumption being crucial to the development of gender-equitable sustainable development and climate-change mitigation strategies. It helpfully explains terminology, sets out the pros and cons of the production of biofuel for women producers, and makes a series of recommendations, including calling for the involvement of women in the development and implementation of biofuel policies, as current policies may be undermining food security, are degrading ecosystems, and preventing rural farmers, especially women, from benefiting from biofuel markets.

Gender And Equity Issues In Liquid Biofuels Production: Minimizing The Risks To Maximize The Opportunities (2008), Andrea Rossi and Yianna Lambrou, FAO, www.fao.org/docrep/010/ai503e/ai503e00.HTM

In this 30-page paper the authors examine the potential socio-economic risks for women and men of the large-scale production of liquid biofuels in developing countries. These risks include the exacerbation of existing gender inequalities in access to and control of land and associated decision-making power; the gendered impact of large-scale monocultures on the environment – for example, if biofuels production competes for water and firewood supplies, it would negatively affect women, who already bear the burden of collecting water and firewood for the family; the potential for the growth of gender-discriminatory working conditions on biofuel plantations; and increased food insecurity for women and men. The paper makes a series of recommendations, including; that more research be carried out on the potential gender-differentiated risks and opportunities associated with second-generation liquid biofuel production (wherein fuel is produced from agricultural waste, wood, and grasses, rather than from agricultural crops); and that rules governing the international liquid biofuels market should be adopted and the social and environmental sustainability of biofuels productions should be ensured at the international level.

Water

Biopolitics, climate change and water security: impact, vulnerability and adaptation issues for women (2007), Nidhi Tandon, Agenda 73, www.siyanda.org/search/summary.cfm?nn=3560&ST=SS&Keywords=biopolitics&SUBJECT=0&Donor=&StartRow=1&Ref=Sim

Focusing on Africa, with examples drawn from other developing countries, this paper examines the impact of climate change on water security, in a context in which the increased degradation of ecosystems, excessive consumption of water, contamination and salinization, and the privatization of water utilities has already had profound effects on the availability of drinking water. The paper considers what needs to be done at community levels to enable women to articulate their needs and priorities as the collectors and managers of water; why it is important for women, as a matter of urgency, to get involved in the protection of water in solidarity with each other; and how women are adapting to change at the local level, and the implications for local, national, and international water policies. For the author, the danger is that with relation to climate change, policy and aid decisions will go the way they usually have done, leaving women with the responsibility of managing local change but without the required resources. For this to be avoided, women need to be better informed, but also need to have their own information, experiences, and ideas valued and organized into voices for change.

Security and disaster risk reduction

Gender, Climate Change and Human Security: Lessons from Bangladesh, Ghana and Senegal (2008), Irene Dankelman and Khurshid Alam, Wahida Bashar Ahmed, Yacine Diagne Gueye, Naureen Fatema, Rose Mensah-Kutin, WEDO with ABANTU for Development in Ghana, ActionAid Bangladesh and ENDA Senegal, www.wedo.org/files/HSN%20Study%20Final%20May%2020,%202008.pdf

In April 2007, the UN Security Council, for the first time, addressed the issue of climate change as a challenge to human security. Climate change could bring about crop failures that cause intensified competition, and conflict, over food, water, and energy, and prompt migration on unprecedented levels. In this excellent 71-page paper, the authors survey the gender aspects of natural disasters; outline the existing international policy framework which can address the human security challenges of climate change from a gender perspective (for example, CEDAW, UNFCCC, NAPAs, or National Adaptation Plans of Action); and present an analytical framework for looking at gender, climate change and human security, in which they define human security as 'security of survival (mortality/injury, health), security of livelihood food, water, energy, environmental, shelter, and economic security), and dignity (basic human rights, capacity, participation)'. The paper provides valuable, and detailed, case-studies from Bangladesh, Ghana, and Senegal, providing in each case an overview of the climate change situation in that country, drawing out the implications for women's livelihoods, security, and gender equality, and reviewing from a gender perspective national strategies and adaptation measures. What is clear from these case studies is that women are already actively engaged in implementing adaptation strategies in order to protect their families' and their communities' assets and livelihoods, and that natural disasters could provide women with a unique opportunity to challenge and change their gendered status in society. On the basis of the outcomes of their study, the authors make a set of recommendations, which include: the application of a human security framework to climate change at all policy levels; the acknowledgement across all sectors that women are among the most affected by climate change because of their social and economic situations and because of their role in the family; the construction of a legal regime that safeguards the security of women affected by climate change, including mechanisms to review land-use planning and infrastructure work; empowering women as agents of adaptation, and provide women with opportunities to control greater percentages of resources (including land) and services to make independent decisions; and the integration of human security for women into climate change funding mechanisms, to ensure that poor women get a fair share of funds

Gender Perspectives: Integrating Disaster Risk Reduction into Climate Change Adaptation-Good Practices and Lessons Learned (2008), UN/ISDR, www.unisdr.org/eng/about_isdr/isdr-publications/17-Gender_Perspectives_Integrating_DRR_CC/Gender_Perspectives_Integrating_DRR_CC_Good%20Practices.pdf

This well set out paper, from the UN-International Strategy for Disaster Reduction, presents examples of successful projects from around the world, which, for the authors, demonstrate how disaster risk reduction (DRR) can be integrated into gender-sensitive climate change adaptation initiatives, so as to reduce people's vulnerabilities to the impact of climate change and weather-related disasters. The project case studies are organized under three headings; Women as natural and environmental resource managers; Women as leaders, decision-makers and full participants; and Gender sensitive tools for climate change adaptation and disaster risk reduction. Each case study is laid out in the same format; an abstract, a description of the project, a brief explanation of how the project links gender, DRR, and climate change, why the project is considered an example of good practice, lessons learnt, impacts and results, the challenges, and the potential for replication. Such a survey will be of great use for those looking for concrete examples of the kind of gender-sensitive DRR and climate change adaptation work already being undertaken in a variety of environments across the globe.

The tsunami's impact on women (2005), Oxfam Briefing Note, Oxfam International, http://www.oxfam.org.uk/resources/policy/conflict_disasters/downloads/bn_tsunami_women.pdf

It is expected that the number of natural disasters caused by climate change will continue to increase over time. Although not a climate-change related event, the tsunami of December 2004 constituted a major natural disaster, of which we are likely to see more and more. This valuable 14-page paper from Oxfam, produced a few months after the tsunami hit, looks at the gender-differentiated impact of the tsunami in India, Indonesia, and Sri Lanka, in an attempt to understand the social impacts of the disaster so as to ensure effective and equitable responses and long-term policies. Oxfam found that in each country, the tsunami had a greater impact on women than on men, not only in terms of loss of life (with many more women than men being killed), but also in the lack of attention given to women's livelihoods activities in the response, and in the increased levels of sexual harassment and violence experienced by women. The paper ends with a list of recommended actions, which include; the collection and use of sex-disaggregated information by all those involved in humanitarian assistance and policy making; ensuring that earning opportunities are accessible to both men and women, whether in immediate cash-for-work programmes or in more sustainable livelihood programmes; the prioritization of the protection of women from sexual violence and exploitation; and the genuine participation of women when assessing needs, delivering aid, or in programme evaluation, an associated benefit of participation being a move away from a view of women as 'vulnerable victims' to one of them as rights-holding citizens with specific perspectives and capacities.

Financing

Gender: Missing Links in Financing Climate Change Adaptation and Mitigation – Position Paper prepared for UNFCCC COP 13, Bali, Indonesia (2007), genderCC Network-Women for Climate Justice, www.gendercc.net/index.php?id=70&auswahl=29

This short paper prepared by gendercc for the United Nations Framework Climate Change Convention, Conference of the Parties 13, held in Bali in 2007, is a call for the inclusion of gender budgeting and gender audits in all funding for climate change adaptation and mitigation and for investments in programmes for adaptation and mitigation, technology transfer, capacity building, etc. to contribute to social justice, and gender justice in particular. The paper reviews the funding mechanisms under the UNFCCC and Kyoto Protocol from a gender perspective, and criticises market-based financing approaches.

Compensating for Climate Change: Principles and Lessons for Equitable Adaptation Funding (2007), Ilana Solomon, ActionAid USA
www.actionaid.org/assets/pdf/Compensating%20for%20Climate%20Change.pdf

Included in this 26-page discussion paper from ActionAid is a very helpful, clear and comprehensive explanation of the current climate change adaptation-funding mechanisms currently operating through the UNFCCC. These mechanisms are reviewed using ActionAid's proposed five principles for effective adaptation funding, which are; democratic governance, civil society participation, sustainable and compensatory financing; no economic policy conditionality, and access for the most vulnerable. The paper also assesses alternative channels for adaptation funding, using the examples of the Global Fund to Fight AIDS, Tuberculosis and Malaria, and the Multilateral Fund for the Implementation of the Montreal Protocol. The paper explicitly addresses the gender-differentiated impacts of climate change, and one of the seven recommendations made in the report is that a Women's Rights Desk should be created within the Adaptation Fund, which would review all proposals to the Fund, and which would have decision-making power with regard to funding priorities.

Turning Carbon into Gold: How the international community can finance climate change adaptation without breaking the bank (2008), Oxfam Briefing Paper No.123, Heather K. Coleman in collaboration with David Waskow, Oxfam International, www.oxfam.org.uk/resources/policy/climate_change/downloads/bp123_turning_carbon_gold.pdf, also available in Spanish, www.oxfam.org.uk/resources/policy/climate_change/downloads/bp123_turning_carbon_gold_sp.pdf, and a seven-page summary is available in French, www.oxfam.org.uk/resources/policy/climate_change/downloads/bp123_turning_carbon_gold_summary_fr.pdf

The Bali Action Plan (issued at the 2007 UN climate change conference – COP13) called for new and additional resources, and innovative finance mechanisms, to address urgent climate adaptation needs. In this detailed 36-page briefing paper, Oxfam International proposes that establishing limits on emissions in the international aviation and shipping sectors – already identified as sectors where it is possible to reduce greenhouse gas emissions while generating new adaptation financing – could be the way forward in the post-2012 climate negotiations. The authors calculate that establishing such limits (focused on developed countries only) and auctioning off emission allowances in these sectors, could generate more than $12 billion and $16.6 billion, respectively. While this paper is primarily concerned with explaining how this proposed financing mechanism would work, the authors recognize the gender-differentiated impact of climate change. They argue that as a key principle, the Adaptation Fund of the UNFCCC should ensure that adaptation planning should involve the identification of the most vulnerable people, prioritizing their adaptive capacity, and as part of this emphasis on vulnerable populations, the particular challenge facing women should be specifically addressed.

Gender and Financing for Climate Change in the Philippines; Gender and Climate Change in Nepal, case studies, http://www.wedo.org/learn/campaigns/climate change/case-study-gender-and-climate-change-in-nepal and http://www.wedo. org/learn/campaigns/climatechange/new-climate-change-case-study

Organizations

ENERGIA – International Network on Gender and Sustainable Energy, postal address: ENERGIA Secretariat, c/o ETC Netherlands, P.O. Box 64, 3830 AB Leusden, The Netherlands, tel: +31 (0)33 432 6044, office address: Kastanjelaan 5, 3833 AN, Leusden, The Netherlands, email: energia@etcnl.nl, website: www.energia.org

The ENERGIA network was established in 1995 'in response to the inadequate recognition of gender issues as a legitimate area of concern in mainstream energy policy, practice, and advocacy at that time.' With its international secretariat based in The Netherlands, the larger network works through regional and national 'focal points', which initiate gender and energy activities within their own networks. Working to mainstream gender into energy policies and energy programmes, ENERGIA focuses its efforts around four main strategic activities: capacity-building; gender in energy projects/markets; policy influencing; and networking. Capacity-building aims to build a critical mass of in-country gender and energy experts who can integrate and mainstream gender into energy projects and policies. Gender in energy projects/markets works on mainstreaming gender approaches in rural energy markets and rural energy-access projects. Policy influencing seeks to promote gender-sensitive national energy policies in countries where the ENERGIA network is present. Networking activity seeks to strengthen energy and gender networking at regional, national, and international levels. Strong networks already exist in Africa and Asia, and ENERGIA is building up its networks in Latin America and in the Pacific. The network's website provides contact lists of its focal-point members in Africa and Asia, and a useful 'related links' page.

Food and Agriculture Organization of the United Nations (FAO), Viale delle terme di Caracalla, 00153 Rome, Italy, tel: +39 06 57051, email: FAO-HQ@fao.org, Climate-change@fao.org, Gender, Equity and Rural Employment Division, ESW-Director@fao.org, website (in Arabic, Chinese, English, French, and Spanish): www.fao.org (gender and climate change: www.fao.org/climatechange/49379/en/)

Working in the areas of agriculture, forestry, fisheries, and natural resources management, FAO supports its member countries in the creation of agricultural policies and national strategies to achieve rural-development, hunger-alleviation, and food-security goals, and provides a forum where agreements on major food and agriculture issues can be made. The Gender, Equity and Rural Employment Division within FAO is responsible for producing normative work and mainstreaming gender issues throughout the organization, in collaboration with gender focal points in other divisions of the FAO. Gender-equality gains are seen as essential to the fulfilment of FAO's mandate of raising levels of nutrition and standards of living, and improving agricultural productivity and livelihoods of rural populations. On gender and climate change, recognizing that women and men's ability to protect themselves from climatic changes threatening their food security depends on the resources they have, FAO is addressing gender inequality in access to resources through its work in fisheries, forestry, and agriculture, so that better adaptation practices and better coping strategies can be developed.

genanet – focal point gender, environment, sustainability, Life e.V., Dircksenstr. 47, D-10178 Berlin, Germany, tel: +49 30 308 79835, email: leitstelle@genanet.de, website: www.genanet.de

Based in Germany, genanet is an online network which promotes gender equity in environmental and sustainability policies, the integration of gender equity in research, and the implementation of gender mainstreaming into environmental policy making and the activities of environmental organizations. Its website (in German and English) provides free resources on gender and climate change; gender and biodiversity; gender and energy; gender, agriculture, and nutrition; gender, mobility, and transport; gender and sustainability; gender, environment, and health; and gender and water.

Gender and Disaster Network, Disaster and Development Centre, Northumbria University, School of Applied Sciences, Newcastle upon Tyne, NE1

8ST, UK, tel: +44 (0)191 227 3108, email: gdn@gdnonline.org, website: www. gdnonline.org

Working through its website, GDN seeks to share knowledge and resources on gender relations in the context of disasters. This includes not only work on gender in disaster risk-reduction (DRR), but also in the areas of climate change, pandemics, and conflicts and displacement. The website hosts and maintains the Gender and Disaster Sourcebook – an electronic guide providing information on such things as planning and practice tools, best practice, and case studies on gender and DRR – and gives updates on relevant upcoming events. Members contribute resources, and there are up-to-date additions on the subject of gender and climate change in the context of DRR and adaptation.

Gender and Water Alliance, PO Box 114, 6950 AC Dieren, The Netherlands, tel: +31 313 427230, email: secretariat@gwalliance.org, website: www.genderandwater.org

GWA is a global network dedicated to mainstreaming gender in water resources management and has more than 1000 members in 104 countries. Its membership is diverse and represents a wide range of capacities and expertise across all water sectors as well as from different stakeholder groups including government, grassroots organizations, NGOs, universities and research institutes, international agencies, and individual consultants. More than 80 per cent of the membership comes from countries in Asia, Africa, and Latin America. Financed by the Dutch and UK governments, the Alliance's mission is to promote women's and men's equitable access to, and management of, safe and adequate water for domestic supply, sanitation, food security, and environmental sustainability. GWA believes that equitable access to and control over water is a basic right for all, as well as a critical factor in promoting poverty eradication and sustainability.

gendercc – women for climate justice, c/o LIFE e.V, Dircksenstr. 47, D-10178 Berlin, Germany, tel: +49 30 308 79831, email: info@gendercc.net, website: www.gendercc.net

Established during the UNFCCC COP (United Nations Framework Convention on Climate Change, Conference of the Parties) 13, in Bali, in 2007, gendercc is a networking platform for organizations, institutions, and gender and climate-change experts. It serves to provide information and resources for those wishing to gain familiarity with the issues, as well as those who are already more deeply engaged in research and action in the area of gender and climate change. Registered users of the website can add literature and case studies to the databases and information is downloadable to all website visitors, at no charge. The website gives useful summaries of all the UNFCCC COPs that have taken place so far in terms of the activities undertaken during the conferences around the issue of gender.

The Global Gender and Climate Alliance (GGCA) is a partnership between 25 UN agencies and international civil-society organizations that was launched at the Bali climate-change negotiation in 2007. The core partners of the GGCA are United Nations Development Programme (UNDP), International Union for the Conservation of Nature (IUCN), and United Nations Environment Programme (UNEP). The GGCA works to ensure that climate-change policies, decision-making, and initiatives at all levels are gender-responsive. Currently the GGCA is providing gender training to climate-change negotiators, developing gender guidelines on climate-change finance mechanisms, and partnering with the UNFCCC Secretariat to develop a gender strategy. For more information about the GGCA, or to become an institutional member, please contact info@gender-climate.org.

International Union for the Conservation of Nature (IUCN – The World Conservation Union), Rue Mauverney 28, Gland, 1196, Switzerland, tel: +41 (22) 999 0000, email: webmaster@iucn.org, website: www.iucn.org, IUCN Gender and Environment website: http://genderandenvironment.org/

The IUCN was founded in 1948 as the world's first global environmental organization, and today has more than 1000 member organizations, including over 200-plus government, and 800-plus non-government organizations, in 140 countries. The IUCN supports scientific research on the environment and sustainable development, managing field projects across the world, and seeks to bring governments, NGOs, UN agencies, companies, and local communities together to develop and implement environmental policies, laws, and best practice. The organization also produces the IUCN Red List of Threatened Species, which catalogues plant and animal species which are at risk of extinction. The IUCN works on gender and environmental issues, including gender and climate change – Lorena Aguilar, IUCN's senior gender adviser, is an expert on the issue – and there is a dedicated IUCN gender and environment website, in English and Spanish, which contains free-to-download IUCN resources on gender and climate change, some in Spanish and French, as well as English.

Women's Environment and Development Organization (WEDO), 355 Lexington Ave., 3rd Floor, New York, NY 10017, USA, tel: +1 212 973 0325, email (general enquiries): wedo@wedo.org, email (publications and resources): anna@wedo.org, website: www.wedo.org

Founded in 1991, WEDO is an international, US-based organization advocating for women's equality. It works in four programme areas: economic and social justice; gender and governance; sustainable development; and US global policy. The focus of its sustainable development programme is gender and climate change, and the organization's stated goal of its advocacy work on this issue is 'to help achieve a gender-sensitive, rights-based binding global agreement of climate change, fully financed and implemented.' With international negotiations to replace the Kyoto Protocol (which expires in 2012) ongoing, WEDO is seeking to influence decision-makers through a variety of

approaches: an advocacy campaign with partners in five developing countries, to ensure integration of a gender approach and women's participation
into national adaptation planning; in the USA, a media and public awareness
campaign – Women Demand US Action on Climate Change (WDACC) – to
persuade the US government to change its unilateralist stance on global climate-change policy, and to enlist women as leaders on this issue; and work
with the UN agencies and other civil-society organizations comprising the
Global Gender and Climate Alliance (GGCA) to ensure that climate-change
policies, decision-making, and initiatives at the global, regional, and national
levels are gender-sensitive. The WEDO website contains an online resource
guide, providing links to free-to-download resources, including WEDO-
authored papers and factsheets.

Index

Oxfam GB is a development, relief, and campaigning organization that works with others to find lasting solutions to poverty and suffering around the world. Oxfam GB is a member of Oxfam International.

As part of its programme work, Oxfam GB undertakes research and documents its programme and humanitarian experience. This is disseminated through books, journals, policy papers, research reports, and campaign reports which are available for free download at: www.oxfam.org.uk/publications

www.oxfam.org.uk
Email: publish@oxfam.org.uk
Tel: +44 (0) 1865 473727

Oxfam House
John Smith Drive
Cowley
Oxford, OX4 2JY

The chapters in this book are available for download from the Oxfam GB website: www.oxfam.org.uk/publications

The *Working in Gender and Development* series brings together themed selections of the best articles from the journal *Gender & Development* and other Oxfam publications for development practitioners and policy makers, students and academics. Titles in the series present the theory and practice of gender-oriented development in a way that records experience, describes good practice, and shares information about resources. Books in the series will contribute to and review current thinking on the gender dimensions of particular development and relief issues.

Other titles in the series include:
Gender-Based Violence
HIV and AIDS